Why Afterschool Matters

The Rutgers Series in Childhood Studies

The Rutgers Series in Childhood Studies is dedicated to increasing our understanding of children and childhoods, past and present, throughout the world. Children's voices and experiences are central. Authors come from a variety of fields, including anthropology, criminal justice, history, literature, psychology, religion, and sociology. The books in this series are intended for students, scholars, practitioners, and those who formulate policies that affect children's everyday lives and futures.

Edited by Myra Bluebond-Langner, Board of Governors Professor of Anthropology, Rutgers University and True Colours Chair in Palliative Care for Children and Young People, University College London, Institute of Child Health.

Advisory Board
Perri Klass, New York University
Jill Korbin, Case Western Reserve University
Bambi Schieffelin, New York University
Enid Schildkraut, American Museum of Natural History and Museum for African Art

Why Afterschool Matters

INGRID A. NELSON

Rutgers University Press

New Brunswick, New Jersey, and London

Library of Congress Cataloging-in-Publication Data
Names: Nelson, Ingrid A., author.
Title: Why afterschool matters / Ingrid A. Nelson.
Description: New Brunswick, New Jersey : Rutgers University Press, [2016] | Series: Rutgers series in childhood studies | Includes bibliographical references and index.
Identifiers: LCCN 2016012310 | ISBN 9780813584942 (hardcover : alk. paper) | ISBN 9780813584935 (pbk. : alk. paper) | ISBN 9780813584959 (e-book (epub)) | ISBN 9780813584966 (e-book (web pdf))
Subjects: LCSH: Student activities—Social aspects—United States—Longitudinal studies. | Student aspirations—United States—Longitudinal studies. | Mexican American students—Longitudinal studies. | Mexican Americans—Education, Higher—Longitudinal studies. | Educational attainment—Social aspects—United States—Longitudinal studies. | Academic achievement—Social aspects—United States—Longitudinal studies.
Classification: LCC LC205 .N45 2016 | DDC 371.829/68073—dc23
LC record available at https://lccn.loc.gov/2016012310

A British Cataloging-in-Publication record for this book is available from the British Library.

Visit our website: http://rutgerspress.rutgers.edu

Manufactured in the United States of America

To my parents for giving me roots and wings
And to Allyson for being with this project from the beginning

Contents

Preface

Why Does College Matter?

In order to talk about the role of extracurricular activities on the pathway to college, it is important to begin with the question we too often take for granted: Why would anyone want to go to college? You probably already know the answer: College matters because it is a key element in the class structure of the United States. Attainment of the relatively secure, well-compensated jobs held by the upper middle class virtually requires a college education these days.

The typical young worker with a bachelor's degree earns significantly more than those who did not pursue any education beyond high school. In 2009, the average twenty-five- to twenty-nine-year-old with at least a bachelor's degree earned almost $50,000 per year, while those who finished high school earned only about $31,000 per year. The earnings of workers with less education, when compared to those of their more educated counterparts, tend not to grow as much as careers unfold. As a result, the difference in average earnings across education groups gets even larger as workers age. The typical adult with a bachelor's degree will earn $1.42 million during a forty-year career, compared with $770,000 for a typical high school graduate. That $650,000 difference narrows only marginally to $550,000 after factoring in the expenses of going to college and the four years of potential earnings that college graduates give up while they are in school (Taylor 2011).

This is the crux of the American Dream. This is how you get ahead—you work hard in school, you get good grades, you go to college, and you get on your way to living the good life. This is the story many of us heard growing up, and this, in turn, is the story we tell our children. In fact, among parents of a child age seventeen or younger, 94 percent say they expect their child to go to college (Taylor 2011).

So how does one get there? Before becoming a sociologist, if you had asked me how I got to college I would probably have begun the story with my senior year in high school when my mom took me to the bookstore and bought me a guidebook to the best three-hundred-and-something colleges in the United States. She instructed me to go through the book and, based on the profile of each school, pick five schools to apply to. I grew up in Oregon and was ready to try on a new place; thus, all of the schools I applied to were on the East Coast. I applied sight unseen. No one read over my personal essay or suggested I take a test preparation class for the SAT. After I learned where I had been admitted, my dad and I traveled east to tour the campuses. That is the story of how I got to college through the eyes of my seventeen-year-old self. I got good grades, I got good SAT scores, I wrote an essay, I went for a visit, and I made a choice. I worked hard, and I got ahead. This is the American Dream.

Unfortunately, my story suffers from a complete lack of what esteemed sociologist C. Wright Mills (2000) would call a "sociological imagination." Applying your sociological imagination means seeking out connections between your own life and the social context in which you are embedded. This is also spoken of as identifying the links between biography and history. For example, Mills cautions that rather than feeling like a personal failure for getting a divorce, use your sociological imagination to recognize that you live a society where half of all marriages end in divorce. How does our social structure make this possible? Historically speaking, how did we all come to be at this place together? As Mills wrote, "The first fruit of this imagination—and the first lesson of the social science that embodies it—is the idea that the individual can understand his own experience and gauge his own fate only by locating himself within his period, that he can know his own chances in life only by becoming aware of those of all individuals in his circumstances. In many ways it is a terrible lesson; in many ways a magnificent one." How then do we apply our sociological imaginations to this question of getting to college?

First, we go back to the American Dream—that story about how the key to making it in this country is getting a bachelor's degree, that story about how 94 percent of parents expect their child to attend college (Taylor 2011), that story we have all heard about how if you just work hard enough you can make it in this country. But that story is not as true as some of us are taught to believe. Of any developed country, the United States has the greatest gap between expectations for college attainment and actual college attainment (Jerrim 2014). Most other countries are fairly well matched in terms of expectations and reality. But not the United States—our dearly held belief that anyone can achieve if they just work hard enough is not matched to our societal institutions. Rather, the American Dream masks drastic and growing inequalities.

We do not actually reside in a country where anyone who works hard enough can get ahead or where the most successful people in the room are always the most talented or the hardest working. We live in a country that was built through genocide, colonization, and slavery and has been largely governed through a system of upper-class white supremacy since its establishment. The list of government policies that have used socially constructed racial categories to selectively prohibit accumulation of income, wealth, property, health, human rights, safety, justice, and more is long and growing every day.

Our educational system is at the crux of this contradiction between our belief that anyone can get ahead and the ways our institutions practice stratification by race and class. Public schools were officially desegregated by mandate of the Supreme Court in the iconic *Brown v. Board of Education* decision of 1954. But it took two more decisions by the Supreme Court and nearly twenty years to actually begin to achieve integrated schools in the United States. And the public—particularly white homeowners—continues to gravitate away from integration. Since the 1970s, schools, especially those that are no longer under court order to desegregate, have steadily resegregated (Reardon et al. 2012). Currently the most segregated group in our society is white families with children (Frankenberg, Lee, and Orfield 2003).

As a result, racial inequality in our school system produces enormous differences in educational outcomes. Only 75 percent of Latino/as ages twenty-five to twenty-nine have a high school diploma, compared to 89 percent of blacks and 95 percent of whites, and only 15 percent of Latino/as have earned a bachelor's degree, compared with 23 percent of blacks and 40 percent of whites (Fry and Parker 2012). In other words, whites are nearly twice as likely as African Americans and almost three times as likely as Latino/as to attain a bachelor's degree or higher.

Part of this disparity, of course, is owing to other factors. The most reliable way to know how likely it is that a child will attend college is to learn their parents' level of educational attainment. If your parents did not go to college, regardless of your race, it is most likely that you will not go to college either (Reardon 2011).

Although race and class are intertwined, they are not the same thing. Each has independent effects. In comparison to white students whose parents did not go beyond high school, African American and Hispanic students drop out of college at higher rates—34 percent versus 27 percent of whites—and do not attain a bachelor's degree as often—8 percent versus 14 percent of whites. At the other end of the parental education spectrum, racial differences are even more profound. Among students whose parents have attained at least a bachelor's degree, the statistics are even more striking: African American and Hispanic students do not attend college at twice the rate of similarly situated white students (15 percent versus 7 percent of whites), drop out of college much more often (37 percent versus 25 percent of whites); moreover, only 35 percent graduate with a bachelor's degree, relative to 58 percent of whites (Carnevale and Strohl 2013).

On top of race and parental education, growing segregation by income also contributes to unequal educational outcomes. In 1970, only 15 percent of families lived in neighborhoods classified as either affluent or poor; by 2007, 31 percent of families lived in such neighborhoods (Reardon and Bischoff 2011). Along with growing residential inequality we see a growing achievement gap. The gap between the children with family incomes in the top 10 percent and children with family incomes in the bottom 10 percent was about 40 percent wider in 2001 than in 1975, and twice as large as the black-white achievement gap. (For reference, the 90th income percentile was $165,000 per family per year. The 10th income percentile was at $15,000 per family per year.)

Given these data, it is perhaps unsurprising to see how we as Americans compare to other countries with regard to the difference between professional and working-class children's plans to complete college versus the difference in their test scores. While professional and working-class children show very small differences in their plans to attend college, the differences in their academic achievement are quite large. Children of professionals on average score eight-tenths of a standard deviation higher than working-class children in the United States. While other countries have even larger class-based differences in achievement, they are matched by differences in expectations (Jerrim 2014).

So how did I get to college? While hard work might be part of the equation, the fact that our societal institutions favor people like me made my journey much easier. I am white, I grew up in a middle-class family, in a home my parents owned, and in a neighborhood with very low rates of poverty and violence. I went to a very good public school with other middle- and upper-class white kids, and both of my parents are college graduates. In addition, I am a US citizen and had access to federal financial aid. I had no control over any of these things, and all played a large role in how I got to college.

It is no accident that our institutions of higher education are filled with people like me who have benefited from legacies of educational attainment. But why is there such a strong relationship between children's educational outcomes and parental race, education, and income? Why is there such a strong relationship even though we are taught to believe that everyone can achieve a college degree by applying a bit of effort?

One theory suggests that variation in educational attainment is essentially a cloak for preexisting class inequalities. This theory builds on Karl Marx's insights about the ways powerful groups in a society create systems that legitimate their own advantage. From this perspective, bachelor's degrees (and the coursework they represent) provide an appealing justification for the propensity of well-off parents to pass privilege along to their offspring. What about those who do not fit this pattern—the homeless-to-Harvard stories? Reproduction theorists argue that those stories are actually essential to public acceptance of the whole regime; that is, the exceptions give the system the appearance of class neutrality.

Another answer to the question of why there is such a strong relationship between parental social class and children's educational outcomes harkens back to the work of sociologist Max Weber. This theory argues that modern societies have replaced traditional hierarchies of caste or tribe with hierarchies based on individual achievement. Thus, the ultimate worth of the college degree lies in the educational institution's ability to bestow advantages totally independent of a student's social background.

So which one is it? Does higher education simply sugarcoat existing inequalities in order to make privilege-laundering look legitimate? Or is the college degree a valid measure of individual merit? Lucky for us, many scholars have worked on these questions, and it turns out their findings are very consistent across datasets and methodologies. The answer is yes and yes: schooling does have independent effects on an individual's life chances, and at the same time educational credentials act as the paramount mechanism through which parents hand privilege down to their children (Stevens 2007).

But the landscape of higher education is changing, and mainly it is expanding. This means that the hoops privileged parents have to jump through to pass their privilege onto their children—and make it look like their kids earned it in a class-neutral system—are becoming more elaborate and more costly. Admissions offices' development of clear measures of accomplishment—standardized test scores, high school grade-point averages, athletic win records, counts of Advanced Placement classes, demonstrated artistic accomplishment, and formally recognized community service—have transformed the organization and culture of how we raise our children from the day that they are born. Indeed, the admissions criteria developed by elite colleges now act as the blueprint for childrearing in middle- and upper-class America (Lareau 2003; Stevens 2007). Parenting has become more competitive, more expensive, more structured around the production of demonstrated accomplishment, and, perhaps most consequential for the ideal of the American Dream, more and more difficult for middle- and lower-class families to match.

Not only is there growing income inequality, and upper-class families simply have more money than before—though that is part of the equation (Fry and Kochhar 2014)—the rub centers on how upper-class families are spending their money: they are increasingly dedicating their resources to ensuring their children's educational success—they are buying books, iPads, high-quality child care, summer camps, private lessons, tutors, traveling sports teams, and the list goes on. Over the last forty years, families in the top income quintile have increased the amount they spend on enrichment activities each year from $3,536 to $8,872 (in 2008 dollars)—an increase of nearly 150 percent. Meanwhile, families in the bottom income quintile have increased their spending on educational enrichment from $835 to $1,315 (in 2008 dollars)—a substantially smaller increase (less than 60 percent) and a much smaller dollar amount overall (Duncan and Murnane 2011).

And why? College admissions offer a system, a game if you will. Like every other game, if you want to win you have to know not only the formal rules but also the strategy—that is, the unspoken rules. While the official rules of college admissions declare the importance of purportedly unbiased measures like standardized test scores, grades, and extracurricular accomplishments, privileged parents do things to put their children at the front of the pack. They make sure their kids are attending good schools in good neighborhoods, they purchase athletic gear and art supplies, they shuttle their minivans from band practice, to Girl Scouts, to ballet. They start early—in preschool even—intervening on behalf of their children in schools and other institutions to ensure the best possible outcomes and teaching their children that there is an exception to every rule (Lareau 2003).

Think about your own pathway to college. Who showed you the ropes? Did you consider not going to college? What kind of help did you get with preparation for standardized tests or essay writing? Did you participate in athletics? Arts? Yearbook? What kind of resources and transportation did these activities require? I was required to play team sports every season starting in elementary school, not to mention piano lessons, Sunday school, and summer camps. I did not have to give up extracurricular opportunities to care for my siblings, and I did not have to work for pay to keep my family afloat. When it came time to apply to colleges, my mom did not mention community college as a possibility. Instead, she bought me that book about the three-hundred-and-something best colleges, not coincidentally all four-year schools.

Thus, what are we to make of the fact that we are taught to believe that if you work hard, then you will get ahead—that those young people who do well in school are the smartest and hardest working kids in the crowd—when we live in a country where higher education is doing more to replicate existing inequality than to eliminate it?

Is this a problem? I argue yes, partly for moral reasons. We, as a society, claim to value equal opportunity. But if that doesn't convince you, look at the data. Our society is becoming increasingly socioeconomically unequal and increasingly ethnically and racially diverse (Frey 2011). In 2010, among children age five and under, whites made up only about half of the population. Among school-aged children, one in four were Latina/o. The number of white students in our schools will continue to shrink as time passes.

Increasing the number of black and Latina/o college graduates and the number of low-income college graduates must become a national priority.

For decades policy analysts and researchers have been trying to alleviate these troubling academic attainment gaps by focusing on schools—class size, teacher training, curriculum innovations, school choice—but with little success. The problem with this approach is that kids actually do not actually spend that much time in school; even counting homework time. Reed Larson and Suman Verma (1999) estimate that youth spend only 25 percent of their waking hours on school work. While public schools are incredibly unequal, what happens outside school accounts for much more of the variation in educational outcomes than what happens on the inside (Entwistle and Alexander 1992).

This book takes a closer look at the role extracurricular activities play in academic attainment. Researchers have linked participation in extracurricular activities to a plethora of positive outcomes, ranging from increased academic achievement to lower drop-out rates to stronger self-image. Most promising about extracurricular activities, however, is that disadvantaged students actually gain more from participation than their advantaged peers. Therefore, when disadvantaged youth participate, the attainment gap between students of high and low socioeconomic backgrounds begins to shrink. In other words, by giving disadvantaged students access to the same kinds of enrichment opportunities that privileged kids have, we can actually chip away at the educational attainment gap.

How do extracurricular activities—where youth arguably spend far less time than the formal school day—influence on educational outcomes? This book explores that question. By bringing to life the challenges that some Mexican American students face when navigating the intersections of drastically different home, school, and community spheres on their pathways to college, this book highlights the processes through which extracurricular contexts might play an important role in educational attainment for disadvantaged youth by whittling away at race- and class-based academic attainment gaps—gaps that have important implications for our society in the decades ahead.

Acknowledgments

My deepest appreciation goes to all of the individuals who helped make Students Together the welcoming, empowering, and transformative program that it was for so many young people over the years. From the visionary and founder, to the staff members, Americorps volunteers, undergraduate and graduate students, curriculum designers, and those in administrative roles behind the scenes, you have made a lasting impact. I would also like to thank the young people who worked through this program and beyond to make their communities and the world a more just and compassionate place. I owe a particular debt of gratitude to the students who gave their time over and over again being interviewed for this project. This book would not exist without you. You have been so generous, tenacious, and inspiring.

I am fortunate to have worked with outstanding faculty members who saw me through the beginnings of this book at Stanford University. I am especially grateful to my advisor Michael Rosenfeld for being a tireless sounding board and sage mentor, and for providing practical advice and genuine encouragement. I am also grateful to Milbrey McLaughlin for taking me under her wing and always expecting the best and to Monica McDermott for her guidance, intellect, and unending kindness.

In addition, I have had wonderfully supportive colleagues and mentors. I am thankful for Professors Susan Silbey and Barbara Beatty at Wellesley College for first inspiring my sociological imagination. Anahi Aguilar,

Maria Fernandez, Jon Norman, Mary Hofstedt, and Sarah Miles deserve special mention for their critical contributions to research design and data analysis. Craig McEwen and Karen Strobel have been patient mentors and irreplaceable and ongoing supports. I am grateful to Stanford University and the Robert Bowne Foundation for the financial assistance that made this research possible, and to Bowdoin College for the research leave that allowed me to complete this book. I would like to thank my editor at Rutgers University Press, Peter Mickulas, for his support and for working so efficiently to see this manuscript through to publication. Richard Lerner and an anonymous reviewer generously read and provided feedback on a draft of this manuscript. I also want to express my gratitude to a community of scholars and friends that have made the writing process more bearable: Shaun Golding, Natalie Privett Yu, Erin Schenck, and Kelly Tuomokoski. And, of course, I owe many thanks to countless others who have supported this project and my development as a scholar in so many ways.

Finally, I am grateful to my immediate and extended family, for all that they are and all that they do. I have been beyond fortunate to grow up with the love and encouragement of amazing grandparents, aunties, uncles, siblings and cousins. My parents have been my biggest cheerleaders since the beginning. My wife, Allyson, has been there for me in the good and the bad, every single day. Words cannot express my gratitude for her love, support, and humor. Lastly, I am grateful to Miles for his unending spirit and love of books, and to Lydia for being the best kind of deadline.

Why Afterschool Matters

1

Extracurricular Activities and Pathways to College

Born in Mexico City, Ana immigrated to the United States at the end of first grade with her mother and sister, Victoria. Ana's father, seeking a better life for his family, had previously immigrated and established a home in Bayside, a diverse urban community thirty minutes outside a major California city. Ana spoke no English when she enrolled at Jackson Elementary School. The transition was difficult, but Ana was placed in an English Language Learner class. Her parents worked diligently to help her become a proficient student, and she loved school and made friends quickly. Outside school, she enjoyed Jackson's afterschool program and spending time with her family.

At the beginning of sixth grade, Ana transitioned from Jackson to Adams Middle School, an eight hundred-student magnet school drawing students from across Bayside. Although her transition to middle school was somewhat scary, she had no trouble making friends and adapting to the new environment. While participating in Adams's afterschool program during sixth and seventh grades, she relished the time to complete her homework. Ana remained a strong student and continued to draw on her family for encouragement and support.

As an eighth grader, Ana joined Students Together—a twice-weekly extracurricular program that trained young people to become civic leaders—because she enjoyed staying after school for activities and wanted to help out in her community. She really liked the program, partly because of the opportunity to be active in local affairs but primarily for the "really great people" she met through participating.

Teresa was born and raised in a mobile home park in the industrial area of Bayside. A self-described "shy and nerdy" child, she had a good experience at Harrison Elementary and participated in a variety of afterschool activities. She learned so much in school, "not only about regular school, but just being with the people." In her down time she enjoyed playing with friends from her neighborhood, ice skating, and spending time with her family.

When Teresa transitioned to Adams Middle School as a sixth grader, academics continued to come easily, but the social aspects of school grew increasingly difficult. Her fellow students were "annoying" and "mean," so much that she did not want to go to school at all. As often as her parents would permit, Teresa stayed home and pretended to be sick. Outside school, however, she continued to enjoy the company of her family and neighborhood friends.

As an eighth grader, Teresa joined Students Together because "it sounded like a cool program" and a "positive place to be," and, for her, it really was. Adult staff members made her feel cared about, and Students Together became a place where she felt she belonged. Her confidence multiplied, and her college ambitions strengthened.

Maria attended preschool in Mexico before moving to the United States. Soon after arriving in California, her parents separated. Maria grew up with her mother, moving frequently between different homes, changing schools nearly every year, and subsisting below the poverty line. She witnessed her mother surviving violence and abuse at every turn. Bright but uninterested in academics, Maria had little ambition.

When Maria began at Adams Middle School her sixth-grade year, she fell in with the wrong crowd. According to Maria, "My sixth-grade year I was a little troublemaker in school. I would always be in fights with other people—girls and guys." With each passing year, Maria crept closer to gang involvement and pregnancy. Her grades were poor, and she felt little connection to school. By the beginning of eighth grade she was on the verge of dropping out.

When she heard a presentation encouraging eighth graders to apply to Students Together, she believed the program would offer her an opportunity to make a change in her life for the better. Her older friends had moved on to high school, and she was ready to "expand herself in a different way." The adult staff members inspired Maria, the diverse peer group taught her to see the world in new ways, and the leadership opportunities helped her discover her passion for social justice advocacy.

Research has shown that participation in organized out-of-school time activities is associated with an array of benefits, and Ana, Teresa, and Maria are examples of this trend. But how exactly do such programs influence participants' educational trajectories? And why do programs seem to matter for some students more than others? Can the differential outcomes be traced to the preexisting attitudes and experiences of those who choose to participate, or does the act of participation contribute uniquely to students' trajectories? By drawing on in-depth interviews with former participants in a high-quality extracurricular program at an urban California middle school, this book takes a longitudinal look at structured out-of-school time activity participation in the lives of Mexican American youth.

Very little research has been conducted on the experiences of Mexican American students in out-of-school time programs and, in particular, how those experiences might influence their educational pathways over time. Existing large-scale longitudinal studies of academic attainment collect only limited measures of extracurricular participation (Vandell et al. 2015). Meanwhile, Mexican American students tend to have limited access to organized activities and participate at lower rates than their peers (Covay and Carbonaro 2010; Dumais 2006; Simpkins et al. 2011). Yet as the proportion of Mexican American children in our public schools continues to rise and the importance of organized activities for school success continues to increase, practitioners, policymakers, and researchers will require a better understanding of how such programs might influence educational attainment.

Through an in-depth longitudinal look into former participants' lives across school, home, and community contexts, this book not only illuminates the processes through which out-of-school time participation is associated with improved educational outcomes, but it also highlights the complex reasons why some adolescents benefit more than others. All of the young people profiled in this study attended the same middle school, and five to seven years later all attend a higher education institution of some kind. Yet each participant's path to college was unique, including substantial variation in family support, peer influences, teacher interventions, and extracurricular participation. Participation did not work in the same way for all students, nor should we expect uniform results. For some adolescents—both high and low achievers—program participation did not significantly alter their predicted pathway. Already successful students opted for additional enrichment opportunities and continued along their road to college. Struggling teens got drawn in by guidance counselors or parental mandate, yet they still dropped out of school or got in trouble with the law. For some adolescents, however, program participation became a life-changing experience. While existing studies of out-of-school time posit that participation is universally beneficial, the case study of the Students Together program presented in this book instead spotlights variation in the ways an extracurricular program might influence adolescents' educational trajectories.

Building on a detailed exploration of how and why this influence varies, *Why Afterschool Matters* sounds a call for more holistic considerations of the role of organized activities in adolescents' lives. This book highlights three factors that interact to explain the differential impact associated with Students Together: the strength and nature of the relationships students have outside the program, the multiple school and community structures they are embedded in, and personal agency. I argue that researchers, practitioners, and policymakers must take into account the complex individual and structural factors contributing to varied outcomes as we consider the powerful ways through which out-of-school time programming can influence students' pathways to college.

Students Together

Since the widespread advent of community-based out-of-school time programs in the early 1900s, disadvantaged urban youth have been viewed by philanthropists and policymakers as problems to be fixed (Halpern 2003). A sea change in the late 1980s, spurred in part by a Carnegie Corporation report titled *A Matter of Time: Risk and Opportunity in the Nonschool Hours* (1992), reoriented the purpose of organized activities toward offering positive youth development opportunities—helping keep kids out of trouble rather than intervening after the fact (Eccles and Gootman 2002).

Proponents expanded these goals to emphasize the potential contribution engaged young people could make to community affairs (Pittman et al. 2003), and philanthropic funders followed suit (Kwon 2013).

The Students Together program grew out of this movement. Founded in 2000 as a partnership between Adams Middle School and a nearby university, Students Together was an afterschool youth leadership program for eighth-grade students. Program activities focused on teaching communication and interpersonal skills, critical reflection, and positive involvement in school and community affairs. The program year was divided into three curricular units, each building on the previous unit. In the first unit, students learned communication skills, such as active listening, debate, decision making, compromise, and group facilitation. In the next unit, participants developed and deepened their concepts of leadership by thinking critically about their personal leadership style, strengths and areas for growth, and the broader purpose of leadership. In the final unit, participants designed and implemented research and action projects, which began by thinking critically about challenges in their community and identifying research questions. They subsequently employed social science research methods—such as surveys, interviews, and focus groups—to gather data, analyze findings, and develop recommendations. While focusing explicitly on youth leadership, Students Together also sought to impart a strong of sense of efficacy and potential, while building a culture of respect and belonging.

On any given Tuesday at 3:36 p.m., the door to room 211 at Adams Middle School was propped open and a warm breeze wafted in. The open-air corridors, typical of California schools, bustled with the shrieks and footsteps of young people just released from classes and shuffling to catch their rides or jostling to keep up with friends. Amid the chaos, fifteen eighth graders stepped into room 211, dumped their backpacks and, newly unburdened from the weight of the day, ambled over to inspect the snack options. Munching on pretzels or Sun Chips or apples, some students lounged on the well-worn couches while others, reliving the events of the day, continued to bounce and chatter. Carolina and other staff members—primarily students from the nearby university—mingled, inquiring about upcoming school events and checking in on life at home.

Every meeting proceeded in the same manner. Once all the participants had arrived and enjoyed a few minutes to snack, chat, and decompress, Carolina invited everyone to come together in a circle. Some students dove for spots on the couch while others pulled up chairs from disparate corners of the room. The classroom had no desks, and the walls were adorned with posters proclaiming the group's behavioral agreements, photos of Students Together participants at a recent retreat, and artwork created by the students. Carolina welcomed the group, pointed out the agenda on the whiteboard, and called on one student to read aloud the group agreements and the agenda.

First, opening circle time set the tone for the session and connected students to the lesson of the day through personal reflection. One at a time, each participant shared an opinion or experience on a given topic. For instance, as part of a session on communication, the facilitator asked students to share a rule they strongly favored or disliked. The opening circle was followed by a team-building activity. On this day, Carolina pretended to be an alien and had the students give her step-by-step directions for making a peanut-butter-and-jelly sandwich. The group expressed frustration at having to relay even the smallest details, like how to open the jelly jar and which end of the knife to use, and the conversation seamlessly shifted to the difficulty of engaging in good communication. The main lesson considered the role of debate in decision making. The group began by watching a clip of a presidential debate and then divided into teams to enact their own debate on the pros or cons of wearing matching socks. After a lively deliberation, the students debriefed the experience. How could the speakers have been more effective? What did they do well? Each session ended the way it began, with a group circle. The closing question asked students to share how debate might be applicable to their daily lives with family and friends. After everyone had a chance to share, Carolina thanked the students for their participation and offered a sneak peek at the next session.

The group met for ninety minutes, twice each week, and sessions were kept interactive through a combination of games, movement, discussion, and reflection. For example, participants often used a fist-to-five voting system, where each student held up one to five fingers to show how strongly they felt about a topic. Alternately, students might have weighed in on hot topics by placing stickers on a large piece of butcher paper next to ideas they supported. Sometimes facilitators used sticky notes to gather feedback from less vocal students. Sometimes they called for a snowball fight, where students wrote an idea on a piece of paper, wadded it up, and tossed it into the air. Each student then picked up a snowball and read aloud what one of their peers had written. At any point in a session, group leaders might have asked everyone to stop what they were doing and say something positive to the person standing next to them. Each session was organized around a concrete leadership skill or disposition, while each session also sought to engage a diverse audience of participants and maintain an affirming, empowering, and constructive environment. By the end of their year in the program, participants would have decided on an issue to work together to address. One cohort researched students' experiences of bullying and stereotyping at Adams and presented the findings to school leaders. They made several recommendations, including a peer mediation program and teacher training in positive classroom management. Other cohorts addressed other issues, such as the cleanliness and physical appearance of their school and the need for youth hangout spaces in the community.

Ana, Teresa, and Maria were members of the first three cohorts to participate in the Students Together program, between 2000 and 2003. In 2008, I sought to track down former participants—now young adults—to find out what had become of them after their year in the program.

After their eighth-grade year was over, Ana, Teresa, and Maria went their separate ways. At the end of Ana's eighth-grade year, her mother died. The death took a toll on the family. During high school, Ana's father, who was often working, assigned Ana and her sister responsibility for all household chores. As a sophomore, Ana got a part-time job. Although she did not participate in afterschool activities in high school, she joined two lunchtime clubs, one for community service and the other a support group for politically conscious Latinas.

Upon graduation, Ana enrolled at a local community college while working full-time. During this time she learned she was pregnant. She took one term off from school while she gave birth to and cared for her child. Two months later, she returned to working days and going to school at night, while leaving her baby in the care of her aunt. After two years of taking classes she was still unsure of her major, but she enjoyed attending college and maintained a commitment to eventually attaining a bachelor's degree. As a college student, Ana's recollections of Students Together had faded. She remembered liking the program because she got to help the community, meet new people, and work on a project, but she had no recollection of the project and no lasting ties to the program.

After eighth grade, Teresa opted to attend a different high school from her middle school peers in order to have a fresh start socially. Again, academics came easily. Now, for the first time, the social aspects of school were less daunting. Outside school, Teresa spent most of her time volunteering—at the senior center, the public library, or Students Together. Starting in her sophomore year, Teresa also worked part-time. After graduating from high school, Teresa moved into her own apartment and enrolled in community college to pursue a degree in nursing. She liked nursing because, as in many of her high school activities, "you get to help people." Two years out of high school, Teresa was halfway through the nursing program and ready to transfer to a four-year university to complete her degree. She worked full-time and continued to volunteer every week.

For Teresa, Students Together stood out as a turning point and as the one part of middle school where she felt as if she belonged. Thanks to the supportive environment and adult staff members, she started to become more outgoing and confident, a trend that continued throughout her high school and college years.

For Maria, Students Together connected her with resources and relationships that pointed her in a new direction. As a high school student, Maria continued to participate as a mentor in Students Together and through her continued ties to the program she had the opportunity to travel to national youth development conferences. She also volunteered as a tutor for elementary school children and cofounded a support group for Latinas. Maria reflected, "If I didn't keep going in Students Together, I would be a different person right now. I have a lot of friends who are in jail, some of my friends are pregnant and they have babies, some are married already." As an eighth grader, Maria was on the same path. Instead, by the time she graduated from high school Maria had earned a prestigious community leadership award and a college scholarship. Two years later, she was sharing an apartment with a friend, working full-time, and attending community college.

For Maria, Students Together brought about an academic and personal transformation. Over the course of the year, she went from the verge of dropping out to achievement as a star student. Maria's commitment to her education prompted her teachers and peers to begin to see her differently and put her on a pathway to becoming a college graduate.

Though Ana, Teresa, and Maria all enjoyed participating in the same extracurricular program as eighth graders, five to seven years later each remembered different aspects of the experience. Ana remembered Students Together positively—even calling it the best "one of those programs" in which she took part. Over the long run, however, her own dedication and aptitude coupled with support from friends and family carried her through school and onto higher education, in spite of tragedy and complications. For Teresa, her academic aptitude, attitudes toward college, and support from home placed her on a college path before joining Students Together. Yet participation made an impression on Teresa that was distinguishable from other experiences, primarily because the positive environment and relationships with adult leaders influenced her sense of self. For Maria, participation had a transformative influence; while Students Together did not single-handedly change her life, the skill-building, peer networks, and relationships with adults began a cascade of opportunities that helped shift her path from gang involvement to college.

Ana, Teresa, and Maria each benefited from participating in Students Together, yet they benefited in different ways and to different degrees. Their stories illuminate the ways that variation in adolescents' family, peer, and community support systems, as well as their personalities and interests, leave different openings for organized activities to influence their educational trajectories. By examining multiple contexts over an extended period of time, this book documents the distinct differences among the roles Students Together played for each participant. Building on a critical examination of the Students Together program, this book suggests a new framework for understanding the relationship between extracurricular participation and academic attainment by depicting that relationship as predicated on preexisting resources and supports and having the potential to alter future availability of resources and supports through new attitudes, behaviors, and social networks.

Educational Inequality and Shifting US Demographics

Latino/a youth are one of the fastest growing segments of the US population. Between 1997 and 2013, the number of Latino/a students in public schools nearly doubled (Krogstad and Fry 2014). Currently one in four school children is Latino/a, and by 2036 this number is predicted to rise to one in three. The rapid growth of the Latino/a population is especially pronounced in California where Latino/as already constitute 51 percent of all K–12 students and 38 percent of the overall population (Pew Research Center 2011).

Given these projected numbers, the strength of the US economy will increasingly depend on Latino/as in the decades ahead—and on their school achievement. During the last century, a marked shift has amplified the level of education necessary to compete in the US job market. In 1900, only 6 percent of American youth finished high school (Mondale and Patton 2001). In 1973, 72 percent of all jobs required no more than a high school diploma. By 1992, this number had dropped to 44 percent, and by 2007, to 41 percent. Scholars estimate that by 2018, 63 percent of all jobs will require postsecondary education (Carnevale et al. 2011). Thus, America's ability to enable and prepare Latino/a students to attend college has captured public policy interest and growing national concern.

As of 2012, academic attainment among Latino/as lagged far behind that of other ethnic groups. The ways that racial categories have been socially constructed and structurally enforced has led to unequal educational attainment, particularly with regard to postsecondary outcomes. Only 75 percent of Latino/as ages twenty-five to twenty-nine have earned a high school diploma, compared with 89 percent of blacks and 95 percent of whites in the same age group (NCES 2013). Unlike their peers, Latino/a students may drop out of school even when they earn average grades and are not considered at-risk students (Fernandez and Shu 1988). Following high school, Latino/a students are more likely than whites to attend two-year colleges, decreasing the likelihood they will attain a bachelor's degree. As a result, the college completion gap is increasing even though Latino/a college enrollment is rising (National Research Council 2006b). Only 15 percent of Latino/as have earned a bachelor's degree, compared with 23 percent of blacks and 40 percent of whites (NCES 2013). Opening Latino/a students' pathways to college would increase their ability to contribute to and share in our national prosperity.

While Latino/as differ from other ethnic groups, especially with regard to rapid growth and regional concentration, significant socioeconomic and educational variation by national origin exists within the Latino/a population (Bean and Tienda 1987). Mexican Americans constitute two-thirds of the US Latino/a population and face the greatest educational challenges (Stanton-Salazar 2001; Valencia 2002; Valenzuela 1999). Mexican Americans drop out of school at nearly three times the rate of their Cuban American counterparts, score significantly lower on achievement tests than Cuban, Nicaraguan, and Colombian Americans, and exhibit the lowest college completion rate of all Latino/a students admitted to college

(Ream 2005). Some of these gaps can be attributed to the fact that, among adult immigrants to the United States in the 1990s, 86 percent coming from South America had a high school degree compared to 44 percent of those from Mexico (Lowell and Suro 2002).

Ethnicity and class interact to create even larger challenges for many Latino/as, as well as other economically and culturally marginalized students. Socioeconomic status predicts educational outcomes more strongly than place of birth, native language, or family headship (Bean and Tienda 1987). Contemporary US society places a premium on reasoning, assertive action, and negotiation skills. Annette Lareau (2003) argued that students benefit from being raised in the culture of the middle class where they learn that they are special, that their opinions matter, and that adults should adjust situations to meet children's wishes. Disadvantaged youth must find ways to accumulate the institutional advantages that come more easily to middle-class children.

For decades past and continuing into the early twenty-first century, educators, policy analysts, and researchers have sought to pinpoint the causes of the academic attainment gap between low-income students of color, including Latino/as, and their middle-class white peers (Coleman et al. 1966; Kao and Thompson 2003). Competing and complementary explanations exist, but no theory yet predicts why many disadvantaged students follow national patterns of low achievement while others buck the trend.

Extracurricular Activities and Educational Outcomes

Myriad studies point to the perpetuated problems and potential solutions found within the public school system, such as recent attention to the Common Core initiative or class-size reduction; such research, however, largely ignores the fact that young people spend only 25 percent of their waking hours on schoolwork (Larson and Verma 1999). While the best teachers are able to go beyond the basic cognitive tasks of schooling and work to meet children's physical, social, and emotional needs, more often these requirements must be attended to outside the school day. After-school programs, summer camps, and other extracurricular activities seek to supplement formal schooling by emphasizing multiple aspects of adolescents' development. Out-of-school time programs are free from the pressures of standardized testing, report cards, and mandated attendance, and they are often more active, team-oriented, and creative than the traditional school day (Vandell et al. 2015). Many studies of academic success among disadvantaged students touch on the role of extracurricular activities but focus the bulk of their argument on school and home life (e.g., Gandara and Contreras 2009; Perez 2012). Accounting for the influences of non-school settings could be a critical factor to understanding pathways to college among Mexican Americans and other disadvantaged youth.

Organized activities have been associated with benefits for participants both in and out of school. Studies link participation to numerous positive outcomes, including increased academic achievement (Broh 2002; Durlak, Weissberg, and Pachan 2010; Lauer et al. 2006; Schreiber and Chambers 2002), lower drop-out rates (Mahoney 2000; Mahoney and Cairns 1997), and psychosocial improvements such as stronger self-image, positive social development, and reductions in risk-taking behavior (Durlak, Weissberg, and Pachan 2010; Eccles et al. 2003; Gordon, Bridglall, and Meroe 2005). Involvement in out-of-school time programs is also associated with positive school-related attitudes and behaviors such as school connectedness and reduced truancy and delinquency (Darling, Caldwell, and Smith 2005; Durlak, Weissberg, and Pachan 2010; Fredricks and Eccles 2006a, 2006b; Jordan and Nettles 2000; Thompson et al. 2006). The more time students spend in organized activities—both within a given week or year (intensity) and across multiple years (duration)—the larger the benefits become (Bohnert and Gardner 2007; Darling, Caldwell, and Smith 2005; Dotterer, McHale, and Crouter 2007; Fredricks 2012; Gardner, Roth, and Brooks-Gunn 2009; Mahoney, Cairns, and Farmer 2003; Mahoney, Harris, and Eccles 2006; Mahoney and Vest 2012; Zaff et al. 2003).

Although whether a program is school- or community-based has not been linked with differential youth outcomes (Gardner, Roth, and Brooks-Gunn 2009), the nature of the program appears to matter. Different types of activities provide qualitatively different experiences for participants. For example, sports stand out as settings with high rates of initiative-taking experiences, emotional regulation experiences, and stress (Larson, Hansen, and Moneta 2006). Arts activities facilitate spontaneity, creativity, and social unity (Shernoff and Vandell 2008). Further, different activities are associated with different educational outcomes (Barber, Eccles, and Stone 2001; Fredricks and Eccles 2005; Hansen, Larson, and Dworkin 2003).

In particular, studies have examined the impact of high school sports and have found that participation is linked with better grades and test scores (Broh 2002; Hanson and Kraus 1998). Ralph McNeal (1995) found that, once all kinds of extracurricular participation are controlled for, only sport participation is significantly related to a reduced risk of dropping out of high school. The few empirical studies that have investigated whether the effects of activity participation are moderated by race and ethnicity have focused on sports, and they tell a different story. Longitudinal studies of black and Latino/a high school students have found no evidence that sports participation improves grades, test scores, or college-going behaviors (Melnick, Sabo, and Vanfossen 1992a, 1992b; Sabo, Melnick, and Vanfossen 1993; Spreitzer 1994). Kathleen Miller and her colleagues (2005) found that black adolescents who identified themselves as "jocks" reported lower grades than those who did not. Rather than acquiring valuable knowledge and skills from sports participation, black and Latino/a adolescents seem to be impacted by the pervasive cultural stereotypes regarding "dumb jocks."

For other types of school-based activities, the evidence is mixed. Beckett Broh (2002) examined nationally representative National Education Longitudinal Study of 1988 data and found that, in addition to sports, school music group participation was associated with consistent positive effects on grades and test scores. Student council, drama club, and yearbook or journalism clubs were linked with limited benefits, and participation in intramural sports and vocational clubs was linked with impaired academic achievement. Christy Lleras (2008) examined the same dataset and found that participation in academic or sports activities, but not fine arts, was related to greater educational attainment and higher earnings ten years later. Fine arts participation was related to lower earnings, except for in the case of minority students, who had higher earnings ten years out. On the contrary, Jacquelynne Eccles and her colleagues (2003) examined Michigan Study of Adolescent and Adult Life Transitions data (primarily white, middle-class and working-class respondents) and found that all activity types were related to better educational outcomes in young adulthood, but only sports and academic clubs were related to higher occupational status. In sum, studies agree that activity type matters, yet different datasets yield varying accounts of exactly how these differences play out. Part of this lack of clarity may be attributed to the fact that many adolescents participate in more than one type of activity, either simultaneously or in succession.

Because students become hypernetworked into organized activities, it is important to examine participation in different kinds of activities simultaneously to understand the effects of specific activity types (Quiroz, Flores-González, and Frank 1996). Breadth of participation—the variety of different types of activities an individual participates in during a year—has been linked to positive development over time (Bohnert and Garber 2007; Busseri et al. 2006; Busseri and Rose-Krasnor 2009; Denault and Poulin 2009; Fredricks and Eccles 2006a, 2006b; Rose-Krasnor et al. 2006). Participation in a breadth of activities may benefit adolescents by either exposing them to qualitatively different experiences in each activity and thus accumulating a wider repertoire of skills and competencies or by weaving a wider network of peers and adults who provide access to social capital (Bohnert, Fredricks, and Randall 2010; Eccles and Barber 1999; Hansen, Larson, and Dworkin 2003; McGee et al. 2006).

Amy Feldman and Jennifer Matjasko's (2005) review of the literature on out-of-school time activities called for researchers to distinguish whether benefits of participation breadth stem from a larger number of activities or from participation across activity types. To explore this question, researchers have used cluster analyses to examine the relationship between participation patterns and educational outcomes. In a general sense, cluster analyses seek to group a set of objects (in this case students) in such a way that objects in the same group—or cluster—are more similar to each other than to those in other groups. Feldman and Matjasko (2007) used data on structured activity participation from the National Longitudinal Study of Adolescent to Adult Health to identify six clusters of participants. The authors concluded that multiple-activity participants tended to be a unique and high-functioning group, thus underscoring the theory that participation across activity types may garner additional benefits. Their study, however, lumped together all multiple-activity participants, regardless of the activities in which they participated, such that a student who participated in her school's soccer and softball teams would be grouped into the same cluster as a student who was part of the French club and the yearbook committee. In addition, this study was cross-sectional, descriptive, and did not explore links between the variety of activities students participated in and long-term educational outcomes. Using data from the Panel Study of Income Dynamics, Miriam Linver, Jodie Roth, and Jeanne Brooks-Gunn (2009) distinguished between sports and other types of activities and came to similar conclusions: those who participated in sports demonstrated more favorable outcomes than those who did not participate in any activities, but less favorable outcomes than those who participated in sports alongside other activities. In their analysis of Educational Longitudinal Study of 2002 data, which includes both structured and unstructured out-of-school time pursuits, Billie Gastic and I (2009) found five clusters of activity participation. Each cluster or "activity portfolio" was linked with different educational outcomes. This study showed an important finding: not only is breadth of activity participation important, but also each specific combination of activities can be linked with different short-term outcomes.

Overall, studies of the relationship between structured extracurricular participation and academic outcomes show a generally positive relationship with regard to a range of short- and long-term indicators. Studies further indicate that type of activity and combination of activity types seem to matter, but researchers have yet to unravel the ways that distinct "participation portfolios" relate to long-term academic attainment. Instead of further detailing links between specific activity combinations and educational outcomes, this book draws on the Relational Developmental Systems paradigm (Lerner et al. 2015) to argue that even considering "participation portfolios" may be too limited of a lens for understanding the influence of organized activities on students' trajectories. Rather, this book outlines a comprehensive framework that highlights variation according to individual and contextual factors.

Extracurricular Activities and Social Reproduction

Studies show that participation in extracurricular programs correlates with positive academic and social outcomes for all adolescents, not just youth from families with high incomes who usually do better in school. Pierre Bourdieu (1986) argued that youth who participate in structured out-of-school time activities accrue cultural capital that they can subsequently employ to garner educational rewards. Bourdieu and Jean-Claude Passeron define cultural capital as "the educational norms of those social classes capable of imposing the . . . criteria of evaluation which are the most favorable to their children" (as cited in Lareau and Weininger 2003, 588). In other words, any piece of knowledge or set of skills that gets systematically rewarded by dominant institutions can act as cultural capital. The competencies most likely to be rewarded are those shared by the people in charge of doling out rewards, and thus they shift with the educational norms of the powerful classes. In recent decades, participation in organized activities has been systematically rewarded by dominant educational institutions, namely in the form of college admissions (Kaufman and Gabler 2004; Stevens 2007).

Yet students do not participate in extracurricular programs at the same rate across socioeconomic lines. Privileged youth are more likely than their peers to participate in nearly all types of organized activities, in greater numbers of activities, and with greater frequency, due to increased opportunities to participate and resources to support participation—such as fees, transportation, flexibility in parents' work schedules, and leisure time (Bennett, Lutz, and Jayaram 2012; Bouffard et al. 2006; Chin and Phillips 2004; Flores-González 2002; Laughlin 2013; Valenzuela 1999). Over and above financial resources, mother's education has been linked with large increases in time spent participating and expenditures on organized activities (Weininger, Lareau, and Conley 2015). Through enhanced access to and participation in extracurricular activities, privileged youth accumulate more cultural capital than their disadvantaged peers (Lareau 2003). The gains in cultural capital associated with participation thus serve to translate social background and class position into academic attainment. When disadvantaged youth participate, however, they demonstrate even greater benefits than their privileged peers (Camp 1990; Covay and Carbonaro 2010; Dumais 2008; Gerber 1996; Holloway 2000; Marsh and Kleitman 2002; Morris 2015). Thus, if disadvantaged students can gain access to and participate in such activities, the cultural capital gained from participation can begin to narrow the academic attainment gap.

Furthermore, students do not participate in organized activities at the same rates across racial and ethnic lines. Across most activities, whites are overrepresented, and Latino/as are underrepresented (Bouffard et al. 2006; Covay and Carbonaro 2010; Dumais 2006; Simpkins et al. 2011). Although there is little research on why participation rates differ, researchers speculate that racial and ethnic group differences may result from some of the same factors driving socioeconomic gaps as well as linguistic and cultural differences between families and program providers (Bouffard et al. 2006; Simpkins et al. 2013).

Because of the ways that some minorities—particularly blacks and Latino/as—have been systematically disadvantaged by dominant institutions across US history, these groups have generally had fewer opportunities to acquire education-related cultural capital. Returning to Bourdieu's conceptualization, one important attribute of cultural capital is that "these specialized skills are transmissible across generations, are subject to monopoly, and may yield advantages or profits" (Lareau and Weininger 2003, 597). In other words, those who have gathered the skills and dispositions valued by dominant institutions are likely to pass them on to their children. Those who have been excluded from acquiring these skills have to look to sources outside their families to learn the competencies rewarded by educational institutions. Based on this theory, black and Latino/a youth who accumulated cultural capital through participation in extracurricular activities would be more likely to succeed than their coethnic peers and may achieve on par with white students who are more likely to acquire cultural capital at home. In their reviews of the literature, however, Feldman and Matjasko (2005, 2012) and Deborah Lowe Vandell and her colleagues (2015) have noted a gap in research examining how adolescents' racial and ethnic characteristics moderate their experiences in organized activities.

Researchers largely treat out-of-school time programs as black boxes, neglecting to explore or explain their internal workings (Fredricks and Eccles 2005; Hansen, Larson, and Dworkin 2003; Larson, Hansen, and Moneta 2006). To fill this gap in knowledge requires understanding the processes through which such programs influence student trajectories in order to tease apart how and why participation is associated with benefits for students.

Evidence of successful practices is only beginning to emerge. Adult relationships with young people act as one pivotal force (Larson and Hansen 2005; Larson and Walker 2006; Larson, Walker, and Pearce 2005). Staff members in extracurricular programs often cater to smaller groups of students and can thus demand higher standards than classroom teachers. Personal attention from staff members fosters feelings of safety, engagement in program activities, and better work habits, thus increasing efficacy and raising educational aspirations (American Youth Policy Forum 2004; Bodilly and Beckett 2005; Pierce, Bolt, and Vandell 2010; Rutten et al. 2008). By cultivating a culture of youth input and actively monitoring task management, staff members can further facilitate student empowerment (Larson et al. 2004). Relationships with peers matter, too. Positive interactions between program participants not only foster a sense of belonging and encourage program attendance, but they have also been associated with a growing list of desirable developmental outcomes (Blazevski and Smith 2007; Kataoka and Vandell 2013; Simpkins, Eccles, and Becnel 2008).

Additionally, structural elements have been linked with positive outcomes. In a meta-analysis of sixty-eight studies conducted between 1980 and 2007, Joseph Durlak, Roger Weissberg, and Molly Pachan (2010) found that participation in programming that was sequenced, active, focused, and explicitly targeted toward specific personal or social skills was associated with larger effect sizes for positive social behaviors, higher academic achievement, and school bonding. Other studies have suggested that particular program features—such as youth leadership opportunities, chances to reflect and set goals, and projects that engage participants in a sequence of work over time—encourage the acquisition of life skills such as teamwork, communication, and problem-solving (American Youth Policy Forum 2004; Blazevski and Smith 2007; Larson and Angus 2011; Salusky et al. 2014).

The voluntary nature of many out-of-school time programs may also empower youth. Research has shown that while in school, students report high concentration and low intrinsic motivation; during unstructured leisure time, students report low concentration and high intrinsic motivation. Students only report high motivation and concentration simultaneously while participating in structured voluntary activities (Csikszentmihalyi and Larson 1984; Larson and Kleiber 1993; Vandell et al. 2005). The unique environment of extracurricular programs engages students' hearts and minds, thus encouraging internal motivation in the context of developmentally appropriate structures and healthy adult relationships (Shernoff 2013).

In sum, a growing body of research has documented the benefits of involvement in structured out-of-school time activities, and evidence of the processes through which these benefits are achieved is starting to emerge. The majority of these studies, however, fail to consider the ways that the experience of extracurricular participation varies across participants—by relevant social categories such as race and social class, but also in terms of other differences (Vandell et al. 2015). Socioeconomic status, race, gender, and academic achievement are most often used as control variables or occasionally as moderating variables. In other words, researchers have yet to tackle the ways that participation does not influence all students equally, especially over time.

Furthermore, existing studies do not consider the ways that participation is facilitated and constrained by the lived realities of adolescents' family, school, and neighborhood conditions. Regular participation requires free time—time not already committed to paid work or family responsibilities, such as caring for siblings—and parental consent. Participation also requires reliable and safe transportation and often fees or specialized equipment. In addition, the activity must fit the student's tastes and interests, and interactions with peers and adults must feel welcoming. Such contextual factors impact not only why adolescents choose to become involved with an activity but also why they do or do not stay involved and how the program impacts their academic outcomes (Casey, Ripke, and Huston 2005; Hultsman 1992; Simpkins, Fredricks, and Eccles 2012). Expanding our framework for understanding the relationships between extracurricular participation and educational attainment to take into account these contextual factors—before, during, and after participation—will be critical to improving academic attainment among marginalized students.

Extracurricular Activities in the Context of the Life Course

The Relational Developmental Systems paradigm now prevalent in developmental science emphasizes "that the basic process of human development involves mutually influential relations between the developing individual and the multiple levels of his or her changing context" (Lerner et al. 2015, 608; Overton 2015). In other words, at every moment adolescents are embedded in a wide variety of overlapping settings, ranging from microlevel relationships with parents or friends to macrolevel political economies. Neither are these settings static, nor are young people passive recipients of their environments. Rather, both individuals and settings change in reaction to one another and over time, such that the individual-context relationship is bidirectional and reciprocal. Research within this paradigm explores the processes that regulate exchanges between individuals and their layered and changing contexts and seeks to hone in on those individual-context relationships that are mutually beneficial.

Under the umbrella of the relational developmental systems paradigm, life course theory brings together ecological systems theory (Bronfenbrenner 1979; Bronfenbrenner and Morris 2006) with a temporal approach (Elder 1974), to highlight the ways that biography, history, and social contexts impact development over time. In contrast to psychological approaches that parse out distinct facets of the developing individual, such as emotion, cognition, or motivation, life course theory views each person as a dynamic whole playing an active role in his or her own development (Elder, Shanahan, and Jennings 2015). As we experience personal agency, our choices are constrained by the pathways made available by historical and social circumstances. Social pathways, a key concept in life course theory, are defined as age-graded sequences of social positions that reflect the macro- and microlevel contexts of development.

Developmental psychologists have often used Urie Bronfenbrenner's ecological systems theory (1979) and expanded bioecological theory (Bronfenbrenner and Morris 2006) as a framework for examining the role of organized activities in human development (Vandell et al. 2015). Ecological approaches to development argue that context matters. Early iterations of the theory positioned the individual at the center of four contextual layers—much like the smallest piece in a set of Russian nesting dolls— that all play a key role in development. The first layer—the microsystem—refers to face-to-face settings where a young person spends time, such that each extracurricular program (e.g., chess club) comprises a distinct microsystem, as does every other face-to-face setting that individual encounters (e.g., family, school). The next layers contain connections between microsystems, with mesosystems comprised of linkages between settings that include the student, and exosystems comprised of linkages between microsystems where one does not include the student. For example, parents' work schedules may impact participation owing to the availability of transportation. These three layers of context are all nested within a macrosystem, which is comprised of societal beliefs and values.

Recent iterations of ecological theory, recognizing more than just context, argue that development is the product of multiple layers of context interacting with person, process, and time (Bronfenbrenner and Morris 2006). Person refers to individual-level characteristics, including social identities such as age and race, and developmental traits like temperament and personality. Process refers to individuals' experiences within a microsystem or the ways that person and context transact. In the case of extracurricular activities, this includes interpersonal interactions with peers and adults, engagement in activities, the availability of resources, and the roles or identities youth take on (Vandell and Posner 1999; Vandell, Pierce, and Dadisman 2005). Finally, time refers to minute-by-minute exposure to processes within microsystems, duration of participation in a given microsystem, and historical changes in society across generations.

Research on organized activities, framed by ecological perspectives, has focused on features and processes within the microsystem of a particular activity or genre of activities and on the connections between activity participation and other settings, primarily school and home. Studies have also begun to investigate the role of time, in terms of intensity and duration of participation, and macrolevel factors, such as ethnicity and culture. Yet the ecological approach fails to situate adolescents' experiences in organized activities within biographical context.

Life course theory brings together Bronfenbrenner's conception of multilevel social context with sociological understandings of the life course as a pattern of age-graded events and roles. Life course theory positions development as a lifelong process situated in historical time and place and driven in part by human agency. This framework draws attention to the ways that the timing of particular events and transitions drives cumulative effects by underlining the importance of transitions (exit from one role and entry into another) and turning points (marked shifts into new behavioral patterns). While focusing on the ways macro- and microlevel factors shape social pathways (i.e., context) and individuals' behaviors and achievements over time shape their own trajectories, life course theory also recognizes the ways relationships with significant others influence development. Specifically, the principle of "linked lives" highlights how social networks exert informal social control and how intergenerational transmissions contribute to the social reproduction of education, occupation, and beliefs.

Such constructs may be useful for understanding the influence of extracurricular participation on educational attainment over time. Not only are organized activities dynamic microsystems that influence short-term indicators of development, but they are also contexts shaping and shaped by macrolevel social forces, interacting with other microsystems, and intertwined with prior and forthcoming events in each individual's biography. The analysis in this book goes beyond locating, within a particular context, the features and processes that matter while investigating how participation features in the broader arc of individual development over time and contributes to or interrupts the accumulated experiences shaping students' educational trajectories.

Study Setting and Research Methods

The purpose of this book is to map out a theoretical framework for understanding and studying the relationship between extracurricular participation and educational attainment among Mexican American students and other marginalized youth. As Barney Glaser and Anselm Strauss (1967) argued, the intimate connection with empirical reality permits the development of relevant and valid theory. To account for how and why out-of-school time programs influence adolescents differently, I have undertaken an intensive case study of former participants in a single high-quality program. This method allows me to present detailed contextual information on young people's lives while focusing on thick description and developments over time. Rather than aiming for broad generalizability, this exploratory research digs deep within adolescents' life histories to unpack the black box of extracurricular participation and identify the processes through which program participation is associated with student outcomes. Furthermore, such rich contextual data exposes the factors that explain why a program may play different roles for different students.

Following the grounded theory approach, I selected a theoretically useful case for this study. I chose the Students Together program because it has been recognized as a high-quality urban extracurricular program, serving predominantly—though not exclusively—Mexican American students. To have the best chance of observing the processes through which a program might be associated with students' pathways to college it was important to study a high-quality program. Moreover, I selected a program that minimized many reasons why Latino/a youth often choose not to participate in organized activities. Specifically, Students Together served students who were too young to work legally outside the home, the school (where meetings were held) was easily accessible by public transportation, and the program charged no fees and did not require specialized equipment. Rather, Students Together paid students a small stipend for regular attendance. Finally, in accordance with research showing that cultural fit is important for youth from marginalized groups (Ginwright 2010; Kwon 2008; Riggs et al. 2010), Students Together was designed by recognized Positive Youth Development (PYD) practitioners with Latino/a students in mind. The program consistently employed adult leaders who were fluent in Spanish and English and were knowledgeable about the local community. Although the school where the program was based served a largely Latino/a student body, the surrounding community was diverse.

At the time I conducted follow-up interviews in 2008 approximately 75,000 people resided in Bayside, an urban community about thirty miles outside a large California city. Of the community's residents, slightly more than 50 percent identified as white, nearly 33 percent identified as Latino/a, and 9 percent identified as Asian or Asian American. Just under 10 percent of the residents were recent documented immigrants, mostly from Mexico and El Salvador. Meanwhile, 25 percent of the city's residents were children and teens, and only 6 percent of the population lived below the poverty line.

Adams Middle School (AMS) was a magnet school serving sixth, seventh, and eighth graders from neighborhoods throughout Bayside. The student population was not representative of the community as a whole; of the students, about 66 percent identified as Latino/a, 20 percent as white, and about 8 percent as Asian or Pacific Islander. Approximately 30 percent of the students were considered English language learners, and nearly 60 percent qualified for free or reduced-price meals. Although other schools in Bayside School District had been recognized for high marks on standardized tests, AMS's mean scores fell slightly below the state's target mean.

Students Together was a yearlong extracurricular program based at AMS. Started in 2000 as a partnership with a nearby university, the operations of the program were heavily influenced by the Positive Youth Development (PYD) movement. Though PYD programs take on many forms, all share a common allegiance to promoting normal socialization and healthy development (Eccles and Gootman 2002; Quinn 1999). The PYD approach emerged in reaction to decades of deficit-based prevention programs for at-risk youth. The deficit-based approach agreed with the psychological approach to adolescence espoused throughout most of the twentieth century. Beginning with G. Stanley Hall's turn-of-the-century theory of adolescence as a time of "storm and stress," psychologists characterized the teen years as a period during which young people were at risk for behaving in problematic ways and therefore designed programs to prevent problem behaviors, such as teen pregnancy or drug use.

In the 1980s, however, the PYD stance began to gain popularity among three often diverging groups: researchers, practitioners, and policymakers (Catalano et al. 2004). Developmental psychologists began to recognize the influences of multiple embedded contexts—family, school, community—on adolescent development (Lerner 2005). Neuroscientists found evidence of continued and plastic brain development throughout adolescence (Dahl 2005). Longitudinal program evaluations showed that problem behaviors in youth were highly correlated, and thus many of them could be prevented via the same interventions. Meanwhile, federal and state officials were struggling to address the needs of the rising proportion of American children with mothers in the labor force (Willer et al. 1991). Taken together, these findings heralded a call for programming geared to prevent a broad range of problems, instead of specific issue-based interventions (Catalano et al. 2004; Eccles and Gootman 2002; Larson 2000). In the years since, the PYD framework has continued to garner support as a guiding philosophy for community-based youth services.

Numerous scholars have published detailed descriptions of the PYD philosophy (e.g., Blum 2003; Lerner 2004; Roth and Brooks-Gunn 2003), and still more youth programs have adopted this approach (e.g., see Lerner et al. 2015). What exactly does the PYD framework entail? Perhaps the best-known description of the PYD philosophy comes from Jacquelynne Eccles and Jennifer Gootman's (2002) book, *Community Programs to Promote Youth Development,* based on the work of the National Academy of Sciences Committee on Community-Level Programs for Youth. In this volume, the committee identified four domains of individual assets that contribute to well-being in adolescence: physical, intellectual, emotional/psychological, and social development. Although positive development does not require that an individual possesses all of these assets, more assets are considered more beneficial. To develop these assets, young people need to be exposed to positive experiences, settings, and people and have opportunities to develop real-life skills. Rather than expecting a single program to provide all of these things, the committee called on communities to offer a range of programs that collectively offer young people the opportunity to develop all these assets. Within each program, however, physical and psychological safety, appropriate structure, and positive social norms pave the way for supportive relationships, belonging, skill building, and empowerment. In addition, this volume underlined the importance of programs operating in harmony with the efforts and perspectives of participants' families and communities. More recently, in line with ecological and life course perspectives, Kara Dukakis and her colleagues (2009) called for expanding the focus of the PYD approach beyond individual- and setting-level indicators to include system-level factors as well, such as opportunities for youth engagement in policymaking and broad accountability for youth development outcomes.

The Students Together program was launched in 2000, just as the PYD movement was gathering momentum. Drawing together the expertise of community youth development specialists and university-based social science researchers, Students Together was designed to teach social science research and advocacy skills in an environment that promoted teamwork, communication, and confidence. In program design and implementation, staff members prioritized positive social norms that encouraged youth empowerment, supportive relationships, and a sense of belonging. Each year, school and program staffs collaborated to select a cohort of about fifteen eighth graders to participate based on the following criteria: enthusiasm for the goals of the program, ability to get along with others, and diversity in terms of socioeconomic status, neighborhood, ethnicity, academic performance, and gender. After the pilot year, a handful of ninth-grade former participants were chosen to serve as mentors each year. Selection into the program was biased by both the above criteria and student interest and availability; however, because the program paid participants a small stipend each month instead of charging tuition or fees, many low-income youth were able to participate. In addition, the AMS campus was served by a countywide public transit system that provided students with affordable transportation. Although Students Together continues, this book focuses on the first three cohorts of participants.

To develop a case study of the ways that program participation played a role in students' educational trajectories over time, this book draws on interviews that were conducted with eighth-grade participants and high school mentors during their time in the program as well as in-depth life history interviews that I undertook five to seven years later (see Nelson 2010 for a detailed description of the qualitative life history protocol used). During their tenure in the program, participants were interviewed at least twice each year. In 2008, I spent a full year attempting to contact and interview all participants from the initial three cohorts via phone, e-mail, Facebook, MySpace, and word of mouth. Of the twenty-eight Mexican American youth in the first three cohorts, I was able to locate half and interview ten. Of the remaining fifteen participants, I was able to locate seven and interview two. Due to the longitudinal nature of this case study, I have only included respondents who were interviewed both in eighth grade and in young adulthood. In total, my analysis draws on fifty-two interviews with twelve former participants over a seven-year period. All quotations presented in this book have been taken from young adult interviews unless the text indicates otherwise. All names of individuals and organizations have been changed to protect confidentiality, and, in some cases, identifying details have also been modified.

Former participants were difficult to locate for a number of reasons. It was difficult to track down those whose parents had moved since participation and those whose parents were no longer in contact with their children. Some former participants had been deported or had landed in jail. In one instance, multiple interviewees cautioned me not to contact one of their peers given his deep involvement with gang violence. In addition, it became difficult to stay in contact with respondents if their cell phones operated on prepaid plans, as was common to low-income youth. If a respondent failed to recharge the phone account, the cell phone number changed when the respondent opted to pay again. For example, over the course of the year, one respondent's home phone number changed four times, and her cell phone number changed three times. In addition, the climate of fear created by the widespread and unpredictable Immigration and Customs Enforcement (ICE) raids happening in 2008 caused many respondents to be distrustful of unknown callers. It is important to recognize that the group of former participants who chose not to be interviewed as young adults or could not be located most likely included individuals who would not claim to have been positively influenced by the program. It also includes a disproportionate number of young men. This experience suggests that the limited longitudinal research conducted on low-income and Mexican American youth reflects, in part, the difficulty in conducting follow-up interviews.

The sample of interviewees for this book was 75 percent female, 83 percent Mexican or Mexican American, and 17 percent white. Of the Mexican or Mexican American respondents, 80 percent participated in English language learner programs for some portion of their elementary school years. Most respondents attended one of the three local large public high schools, but 17 percent attended small private day schools on full scholarships. All former participants located for young adult interviews were then living within an hour of AMS and were enrolled in some kind of educational institution. About a third was attending a private university full-time, another third was attending community college part-time, and the final third was split evenly between attending community college full-time and attending trade school full- or part-time. Though not representative, this selection of former participants provides a poignant case study for understanding the processes through which participation might play a role in adolescents' pathways to college.

Organization of This Book

This book explores why even high-quality out-of-school time programs vary with regard to how and how much they benefit participants. Employing in-depth interviews with twelve participants in the same extracurricular program—first in eighth grade and again in young adulthood—*Why Afterschool Matters* examines students' experiences at school, at home, and in extracurricular contexts in order to identify the processes through which out-of-school time programs might influence educational attainment over time and why participation matters for some students more than others.

Employing a life course perspective, this book builds on cultural capital, social capital, and role identity theories to incorporate the role of out-of-school time programs into dominant sociological explanations for academic success and failure. Chapter 2 begins by providing a primer on the most prominent sociological accounts of failure and low attainment among disadvantaged students, followed by a primer on the theories accounting for success and high attainment. In addition, this chapter uses empirical data to illustrate the three primary processes through which Students Together played a role in the college pathways of participants: by teaching concrete skills or cultural capital, by helping students develop an identity that bridged school and home contexts, and by building social networks through relationships with supportive and knowledgeable adults. Other studies draw on a single theoretical lens, but this book stands apart by recognizing the multitude of ways that organized activities may support educational attainment.

Chapters 3, 4, and 5 build on this theoretical framework by juxtaposing the processes through which Students Together benefited participants— concrete skills, identity development, and relationships with adults—with the degree of benefit each student experienced. Variation in the degree to which participation played a role for respondents was explained by three factors: the relationships they had outside of the program (e.g., friends and family), the multiple structures in which they were embedded (e.g., other out-of-school programs, church groups, paid work), and their personal agency. Although participation was associated with benefits for all respondents, the program had the opportunity to influence students lacking preexisting supports more than those who were already well supported. In other words, participation was more likely to be associated with a higher degree of influence for students lacking outside supports.

Chapter 3 introduces the concept of *auxiliary influence.* Auxiliary influence depicts participants who had positive experiences in the program but for whom the program was not associated with lasting change in the context of all the other factors determining their educational trajectories. The program neither acted as a primary support system nor brought about personal transformation. Respondents for whom the program had an auxiliary influence relied on a parent or adult mentor and their own determination as the primary forces propelling them to college. Students in this group who attend four-year private universities had significant support during high school from a guidance counselor or college prep program.

To illustrate these themes, chapter 3 profiles Graciela and Julio. Like other participants who experienced an auxiliary degree of influence, Graciela and Julio were well supported when they joined the program. They reported a positive relationship with at least one parent and positive peer ties at the time of participation. In the program, they learned concrete skills, such as public speaking and research methods, which acted as valued cultural capital with employers, admissions counselors, and scholarship committees. In other words, participation acted as a credential that granted youth favor with various social and academic gatekeepers. Their ties to the program, however, were limited to their participation year and the influence of the program faded as they became immersed in other settings.

Chapter 4 introduces the concept of *distinguishable influence.* For this group of participants, the program engendered a critical sense of belonging that they did not feel elsewhere, even though they were academically successful and enjoyed strong family support. In Students Together, these students learned leadership skills, generated strong relationships with adults, and got connected to complementary organizations. Among respondents for whom the program had a distinguishable influence, the strongest forces driving them to pursue higher education were the Students Together program, along with family and self.

Chapter 4 profiles Teresa and Selena. Like other participants who experienced a distinguishable degree of influence, Teresa and Selena were supported at home, but they lacked positive peer ties and did not feel a sense of belonging at school. Because they had fewer preexisting supports, the potential for the program to influence them was greater. In addition, the program was a good fit for their interests. They felt inspired by staff members, reported a high level of engagement with program activities, and used the program as a gateway to get involved with other out-of-school programs. Along with cultural capital, the program provided a supportive environment where these youth were able to develop an identity that was positively received both at school and at home.

Chapter 5 introduces the concept of *transformative influence.* For the respondents in this category, participation was associated with momentous changes in their lives. Prior to joining the program, they possessed no college motivation; instead, they had records of delinquency and emerging gang ties. This group of participants stands out because they changed significantly during their time in Students Together—they generated strong relationships with adults, connected to complementary organizations, and bonded with like-minded peers. For respondents for whom Students Together had a transformative influence the program played a primary role in getting them to college.

Chapter 5 profiles Maria and Victoria. Like other youth who experienced a transformative degree of influence, Maria and Victoria lacked positive family and peer supports so the potential for the program to influence them was the greatest of all. The program was also a good fit for their interests. Like others, they gained cultural capital and developed a positively received identity, yet the youth in this group also sustained deep relationships with staff members. These relationships provided emotional support as well as invaluable social capital for navigating the journey through adolescence and beyond.

Chapter 6 returns to the theoretical framework outlined in chapter 2 and situates the discussion of processes and degrees of influence within the framing of life course theory. This chapter introduces the notion of *embedded influence* to emphasize the ways that relationships, school and community structures, and personal agency wield overlapping influences on young people's pathways to college over time. Thus, the embedded influence of a particular extracurricular program on a student's educational trajectory takes into account a more holistic portrait of the adolescent's experiences and a nuanced understanding of the diverse ways programs exert influence. Although it is neither possible nor desirable for a program to have a transformative influence on all participants, it is critical for improving educational outcomes of disadvantaged students to recognize the potential of high-quality organized activities to impact educational trajectories in a variety of ways. This chapter also highlights implications of this study for researchers, policymakers, and practitioners.

In sum, this book presents detailed case studies of young people who experienced each degree of influence—auxiliary, distinguishable, and transformative—while bringing to life the challenges marginalized students face when navigating the intersections of different home, school, and community spheres. The case studies highlight the ways that educational attainment can be associated with both program participation and the structures and relationships in which youth were already embedded. Examining variation in the influence of extracurricular participation helps us understand the role that such programs can play in eliminating the academic attainment gap between low-income students of color and their peers—a gap that has important implications for US society in the decades ahead.

2

Theorizing Educational Success and Failure

Since the 1966 publication of the landmark *Equality of Educational Opportunity*, more commonly known as the Coleman Report, the achievement gap between low-income students of color and their middle-class white peers has become the focal point of educational reform efforts throughout the United States. The report found that black students scored on average a full standard deviation below white students in academic achievement (Coleman et al. 1966). Although many expected that these disparities in achievement could be chalked up to the different levels of resources available at different schools, the report stirred much controversy as it revealed instead that students' family backgrounds make a sizeable impact on their levels of achievement. Subsequent research has proven that schools actually do matter quite a bit for student learning, but Coleman's main finding still stands: variation between schools in resource levels has little impact on the variation between individual students with regard to achievement (Gamoran and Long 2006).

In the years since the Coleman Report, the achievement gap has narrowed, then widened, and then narrowed again; yet significant differences by race and ethnic background persist. Data from the National

Assessment of Educational Progress (NAEP)—the largest continuous and most nationally representative assessment that is standardized across states and districts—show that, in 1971, the gap in reading scores between black and white seventeen-year-olds was 1.2 standard deviations; by 1996, this gap had fallen to 0.69 standard deviations. Math scores show a similar pattern, with the gap declining from 1.33 to 0.89 standard deviations (Jencks and Phillips 1998). During the 1990s these gaps actually increased, yet by 2012 the black-white test score gap and the Hispanic-white test score gap in reading and math were each about half of what they had been in 1971 (NCES 2013; Perie, Moran, and Lutkus 2005).

Researchers have sought to understand what causes these gaps, why they continue, and ultimately how to eliminate them. In the past, dominant sociological theories focused on factors explaining disadvantaged students' failures, such as lack of ambition or poorly prepared teachers. These theoretical frameworks aligned with intervention strategies seeking to minimize negative outcomes, such as dropping out of school, teen pregnancy, and drug abuse. As a result, myriad prevention-oriented programs emerged, each targeting a specific "problem behavior." During the late 1980s, with the advent of the Positive Youth Development (PYD) perspective, both research and practice began to shift toward explaining and promoting success rather than failure. Scholars, practitioners, and policymakers, countering earlier prevention-oriented strategies aimed at ameliorating problem behaviors with programs that promoted a host of positive developmental outcomes, adopted the slogan: "problem-free is not fully prepared." Emerging theoretical frameworks turned their focus to explaining how and why some disadvantaged students excel.

No extant theoretical framework fully captures why some low-income and minority students succeed while others languish. Data from the case studies in this book suggest that the strongest theoretical orientation may lie at the intersection of existing theories. To build the theoretical framework that situates educational attainment in the context of family, school, and community influences over time, chapter 2 introduces the dominant sociological theories explaining failure and low attainment among disadvantaged youth, as well as the dominant theories accounting for success and high attainment, before advocating for an alternative approach.

Theoretical Explanations for Low Achievement

Deficit Explanations

Deficit explanations account for students' academic failures by looking to factors inherent to individual students, their families, or their culture. In general, proponents of deficit explanations attach academic outcomes to demographic data such that specific traits ascribed to categories of people appear to lead to low achievement in school. Deficit explanations frequently explain low academic achievement among Latino/a students by advancing evidence of what these students lack, relative to their middle-class white peers (Valencia 1997).

Modern deficit theorists primarily assert that a child's ability and desire to learn is impressed upon him or her by his or her surroundings and that negative family and neighborhood influences make it nearly impossible for some kids to succeed. For example, during the 1960s many deficit theorists, citing the "culture of poverty" as an explanation of low achievement among minority students, said that poor people were socialized differently and were therefore likely to pass those values on to their children (Lewis 1966). Patterns of generational poverty seemed to support this theory (Foley 1997). In another example from the same era, familial deficit theories blamed accumulated environmental deficits or cultural deprivation for minority students' underachievement. These theorists argued that minority students were not intellectually stimulated at home, rewarded for academic attainment, or supported in their efforts toward school completion (e.g., Bernstein 1958; Deutsch 1967; Frost and Hawkes 1966; Hellmuth 1967). They supported early childhood education programs as a means of counteracting this familial deficit (Pearl 1991).

More recent work follows this tradition. For example, Jeanne Brooks-Gunn and Lisa Markman (2005) explored racial and ethnic differences in school readiness by assessing parental behaviors. They found significant differences in language use at home, notably that black and Hispanic mothers talk less with their young children than do white mothers. The authors also found that black and Hispanic mothers are less likely to read to their children daily. The authors then assessed parental intervention programs that seek to address such behaviors among parents and improve school readiness among children. They found that parental intervention programs often improve parents' behaviors but only sometimes improve students' school readiness. They also found that such intervention programs were more effective for black and Hispanic parents than for white parents.

Critics of deficit theory advanced evidence to the contrary of both the culture of poverty and accumulated environmental deficit claims. Research showed that minority families highly prized education (Pearl 1997). In addition, there was no evidence that the poor held different values and beliefs from other groups in society. Empirical studies clearly demonstrated poor children could learn and aspired to learn (Foley 1997). Furthermore, data showed that continuous spells of poverty most often lasted less than two years, which dispelled notions that poverty was passed from generation to generation (Harris 1993).

In response to this evidence, a new branch of deficit theory emerged during the 1980s. Children who were previously labeled "culturally deprived" were now labeled "at risk" (Margonis 1992). Researchers focused on risk factors to determine which children were mostly likely to be in danger of which problems, from teen pregnancy to dropping out of school. Some deficit theorists assert that Latino/a students come from unstable families or that their parents are indifferent to education. Other deficit theorists argue students lack motivation or do not sustain appropriate involvement in school activities. Still other deficit theorists have found that low achievers are too often absent or suspended or have friends who are also low achievers (Barrington and Hendricks 1989; Delgado-Gaitan 1988; Flores-González 2002). These theorists argue that such risk factors increase students' chances of academic failure.

As I explained in chapter 1, this deficit-based framework fits nicely with the approach to adolescence American psychologists touted throughout most of the twentieth century. Beginning with G. Stanley Hall's theory of adolescence as a time of "storm and stress," teenagers have been portrayed as emotional volcanoes, perpetually at risk for behaving in problematic ways. Adolescents were treated accordingly; they were problems to be fixed. As early as the 1960s, research began to appear that showed that Hall's idea was not universally true; most adolescents still valued their relationship with their parents enormously, had core values that were consistent with those of their parents, and selected friends who shared these core values. Most adolescents were not necessarily a problem. Nevertheless, the deficit-based model persisted in public policy and research (Lerner 2005).

Most scholars would agree that individual, family, and cultural traits do play a role in students' academic attainment. In fact, in this book you see evidence of individual, family, and cultural traits intertwined in each student's narrative of his or her educational trajectory. Modern deficit theorists, however, are often critiqued because they single out risk factors without attending to the process by which students succeed or fail in school. This approach does not accurately predict academic attainment for a number of reasons. First, this approach obscures the differential effects of individual, family, and cultural factors across ethnic, class, or gender groups. For example, an authoritarian parenting style is generally associated with low achievement and thus is categorized as a risk factor (Baumrind 1966; Brooks-Gunn and Markman 2005). But among Latino/a and African American families this style of parenting often produces high achievers (Gandara 1995; Steinberg, Dornbusch, and Brown 1992). Second, the deficit approach fails to explain why students with similar characteristics, such as siblings, have dissimilar educational outcomes. Finally, deficit theorists fail to explain why many Latino/a students drop out of school even though they do not match the typical at-risk profile (Fernandez and Shu 1988); factors such as misbehaving, changing schools, and making low grades, which increase the odds of dropping out for both black and white students, do not increase the odds for Latino/a students (Rumberger 1995). Labeling children "at risk" often overlooks their strengths and potential and focuses only on what they lack.

Structural Explanations

Instead of blaming the individual, family, or culture, structural explanations claim that certain school traits and practices cause low achievement among marginalized students. Instead of blaming the victim—as critics say deficit theories do—these theorists blame the educational system. While deficit-based theories stemmed from historical periods of colonization, structural theory stems from the functional tradition in sociology. In general, functionalists examine the manifest and latent functions and dysfunctions of societal institutions. According to renowned functionalist Emile Durkheim, these institutions work together like organs in a body, each with essential and specialized functions. Our society depends on the educational system to socialize young people and provide basic training in preparation for the labor market.

Structural theorists view marginalized students' underachievement as a direct result of the ways in which their schools operate. They look at the organization of schools and resource flows in terms of teachers, students, and administrators. They see the heart of the problem as schools' difficulties engaging or socially integrating particular sectors of students. Structural theorists highlight that Latino/a students experience less qualified teachers, fewer expendable resources per student, lowered expectations for achievement from teachers and administrators, more and harsher discipline during school, mismatches between school and home culture, and a high mobility rate of students and teachers (Valverde and Scribner 2001). Structural theorists argue that if schools were set up differently, Mexican American youth would be more likely to succeed.

Some structural theorists pay particular attention to the ways that students are sorted and tracked within each school. These theorists attribute the low academic attainment among minorities to their disproportionate placement in nonacademic tracks (Oakes 2005). Although impermeable vocational and general tracks are largely extinct, more nuanced forms of tracking still exist in most American schools. Students are assigned to differentiated classes by subject area based on their perceived ability. For example, some students might be placed in calculus for math while others are placed in algebra. Some students may be placed in Advanced Placement science or history, while some students may be placed in classes that do not meet the minimal requirements for admission to state universities. Like more rigid forms of tracking, this course-by-course sorting and differentiation of opportunities results in unequal outcomes across tracks. Students in lower tracks often end up with less engaging opportunities to learn (for example, they might not get to use lab equipment in science) and less access to high-status knowledge (such as art history or college-prep material); thus, they have poorer academic outcomes of all kinds. Although tracking appears to be based on students' academic ability, research shows that students of color are disproportionally assigned to lower tracks in mixed race schools and often attend majority minority schools where lower tiered classes are most common. Tracking systems can disguise race-based discrimination as ability-based sorting (Oakes 2005).

Critics argue that the problem with the structural perspective comes from its functionalist roots. Structural theories are based on the assumption that one of the essential manifest functions of the school system is to socialize students to conform to a prescribed manner of behavior and motivational orientation (e.g., Robert Merton). Conformity facilitates integration and engenders social order, one of the greatest pursuits of the educational system. This theory assumes that the goals of the school system are rational and desirable, inasmuch as schools develop essential psychological and cognitive traits in young people. Implicit in this theory is the notion that students' families are responsible for continually reinforcing conformity to the manner of behavior espoused in schools. In the case of disadvantaged and minority youth whose families often deviate from this expectation, the school provides students with second chances to benefit from the necessary socialization program.

In her ethnographic study of a Houston high school, Angela Valenzuela (1999) provides a vivid example of how the condoned structure and implicit values of the school system can impact Mexican American students. Namely, Mexican American students were mainly frustrated by two things: courses that were not challenging, and teachers who, in their view, did not care. Lowered teacher expectations and biases against minority students made schooling a "subtractive" rather than an enriching experience. Subtractive schooling reproduced Mexican American youth as English-speaking monolingual youth, who neither identified with Mexico nor were equipped to competently function in mainstream American life. The structure of schooling stripped them of valuable social and cultural resources and left them vulnerable to academic failure. Valenzuela argued that schooling could be structured differently to create an additive school experience for Mexican American students.

Valenzuela's (1999) study shows and critics agree that structural theorists often overlook the possibility that the attitudes and behaviors inculcated by the school system may not actually be universal and rational values. Instead, this system imposes an orientation that supports the culture and political interests of powerful groups in society without recognizing that conformity to espoused norms requires access to class-based resources and opportunities. Furthermore, imposing this orientation may be detrimental to students because such imposition discourages growth within their home culture. According to critics, much of the research in this tradition does not situate schools in the context of our highly class-stratified and segregated society (Stanton-Salazar 2001). Finally, critics claim that structural explanations fail to account for diversity within the Latino/a population. Although this theory implies that students are merely victims of their schooling, both dropouts and college-bound Latino/a youth emerge from even the most disadvantaged schools. In reality, many students actively participate in their education, recognize inequalities, and challenge the system.

Reproduction Theory

While structural theory grew out of the functionalist tradition within sociology, reproduction theory is a branch of conflict theory. Foundations for this perspective come from the writings of Karl Marx. Although Marx self-identified as an economist, his explanations of how powerful groups create social and cultural systems that legitimate their own class advantage have strongly influenced the sociology of education. Reproduction theorists recognize the concept structural theorists avoided: schools act as instruments of the dominant groups in society. According to reproduction theorists, the upper echelons of society designed schools to foster low achievement among marginalized students. Thus, the educational system continually reproduces social relations by keeping the lower classes in service on the bottom and the upper classes in charge on the top. Proponents of this theory support their argument by citing the unyielding correlation between parents' socioeconomic status and their children's school completion (Bourdieu 1973; Bowles and Gintis 1976).

According to reproduction theorists, variation in educational attainment is essentially a candy coating for preexisting class inequalities. Schools reproduce the social order by rewarding knowledge of the dominant culture. Knowledge of the dominant culture therefore leads to better performance in school. Because upper-class parents participate in and continually expose their children to the dominant culture, upper-class children have a clear advantage with regard to school performance. Better performance in school garners upper-class students their admission to more prestigious universities; upper-class graduates then land higher paying jobs because of their superior academic credentials. This system appears to be based on merit or superior performance in school and thus is commonly considered a meritocracy. Success in the school system, however, is actually based on exposure to and knowledge of the dominant culture.

How does this happen without widespread rebellion from the working class? Seat time in the classroom, hours spent on homework and school projects, weekends and summers committed to honing their skills, and hard-won college degrees provide a palatable justification for privileged families passing privilege to their children. For the public to accept the system, at least some disadvantaged children must be able to make the system work for them. Exceptions to this rule—kids from wealthy families who drop out of high school and students from poor families who graduate from Harvard—help give the educational system an appearance of class neutrality. Just enough exceptions exist to enable our educational system to pass as meritocratic.

In an ethnographic study of twelve families of varying class backgrounds, Annette Lareau (2003) documented the ways in which the different parenting styles practiced by upper- and lower-class parents contribute to social reproduction and academic outcomes. Lareau argued that upper-class parents begin investing in their children's extracurricular abilities at a young age: they drive youngsters from practices to games to recitals; they spend countless hours cheering in grandstands and auditoriums: and they pay countless dollars for league fees and lessons. This style of parenting requires the thoughtful nurturing of children's particular gifts and the paid assistance of expert tutors, coaches, and teachers. Thus, the calendar of activities has become the centerpiece of the middle-class American home, and children are intentionally and repeatedly exposed to knowledge of the dominant culture. Lareau highlights that this style of parenting, which she calls "concerted cultivation," favors the development of the individual child sometimes at the expense of family or group needs.

Meanwhile, parents in lower-class families practice what she calls "the accomplishment of natural growth," a philosophy by which children will grow up regardless of harried schedules and adult intervention. These children often play outside with other neighborhood youth and spend ample time with extended family members. They learn to get along with other kids, engage in imaginative play, and consider the priorities of the group or family; they do not focus solely on their own needs. Yet, despite acquiring these useful skills, lower-class children are not privy to the extensive knowledge of the dominant culture their upper-class peers are soaking up, and because of this they are penalized within the school system.

Because a college degree has become synonymous with the good life in the United States, successfully preparing for the demands of college admissions helps upper-class parents ensure the future affluence of their offspring. When the time arrives for young people to compete for admission to college, upper-class adolescents have a clear advantage because not only have they been groomed for this process since early childhood but also their parents have more resources to invest in the process. Mitchell Stevens's (2007) ethnographic study of the admissions department at an elite college exemplifies how the standards of college admission have become a template for middle- and upper-class childrearing throughout the United

States. The development of clear measures of accomplishment by college admissions committees has made the culture of upper-class parenting more competitive, more expensive, and more structured around the production of demonstrated accomplishment. Keenly aware of the terms of admission, privileged parents do everything in their power to develop their children into ideal applicants, from academics to athletics to community service. Stevens (2007) describes how the transition from high school to college for adolescents from privileged families has become "a seamless web of interdependencies between guidance counselors and admissions officers; between youthful athletic talent and athletic league standings; between high property taxes, large tuition checks, and excellent academics" (Stevens 2007, 247). Just like the terms of academic success throughout primary and secondary schools, the terms of college admission boil down to class-biased standards acting as widely palatable justifications of the upper classes reproducing their dominance in society.

Like structural explanations, however, critics argue that reproduction theory fails to account for success and other challenges to the system among members of subordinate groups. Reproduction theory, casting Latino/as as mere victims of their social status, overlooks the diversity within the Latino/a population and strips marginalized students and their families of any agency within the school system. For example, minorities have overtly questioned the status quo in numerous court cases from *Brown v. Board of Education* to *Williams v. California*. Similar to the *Brown v. Board of Education* case, the Williams class action lawsuit argued that the state of California did not give millions of students—mainly low-income students, immigrant students, and students of color—the basic tools of a decent education: qualified teachers, adequate materials, and decent facilities. The state of California did not fight the case in court and, in the settlement, agreed with every argument raised by the students who brought the case. Recent charter school and small school innovations that consistently produce high-achieving minority students also challenge reproduction theories by showing that schools can be designed to foster success for all children, not just those of the upper classes.

Resistance Theory

Stepping away from the notion that adolescents act as passive recipients to their environments, resistance theory is a branch of conflict theory that recognizes behaviors of low achievement among minority students as active challenges to certain aspects of schooling (Fine 1991; MacLeod 1995; Willis 1979). Resistance theorists argue that marginalized youth are not failing and dropping out at disproportionate rates because they are inferior or because schools have been designed to make them fail; instead, they are failing because they are choosing to challenge the system. For example, when students believe that high school graduation will not improve their life chances—maybe because they believe they will be discriminated against on the job market or they want to pursue a career path that does not require a degree—they develop identities in opposition to school culture. In other words, because they believe school will not get them where they want to go, there is no incentive for them to conform to the standardized attitudes and behaviors demanded by schools.

Similarly, if the behaviors required for academic success contradict students' ethnic identity, then they may also develop oppositional identities. Instead of submitting to the system that seeks to rob them of their home culture, they rebel. Finally, under pressure from their peers who have chosen to resist the norms and values of schooling, those marginalized students who choose to conform to the school culture and become high achievers may mask their achievements in fear of retribution from peers or accusations of "acting white" (Fordham and Ogbu 1986).

John Ogbu (1978) argued that minorities' beliefs about academic and economic success are determined by their mode of incorporation into the United States. Those groups brought involuntarily maintain deeply embedded memories of institutionalized racism, discrimination, and subjugation. By involuntary incorporation, Ogbu means that the group was forcibly required to become part of American society. For example, Africans were brought to the United States as slaves, Native Americans were conquered and nearly exterminated, and Mexicans in what is now the western United States were colonized. Ogbu argues that this experience of slavery, conquest, and colonization indelibly marks a racial or ethnic group. As a result, involuntary minorities tend to establish practices in direct opposition to those of middle-class whites (Ogbu 1978). In essence, his theory posits that historical forces cause entire racial and ethnic groups to adopt a culture oppositional to whites that, in turn, influences educational outcomes in modern times.

Other resistance theorists have developed more nuanced theories. Immigration issues, for example, have been found to play a significant role in educational aspirations and achievement of each successive generation of Mexican Americans (National Research Council 2006a). Researchers posit that often foreign-born youth, given their limited English skills, struggle in school (Kao and Tienda 1995). Second-generation students thrive, however, benefiting from the high expectations of immigrant parents and the English proficiency of being native born (Kao and Tienda 1995). But both first- and second-generation youth outperform their third-generation peers. After seeing their parents and grandparents confined to menial jobs and becoming aware of discrimination against them, third-generation Mexican Americans readily join reactive subcultures as a means of protecting their self-worth (Portes and Zhou 1993). Remaining ensconced in the coethnic subculture may be the best strategy for capitalizing on otherwise unavailable material and moral resources. For example, while society at large discriminates, coethnic communities provide social networks that help young people secure employment. Such material resources may be unavailable outside the coethnic community. In addition, coethnic networks offer emotional support and a sense of belonging that may be hard to find elsewhere. Therefore, if academic achievement is antithetical to ethnic solidarity, entrenchment in coethnic community can also create barriers to upward mobility (Portes and Zhou 1993).

Yet other researchers have shown that academic achievement does not always come at the expense of ethnic identity (Carter 2005; Mehan, Hubbard, and Villanueva 1994). The reality of minority students is not an either-or choice between academic success and ethnic solidarity; students can even benefit from achieving both simultaneously. First, contrary to popular stereotypes of African Americans and Latino/as, members of minority groups actually subscribe to the value of education as much or more than whites do and aspire to become middle class (Flores-González 2002). Thus, academic achievement, seen as a pathway to upward mobility that students' coethnic peers respect, is not a rebuke of the ethnic community. While some minority students assimilate into mainstream culture and others become noncompliant, Prudence Carter (2005) argues that many marginalized youth are "cultural straddlers," who keep one foot in each world. Students' home cultures can serve positive functions by engendering both a sense of belonging and a support for handling inequality. According to Carter (2005) students' presentations of self are thus best understood as neither a reaction nor a submission but as "practices of distinction based on a critique of an undiscerning mainstream culture in schools" (Carter 2005, 6). Finally, critics argue that this theory, like others, lumps all members of a minority group together as if they are the same. There is currently no evidence of any single explanation for how so-called involuntary minorities respond to the belief that middle- and upper-class whites control the institutions of opportunity.

While deficit, structural, reproduction, and resistance theories may partially account for low academic achievement among marginalized students, these explanations do not address the diversity among Latina/o youth. Many Latina/os drop out of school even though they do not match typical at-risk profiles (Fernandez and Shu 1988). Academic achievement does not come at the expense of ethnic identity for all groups (Carter 2005; Mehan, Hubbard, and Villanueva 1994). Moreover, individual agency must be considered in tandem with systemic constraints and opportunities.

Theoretical Explanations for High Achievement

In line with the rise of the PYD approach and asset-based (as opposed to deficit-based) characterizations of youth, recent research has turned the spotlight from stumbling blocks to success stories. Instead of interviewing high school drop-outs, these researchers interview high achievers and college students in search of commonalities and explanatory theories. Many of these theories have been developed as mirror images of the theories of academic failure that I have already reviewed in this chapter.

Asset Explanations

In the same vein as deficit explanations of low achievement among marginalized youth, asset theorists look to individual, family, or cultural traits to explain high achievement. Many of their findings echo the findings of deficit theorists. For example, at the individual level, college-matriculated Latino/a students share a sense of responsibility toward others, a sense of accomplishment, and an openness to new experiences (Cornelius-White, Garza, and Hoey 2004; Zalaquett 2006). Demographic characteristics can also be linked with school success: father's education, equal use of English and Spanish in the home, and parental support of students' growth into areas of their own interest (Cornelius-White, Garza, and Hoey 2004). Asset theorists posit that parents' influences have a stronger impact on Latino/a students' educational aspirations than the students' actual academic achievement or self-perceptions (Trusty, Plata, and Salazar 2003). Asset explanations initially emerged in reaction to the deficit theorists use of the "at risk" label during the 1980s. Although asset theorists focus on the positive influence that Latino/a families can have on their children, much of their research calls to mind the foundations of deficit theory that places blame on the shoulders of parents.

Structural Explanations

Structural theorists seeking to explain academic success bring many of the same assumptions as those mentioned earlier in this chapter who seek to explain academic failure. In this case, they argue that support and critical information can be intentionally combined within a school setting to promote academic success among marginalized students (Sanchez, Reyes, and Singh 2006). In other words, schools serving Latino/a students can be structured differently and produce different outcomes. This model of combining caring with information addresses the most common barriers between Latino/a youth and college: minimal adult supervision, misinformation, and poorly informed choices (Immerwahr 2003; Zalaquett 2006). In other words, schools could be redesigned to better make up for what parents lack when it comes to incorporating all students into the mainstream.

In one example, the school "disrupted patterns of low engagement among Latino/a students" by altering school structures to encourage staff members to keep students better informed and demonstrate that they care about students (Conchas 2001, 27). In another example, the school-based Advancement Via Individual Determination (AVID) program put in place institutional support systems to help students navigate the school's hidden curriculum and establish social supports (Mehan et al. 1996). AVID dubbed this process "social scaffolding," but it too boils down to the intentional interplay of caring adults and critical information. Outside the family, support from friends, school personnel, the community, and scholarship funds were common among college-bound Latino/as (Zalaquett 2006).

Both asset and structural theories fail to explain why students exposed to similar environments achieve varied outcomes. Implicit in these theories is the assumption that personal agency plays no part. The next two theories begin to recognize the intertwining influences of social structures and personal agency. Social capital and role-identity theorists spotlight personal agency within school and home contexts. Unlike resistance theorists who posit that the only way to cope with oppressive systems is to opt out of the mainstream, social capital and role-identity theorists locate opportunities for upward mobility within existing structures.

Social Capital and Social Embeddedness Theory

Ricardo Stanton-Salazar (2001) employs a critical network-analytic view of Latino/a adolescents to explain why some achieve academic success while others do not. This critical network-analytic view sees individuals as embedded within social networks, which are embedded within larger networks, which are embedded within even larger networks. Essentially, an individual's movement within society is limited or enabled by the people with whom he or she is connected across multiple levels: social interactions at the individual level comprise egocentric networks; interactions at the community level comprise cliques; and interactions at the societal level comprise system networks. By mapping and examining webs of interaction, researchers reveal how opportunities to take part in certain contexts or be in relationship to powerful people are unequally distributed based on the kinds of networks people possess (Wellman, as cited in Stanton-Salazar 2001). While middle-class networks facilitate smooth access to the mainstream marketplace, working-class networks are bounded. While middle-class networks function like freeways, working-class networks act more like prisons. In other words, working-class people and middle-class people are most often embedded in very different social networks, and they thus have access to very different social resources (Furstenberg and Hughes 1995).

The emphasis within critical network analysis falls on social embeddedness, a concept highlighted by Mark Granovetter (1985). In this view, individuals decide how to act based on the dynamics of the various relationships in which they participate. The nature of an individual's social embeddedness dictates his or her available courses of action. Individuals constantly negotiate constraints and opportunities via the social networks in which they participate. Adolescents, in particular, experience the tugs of often contradictory forces working to shape their social networks and thus influencing their available actions. They may feel the pull of social, cultural, and ideological forces. These forces mold not only the structure and composition of their social networks but also the resources available by way of those networks. The concept of social embeddedness exemplifies how adolescents are active participants in their own pathways in life, but these adolescents must operate within the constraints and opportunities available to them based on their individual social connections.

In the United States today, upward mobility requires forms of social embeddedness that generate social capital. Social capital refers to the social resources a student brings, which result in the building of networks and relationships that they can use as contacts for future opportunities (Coleman 1988), yet lower-class youth are most often embedded in social networks that prevent or obscure the formation of social capital. Societal-level forces foster dynamics within adolescents' relationships and networks that make it difficult for the adults within those networks to reliably act as sources of social support or transmit institutional resources. For example, race, class, and patriarchy are all societal-level forces that impact adolescents' social networks.

In spite of these social forces, individuals, communities, and school staff members can go against the grain to create relational dynamics that act as conduits for social capital. In other words, adults can act in ways that encourage students to build deeper and more beneficial relationships with supportive adults. For marginalized youth, these relationships are created under the strains of broader societal forces and often first focus on buffering students from the negative effects of their surroundings, such as poverty, segregation, or acculturation stress. While the relationships and networks that middle-class adolescents build have the luxury of focusing on creating access to privileges and power, the relationships and networks of lower-class youth must first help protect them from their environments. In addition, the relationship-building process is a two-way street. Adults must be trustworthy and available, and adolescents must seek them out and engage in relationship building.

Thus, social capital theorists agree that low achievement has structural roots, but they locate the pathway to academic success in the individual's ability to navigate the system and build beneficial relationships. As low levels of school and community social capital place the children of immigrants at risk of dropping out (Perreira, Harris, and Lee 2006), successful Latino/a youth are those who actively seek out supportive adults within their schools, families, and communities (Stanton-Salazar 1997, 2001; Stanton-Salazar and Dornbusch 1995). Peer groups also matter. Students involved in school tend to befriend others who value schooling; in this way friendship networks impact school completion and drop-out rates (Ream and Rumberger 2008). Because extracurricular activities often link students with supportive adults within their schools or communities—such as coaches or directors—and positive peer groups (Bodilly and Beckett 2005), social capital and social embeddedness theory may help account for links between extracurricular activity participation and positive academic outcomes.

Role-Identity Theory

Role-identity theory builds on research showing that successful Latino/a students effectively reconcile the differences and manage the transitions between school and home (Flores-González 2002). Students are most likely to manage these transitions well if their worlds are congruent, but others succeed by adopting aspects of school culture while maintaining their home culture—in other words, accommodating without assimilating (Mehan et al. 1994; Phelan, Davidson, and Cao 1991). Guadalupe Valdes (1996) argued that young people must either manage the transition between worlds or experience compatible worlds. Hugh Mehan and colleagues (1994) posited that high achievers could accommodate without assimilating, taking on a new culture while maintaining the old one. Carter (2005) dubbed young people with these inclinations and abilities "cultural straddlers."

Role-identity theory goes one step further to explain how successful Latino/a students bridge worlds. A role-identity is an understanding of who you are by virtue of occupying a particular social role. To sociologists, a social role is the comprehensive pattern of behavior expected of an individual who occupies a given position or status. A role remains relatively stable even though different people occupy the position; for example, any individual assigned the role of physician, like any actor in the role of Hamlet, is expected to behave in a particular way. Each individual has many role-identities, some of which are more dominant than others. Interrelated role-identities (such as spouse and parent) rank higher than others because an individual is likely to enact those identities more frequently.

When applied to academic achievement, role-identity theory posits that Latino/a youth become successful by adopting an all-encompassing "school kid" identity, which is expressed differently at school and at home and received positively across divergent worlds (Flores-González 2002). What Nilda Flores-González (2002) has dubbed "school kid" represents

what is generally thought of as a good kid: the identity is neither specifically bounded to school, nor does it imply that the student has no critiques
of the educational system. As an aggregate of identities activated across
school, community, and home contexts, the school kid identity becomes
dominant.

Specifically, Flores-González (2002) argues that the school kid identity
is developed in response to the presence or absence of certain conditions.
Developing the all-encompassing school kid identity requires that the role
be socially appropriate both at school and at home. This may be based on
the person's age, gender, past experiences, or competency within the role.
And for that role, adolescents must also have social support, including
emotional ties with others at school and relationships brought about by the
school kid identity. In addition, prestige and rewards for adopting that role
must exist. For example, school kids might receive good grades, popularity,
or privileged access to extracurricular opportunities. Next, students must
have a strong commitment to the identity as exemplified in their relationships with others who support the identity and engagement in activities
that reinforce the identity. Developing the school kid identity also requires
the presence of identity-enhancing events and the absence of identity-
threatening events. Finally, the school kid identity must mesh with the
future possible selves the student hopes to attain (Flores-González 2002).
These processes can be facilitated or hindered by school staff members and
structures. Students are successful in school to the extent that they can
adopt and sustain this "school kid" identity.

One process through which organized activities may promote educational attainment is by helping students develop this bridging identity. First,
the "school kid" role is appropriate and encouraged within organized activities. Second, extracurricular activities provide both peer and adult support
for this role. Third, extracurricular activities provide rewards for sustaining
that role. In some activities, participation is limited to students who maintain a certain grade-point average so participation is a reward in itself. For
others, activities help students see future rewards for academic success such
as college matriculation and novel career pathways. Finally, extracurricular
activities may provide a context where identity-enhancing events can occur
while protecting young people from identity-threatening events.

Both social capital theory and role-identity theory highlight the structural constraints that lower-class Latino/a youth experience at home, in
school, and within society at large. Both theories also emphasize the active

role that Latino/a adolescents play in choosing how to act within those varied and overlapping contexts. Social capital theory spotlights not only the ways that relationships and social networks matter but also the ways that variation with regard to young people's ability to navigate the system and build relationships leads to variation in educational outcomes. Meanwhile, role-identity theory spotlights the ways that crafting a socially appropriate, publicly rewarded, and relationally embedded aggregate identity can help facilitate school success. Students vary with regard to the appropriateness, rewards, and relationships supporting this role within school, home, and community contexts. While these two theories share common foundations, they differ in the ways they see students having agency. Social capital theory locates student agency in the students' desire and ability to make interpersonal connections, whereas role-identity theory locates student agency in the students' desire and ability to cohere an identity seen as positive across divergent spheres.

Processes of Influence

The longstanding debate over how to explain persistent race- and class-based academic achievement gaps in the United States has largely centered on schools and families. In spite of the array of divergent sociological theories jostling to explain educational success and failure among low-income students of color, the role of extracurricular activities has yet to be accounted for. Do the processes through which extracurricular participation influences educational attainment fit within the purview of existing theories? Or are out-of-school time programs exercising their influence through new and different channels?

The case studies presented in this book suggest that participation in a high-quality out-of-school time program does not act through a single process but rather through three distinct processes: by teaching concrete skills, by providing a supportive environment for identity development, and by establishing relationships with supportive and knowledgeable adults. Furthermore, participation did not influence attainment through the same process for all adolescents; instead, students varied with regard to which processes were more influential in their college pathways. In the following pages, I describe each process in detail, setting the stage for later chapters that explore how and why students varied with regard to which processes mattered most.

Concrete Skills

Even when marginalized youth are academically prepared for the pathway to college and higher paying careers, they often lack the cultural capital to effectively navigate the school system and attain a degree. Cultural capital refers to any piece of knowledge or set of skills that is systematically rewarded by dominant institutions (i.e., schools, employers, government) and thus acts as a primary process through which upward mobility is achieved (Bourdieu 1986). For example, middle- and upper-class children often learn from their parents how to negotiate with authority figures (Lareau 2003). At school, these negotiation skills might buy privileged youth extra time to complete an assignment, exemptions from required tasks or courses, or permission to take part in prized activities—advantages that lead to better grades, higher track placements, and resume-building experiences. Adolescents whose families have been systematically excluded from acquiring institutionally valued skills and dispositions—most often due to race- and class-based discrimination—must look to outside sources to accumulate the nonacademic competencies required for educational success. Because extracurricular activities occupy a unique space between schools and families, they have the potential to help students navigate the class-biased expectations of institutional gatekeepers by imparting education-related cultural capital.

Out-of-school time programs vary with regard to their goals, curricula, and pedagogies. For some programs, teaching cultural capital may be an explicitly stated purpose; yet more often students are drawn to a program by its topical focus, and institutionally valued skills are acquired en route to a broader mission. A competitive soccer squad may learn communication and collaboration on their way to the district championship, while the debate club will discuss professional dress codes and public speaking as they prepare for a contest. All extracurricular activities, however, will not automatically convey cultural capital. Rather, programs that are deliberate around this goal—with regard to structures, curriculum, and staffing—more likely offer the kinds of lessons, experiences, and connections that will benefit marginalized students on their way to educational attainment.

Students Together was designed to help participants become community-based researchers, policy advisors, and leaders, by teaching skills for collaboration, communication, and data collection and analysis.

As the curriculum was intentionally developed by experienced practitioners with these goals in mind and the program has since been recognized as a high-quality program, it is perhaps not surprising that participants left the program reporting that they had learned concrete skills, such as learning to work with a diverse group of people, public speaking, and social research methods. These skills were valuable and memorable to participants: first, students continued to use these skills over the years in both academic and out-of-school contexts; second, institutional gatekeepers, such as hiring managers and admissions officers, looked favorably upon these skills. In other words, participants in Students Together attained the kinds of skills that more privileged students acquire through what Lareau (2003) called concerted cultivation.

Looking back on what they learned from Students Together, many participants recalled the challenging yet satisfying experience of working in a diverse group. In Students Together, like in many extracurricular activities, participants from different neighborhoods, different ethnicities, and different academic achievement levels came together for a common purpose. Felicia acknowledged, "I started to realize that you need to share everything with other people who not only are different than you, but think differently. In Students Together there was a whole bunch of people who had different ideas." Rosa agreed: "The collaboration was pretty important—coming together with different students and working on a project." Some participants reported that after having this experience, they could more easily move between friend groups, allowing them to escape negative peer influences in favor of a more studious crowd. Others reported becoming more outgoing and finding it easier to speak up and advocate for themselves, among both peers and adults. Getting to know classmates outside their clique gave students a firsthand experience with how diversity can improve a team's results, while expanding their social horizons.

Participants also reported using activities, structures, and experiences learned over the course of their year in Students Together in the workplace, admissions interviews, and scholarship competitions. Employers and admissions personnel expect applicants to talk about their extracurricular activities—an attitude biased toward the upper and middle classes—but working-class and minority youth often spend their out-of-school time caring for siblings or working minimum-wage jobs. Participating in an out-of-school time program geared toward leadership and social advocacy gave respondents an advantage in both professional and academic settings.

For example, Maria recalled a day when she and her boss were brainstorming ideas for a new employee training session, "[My boss] was like, 'Where in the world do you get all these [ideas] from?' But, honestly, what I was doing was I was bringing everything I learned from Students Together in to work." The ability to make a meaningful contribution to higher-level administrative tasks helped Maria step quickly out of her minimum-wage position into one with better pay and more responsibility. Selena, who attended a private high school and college, agreed, "Honestly, some of the skills I learned in Students Together I totally use now! Like, in writing college research papers and a lot of the inquiry and interview skills." Having been exposed to these skills early on, Selena felt well prepared as she navigated elite educational institutions.

Miguel attended a private four-year university and believes he would not be attending that university if he had not been admitted to a private high school. For Miguel, like many of his peers, extracurricular activities were a critical factor in both high school and college admissions: "When I had interviews or when I met the admissions counselor, they actually specifically asked me about Students Together. They were really interested in it, and I told them about it, and it sounds really good on the application." Participants in Students Together left the program with concrete skills, and these skills were rewarded by a host of institutional agents in ways that enabled educational attainment. When faced with gatekeepers who value middle-class attitudes and skills, out-of-school time programs might help fill the gaps marginalized students experience and create pathways for educational advancement.

Supportive Environment for Identity Development

In addition, high-quality out-of-school time programs may benefit participants by providing an environment that supports students to develop an identity that is positively received across multiple contexts. While some adolescents experience congruent home and school environments and others have already cultivated coping strategies for straddling divergent worlds, some students flounder to develop a sense of self that allows them to successfully navigate such complicated transitions. Flores-González (2002) argued that Latina/o youth achieve school success by adopting an all-encompassing "school kid" identity that is positively received across school, home, and community contexts. Whether students develop and sustain this identity depends upon the available social supports and the perceived rewards for the role. Extracurricular programs can supply the necessary conditions for the school kid identity to take shape, including beneficial relationships with peers and adults, encouragement for college and career aspirations and planning, and opportunities to participate in activities that act as both rewards and identity-enhancing events.

Students Together provided this type of supportive environment for identity development for some participants. Staff members required participants to get good grades, but they also engaged them as active citizens in the broader community. By teaching communication skills and respect across differences, the program structure promoted both peer and adult support. Furthermore, especially for those who continued with the program after their eighth-grade year, Students Together rewarded participants for sustaining that role. For those who moved on to other extracurricular pursuits, such as Bayside's Youth Council (an organization operated by the Parks and Recreation department offering teenagers a voice in local issues concerning young people), school personnel and local organizations similarly rewarded their school kid identity. Finally, through multiple avenues, Students Together provided a context promoting identity-enhancing events, such as making presentations at town council meetings, while protecting students from identity-threatening contexts, including gang-affiliated peers.

For example, before joining Students Together, Maria did not know what her interests were and was confused about what kind of person she wanted to become. The purpose of the program appealed to her, and through participation she was exposed to new activities and ways of seeing herself in which she took pride, such as making public presentations and becoming a peer leader. This new identity was positively received both at school and at home. She recalled, "I didn't know what I wanted. I didn't know who I was. But then along came Students Together. I decided that's where I wanted to be and that was in reality who I was, and I never got a chance to know that until [I joined]. And what if that wouldn't have come up in my life? Then maybe until now I'd still be wondering what in the world it is that I like." Following her time in Students Together, Maria became determined to keep up with her schoolwork in order to maintain the positive self-image she had begun to develop in Students Together. She also started taking an active role in local advocacy organizations. Organized activities played a role in her educational attainment by giving her a positive sense of identity and self that propelled her forward with confidence and direction.

Victoria shared a similar experience, in that Students Together provided a supportive environment where she could develop a strong sense of self that would be positively received at school, at home, and around the community. Once she had the opportunity to solidify her identity around constructive activities, she was able to let go of her gang ties. She acknowledged, "I did a lot of stuff with Students Together. That's why I feel like it was like my savior. Once I joined, I was beyond gangs. I mean, that was an issue in the communities that everyone would talk about, and I just felt like, wow! It's a problem and why was I in it? Soon I started seeing [positive] opportunities that were approaching, and I'm like, I can't just say no. And that's how I started leaving my gang stuff behind." Victoria stayed involved with Students Together as a high school mentor and engaged with other community groups working against gang violence. Students Together provided a supportive environment and captivated her interests by helping her develop a new sense of self rooted in community engagement.

Although not all participants experienced sweeping identity transformations like Maria and Victoria, many took solace in finding a supportive environment away from their everyday peer interactions where they could be known in a different way. For some, this was linked to the types of activities that were part of Students Together, such as data collection or public speaking. For others, it was more closely linked to the themes of the program, such as social justice or community improvement. Overall, because participation in Students Together was positively viewed by respondents' teachers, families, and community members, participation helped young people bridge the school-home divide by instilling in them a critical lens on community issues, listening to and validating their perspectives, and empowering them to speak up and be heard among their peers and elders.

Relationships with Supportive Adults

Finally, fitting with social capital and social embeddedness theory, some students benefit from the relationships they develop with adult staff members as a result of participation in an out-of-school time program. While social embeddedness views individuals as embedded within social networks that limit or enable their movement within society (Furstenberg and Hughes 1995; Granovetter 1985; Stanton-Salazar 2001), social capital refers to the benefits students glean from their networks and relationships (Coleman 1988). Disadvantaged youth are often embedded in networks—from their family, school, and neighborhood—that limit access to the kinds of social capital that would prove beneficial on the college pathway; through their relationships with adult leaders in out-of-school time activities, participants gain new access to social capital. Relationships with staff members offer a buffer from the negative influences some students experience in their immediate surroundings from family members, peers, and broader societal forces, such as poverty and racism. These relationships also connect participants with tactical advice and generous encouragement as they work to navigate the transition from middle school to high school and from high school to college. Finally, these relationships connect young people with subsequent out-of-school time pursuits, which weave a web of ongoing supports as participants grow and mature.

Respondents in this study expanded their social capital thanks to the knowledgeable and supportive adults with whom they built relationships during their time in Students Together. While the staff members varied with regard to race, ethnicity, gender, and age, all were college graduates and well connected within the local community. Especially for adolescents who experienced fewer positive interactions with adults at home, the opportunity to feel supported in an out-of-school time program gave them the feeling of having a second home. According to Felicia, "[The staff members] really taught me to get positive feedback for positive actions. In low-income communities like mine because of a lot of socioeconomic reasons, parents are out a lot. So it's hard for them to teach a child how to be positive and reinforce those positive things, it takes a lot of time. It's a lot of time, which unfortunately, our parents don't have. And if you're out on the street, you're not really going to get, 'Oh, you spoke really good in class last time.' You're going to get, 'Oh, I like your shoes.'" The focused attention from staff members fostered caring relationships with students. Given the small size of each cohort, staff members had the opportunity to get to know students in ways that most teachers and school personnel could not provide. In addition, for students with parents who worked many jobs or long hours, staff members could provide support that their parents were too busy to consistently offer.

In addition to caring relationships, staff members also inspired and advised students as they progressed along the road to college. While many participants possessed college ambitions prior to joining the program, most did not know how to turn those dreams into reality. For students whose parents did not go to college, having a trusting relationship with a college-educated mentor was invaluable. According to Teresa, "At Students Together they're always like, 'Yeah, you know, apply for this college.' I mean, they're even saying apply to Harvard! They were just like always, 'Go to college. Get yourself educated. Education is good.' And that helped pushing out, pushing you, and it's really good because it's good for kids to go get education and succeed in life, and it's good Students Together has helped a lot." Graciela recalled, "I always wanted to succeed, and [the staff members] were like, 'Oh, you know, you've got to do this and do this.' And it was really good." Miguel agreed, "[Staff members] always want you to succeed. They just really cared about the kids and their future." Participants not only gained endorsement for their dreams of higher education, but they also were privy to education-related cultural capital through the college-educated program staff that most lacked at home.

Staff members' intimate knowledge of local resources and sense of possibility intertwined to make them vital sources of information, which connected students with a ladder of extracurricular opportunities. They steered students aging out of Students Together toward similar programs geared toward older youth, such as the Bayside's Youth Council. They encouraged participants to follow their own visions of change, helping one student start a school-based Latina support group and another build an outreach program for eighth graders transitioning to high school. Some former participants stayed in contact with staff members as they transitioned to high school and relied on their guidance for many years. The continued support and infusion of information from knowledgeable adults may be one way that extracurricular activities exerted a long-term influence on participants' educational attainment.

How then does extracurricular participation fit into the decades-long debate about the achievement gap? And do out-of-school time programs contribute to disadvantaged students' college trajectories? While previous quantitative research has shown that adolescents generally benefit from participating in extracurricular activities, the analysis presented in this book offers a portrayal of the processes through which marginalized youth, in particular, benefit with regards to educational attainment. Overall, these case studies of former Students Together participants reveal that programs can become avenues for relationships with supportive and knowledgeable adults, opportunities to see themselves in a new or more positive light, and experiences that expand their skill sets and engender cultural capital. Yet all participants did not benefit through all three processes, nor did they benefit to the same degree. Building on this discussion of the processes through which extracurricular activities promote educational attainment, the following chapters longitudinally examine multiple overlapping contexts—including family, school, peers, neighborhoods, and out-of-school time—to elucidate why participation may influence students differently. In the process, the stories these youth tell interweave multiple sociological explanations for academic success among low-income students of color—specifically cultural capital, role-identity, and social capital theories.

3

Auxiliary Influence

"It Was Fun . . . But I Don't
Remember Much"

Ana, Julio, Miguel, Rosa, Benjamin, and Graciela all participated in the
Students Together program as eighth graders at Adams Middle School in
Bayside. After their year in the program, each graduated from high school
and enrolled in college. Looking back, they each have positive memories
from their time in the program. Miguel remembered the collaboration
on a group project and the genuine care of the adult staff members. Ana
recalled all the wonderful people she met and how she learned so much
about her community. Rosa appreciated learning to notice problems in her
neighborhood and getting to spend time with friends. Overall, participating in Students Together had a measured yet positive influence on these
students' academic trajectories.

Specifically, the concrete skills these students acquired during their
time in the program helped them along the road to college and later in life.
Miguel reflected on the accomplishments of his Students Together cohort
during admissions interviews for private high schools. Rosa employed her
leadership skills to start an antilittering group at her high school. Selena

used her inquiry skills to write college papers. Maria used team-building activities from the program to help her earn a promotion in her human relations job. As these examples relate to skills targeted through the Students Together curriculum—communication, leadership, and community-based research—participants in other programs may acquire different skills. Their stories, however, suggest that, through access to and participation in a high-quality extracurricular activity, marginalized adolescents can pick up the kinds of skills that will help them successfully navigate the educational system.

Chapter 3 introduces the concept of auxiliary influence for structured extracurricular activities. Auxiliary influence depicts young people, like those mentioned above, who have a beneficial experience participating in an out-of-school time program but for whom the program does not create a lasting influence or distinct contribution, in the context of all the other home, school, and community-level factors helping to shape their pathways to college. For example, a program may provide a safe and welcoming place to spend time after school, developmentally appropriate activities with which to engage, supportive adult role models, constructive peer interactions, academic enrichment, and vocational training. Given all the relationships and structures in which a student is embedded, however, the positive aspects of participation do not significantly alter his or her trajectory.

The primary process through which young people who experience an auxiliary degree of influence benefit from out-of-school time program participation is through acquiring institutionally valued cultural capital. Cultural capital is any piece of knowledge or set of skills that dominant institutions, such as schools, employers, or the government, systematically reward. The rewards for possessing these institutionally valued pieces of knowledge or sets of skills help facilitate upward mobility (Bourdieu 1986). For example, schools reward well-written term papers with good grades, yet they tend to reward certain styles of written and oral communication more than others. Knowing how to speak and write in the style of the white upper or middle class is a kind of cultural capital that facilitates academic achievement. Other examples of valued cultural capital include the practice of negotiating in times of disagreement or advocating for oneself with teachers, doctors, and other professionals. These skill sets help young people gain advantages at school and around the community.

Yet these skills are not equally distributed. Through the approach to childrearing that Annette Lareau (2003) called concerted cultivation, middle- and upper-class parents tend to intentionally impart such cultural capital to their children at home, thereby giving them a clear advantage as they navigate social institutions. Meanwhile, lower-class parents tend to abide by an approach Lareau has called the accomplishment of natural growth. Under such a system, children are encouraged to spend time with siblings and extended family members, they learn to play and resolve conflict without adult intervention, and they are trained to respect authority figures and defer to their judgments without questioning. Although prioritizing family time and demonstrating deference to one's elders are often considered admirable traits, schools and other social institutions more often reward students who speak up for their own needs and negotiate for the conditions that are most personally favorable. By learning such skills in extracurricular programs, participants begin to narrow the cultural capital gap between themselves and their more privileged peers.

Furthermore, as college admissions committees demonstrate an increasing preference for lengthy resumes of extracurricular accomplishment (Stevens 2007), middle- and upper-class parents have begun to invest more heavily in their children's hectic line-ups of structured activities (Lareau 2003). From the early 1970s until 2005–2006, families in the top income quintile increased the amount they spend on enrichment activities by 150 percent, while spending on enrichment activities among the bottom quintile grew only by about 50 percent (Duncan and Murnane 2011). Participation in structured out-of-school time programs gives lower-income students an opportunity to mimic the pursuits of their higher-income peers and acts as a credential signaling upwardly mobile intentions to institutional gatekeepers. This evidence supports Pierre Bourdieu's notion that education-related capital acts as a mechanism by which class background affects academic achievement.

So why do the benefits of participation end there for students who experience an auxiliary degree of influence? Why do they walk away with only concrete skills and fond memories? To answer these questions we must look beyond their experiences in a given extracurricular program and return to the other structures and relationships within which each has been embedded over time. In addition, we must keep in mind how students' interests and personalities mesh with the specific goals of the program. Participants who experience an auxiliary degree of influence tend not to be struggling socially or academically at the time they join an extracurricular program and are likely to be embedded in supportive relationships and stable home, school, and neighborhood environments. Youth in the auxiliary influence category tend to have a close relationship with one or more responsible and caring adult mentors, in most cases a parent who supports their educational aspirations and endeavors. Moreover, these participants tend to feel supported by their teachers and exhibit few academic struggles. Finally, before and during their time in the program, students in this category feel a sense of belonging in a positive and fulfilling peer group.

Given the supportive relationships and structures participants in the auxiliary degree of influence category tend to experience outside the program, there are fewer opportunities for the out-of-school time program to bring about a profound change in their lives. Indeed, because their educational trajectories are already college-bound and viewed positively across family, school, and peer contexts, respondents for whom Students Together had an auxiliary influence do not require intervention to get them on the track toward educational attainment. That does not, however, mean the opportunity to participate is wasted on these students. Though the magnitude of influence may be small, the overall effect is positive. Experiences in high-quality programs remain important for healthy adolescent development, even for students who are neither socially nor academically at risk.

Some students who experience an auxiliary degree of influence face little resistance on their pathway to college, while others grapple with significant threats to their educational aspirations. When dealing with obstacles, successful students in the auxiliary group rely on resources other than the extracurricular program to provide a buffer from negative influences and to aid in recovery from setbacks. Depending on the timing and nature of the obstacles a student encounters, such resources may stem from a variety of relationships and contexts, including other out-of-school time programs. Even though one program has an auxiliary influence on a participant, other programs may wield varying degrees of influence because the topical focus of one program might provide a better fit with the student's interests, or the student may have developed stronger relationships with adult staff members or fellow participants. In addition, one program may influence a student more than another due to the timing of participation, especially if the student's support networks have shifted or his or her needs have changed.

In the case of the Students Together participants profiled for this book, we see many examples of relationships, structures, and agency intersecting to support respondents in the auxiliary influence category as they deal with adversity on the road to higher education. For example, five of the six respondents in this category were Mexican American, and, while only four of those five spent part of their childhood living in Mexico, all five entered elementary school in the United States speaking no English. Although this is often considered a risk factor for low educational attainment, respondents in this study experienced support both at school and at home to quickly master the language. Each was placed in a bilingual classroom for at least two years, and all cite their bilingual teachers as very influential during elementary school. In addition, each respondent developed a group of bilingual friends who helped them navigate the school day and engaged in supplemental language and literacy activities with their parents at home. All these factors—the structure of the school system that provided bilingual instruction, the positive relationships respondents experienced with teachers, peers, and parents, and the respondents' personal motivations to acquire English language skilled—joined together to support their educational advancement over time.

In another example, all respondents in the auxiliary degree of influence category moved at least once during their childhood years after their arrival in the United States, and some moved as many as three additional times. While residential mobility has been characterized by the literature as a risk factor for low academic attainment, each of the respondents' families managed to continue living within the same school attendance zone as they moved. Though respondents experienced disruption to their home lives, their school environments remained constant, allowing them to remain embedded within supportive school structures, as well as familiar relationships with peers, teachers, and staff members.

These examples show the ways that students can be buffered from negative influences at a young age and maintain a strong academic trajectory through relationships, structures, and personal agency, without the intervention of extracurricular programming. Organized activities, however, can take on a critical role even for those young people who are already well supported by building cultural capital. Especially as students enter into adolescence and begin to prepare for the transition to adulthood, the institutionally valued skills and experiences instilled by high-quality out-of-school time programs can facilitate access to valuable academic and social rewards.

To better illustrate the ways that family, school, and out-of-school time factors overlap for students in the auxiliary influence group, chapter 3 profiles two Mexican American Students Together participants, Graciela and Julio. The profiles draw on interviews that I conducted when each student was an eighth grader at Adams Middle School and new to the Students Together program and continue until their young adult years. Though Graciela and Julio share many traits, their paths diverge in meaningful ways. At the time of the final follow-up interview, Graciela had completed her first year at a selective private college and was on track to pursue a career in medicine. Meanwhile, Julio worked as a deliveryman to support his girlfriend and young son and pursued fire science classes part-time at the local community college. By taking a closer look at the structures and relationships each former participant was embedded in before, during, and after their time in Students Together, we begin to understand how these factors support and detract from each participant's educational attainment and how the auxiliary degree of influence takes shape.

Graciela

Childhood and Elementary School

Graciela was born in rural Mexico and spent her early childhood there. When she was five, her parents immigrated to the United States, "because it was getting hard over there." Though she does not know the specifics of why her parents chose to immigrate, she believes economic factors were the main cause. She remained in Mexico and attended kindergarten, staying with her grandmother, aunts, and uncles. One year later, she joined her parents in California.

For her first-grade year, Graciela and her parents lived with a large group of extended family members in a house in Bayside. Graciela spoke no English and was placed in a bilingual class at Truman Elementary School. She remembers her first-grade teacher fondly and credits her with helping to ease the transition to a new school and new language. "She was a really good teacher. She was so nice and sweet, and she was there helping me along the way." Even as a young adult, Graciela still recalled the critical importance of that first-grade teacher in her transition to the United States.

Also helpful were her bilingual friends. Though Graciela struggled to learn English, she made friends easily. "I was very social, so despite me not knowing English in my first year I was able to make a lot of friends and that was really helpful." After her first year in the bilingual program, her English skills improved dramatically, and things began to look up. "It was hard learning English, but once I got the hang of it everything was so much easier." Graciela continued in the bilingual program at Truman for two more years, but "after [my first year], I don't really recall struggling much."

In addition to her teacher and her friends, Graciela's parents and extended family also helped sustain her during this difficult transition. Graciela described her parents' unwavering strength and support: "They were always there. They never said you can't do it. They never said I feel sorry for you. No. They were always like you can and this is how it's going to be and that's that. There was never hesitation, no questioning about anything, and that was my main strength." Graciela's parents were attentive to her schoolwork and did not put up with excuses or subpar effort. They lovingly supported her as she worked to overcome the challenges of adjusting to a new place. In the evenings, Graciela worked to advance her English skills by reading books with her mother. She recalls, "It was kind of like a learning process for both of us, because [my parents] were learning [English] as well." The time spent reading together not only brought her closer with her parents, but it also communicated their strong support for her academic progress. Throughout her elementary school years, Graciela cited "my parents—but especially my mom," as the most influential force in keeping her on track.

At the end of first grade, Graciela moved across town with her immediate family, two of her aunts, and their children. Late in her elementary school years, Graciela's parents welcomed another daughter. The bilingual program at Truman ended in third grade so starting in fourth grade Graciela's classes were taught only in English. Graciela was ready for the change and began to blossom into a top student. She continued to feel supported by her teachers and felt especially excited when they noticed how quickly her skills were improving.

Outside school, she remained social and enjoyed playing with neighborhood friends and cousins. She felt safe in her neighborhood and home and spent endless hours outside in the company of other children. "I would spend a lot of time playing. I used to play with the boys a lot, so that was fun. One of my friends had a trampoline, so we would go to his house and jump on it a lot. We used to also race on our bikes and climb trees." During her elementary school years, Graciela did not participate in any structured afterschool programs. Rather, she enjoyed the freedom to play in her neighborhood and the time at home with her family.

Middle School

Graciela continued to excel at school and feel supported at home as she transitioned to Adams Middle School in sixth grade. She took her academic work very seriously and started to think about college. "In middle school was when I actually started caring more about my grades. I got all As. . . . I was determined to go to college since basically I was ten. I knew where I wanted to go and I knew what I wanted to do, at least sketches of it." Her parents had impressed upon her the importance of not only good grades for getting into college but also the importance of college for success in life. Graciela took their advice seriously and developed concrete plans, for both higher education and her subsequent career. "My parents were always behind me. They were like, 'Do you really want to be working your ass off for $9 an hour or $8?' And I'm like, 'No, I prefer to work my butt off for something that's worth it than for something that's not.' That was my mentality throughout high school and all throughout middle school. . . . I always wanted to make [my parents] proud and make myself proud for what I would do or accomplish." Having supportive parents pushed Graciela to keep her sights set on college from an early age.

During middle school Graciela's family moved twice, but they remained in the same school district so she was able to continue attending the same middle school for sixth, seventh, and eighth grades. Each time the family moved to relatively safe and family-friendly areas of town. For example, as an eighth grader Graciela characterized her neighborhood as "pretty okay," saying, "there is nothing I would like to remove—just speeding cars because I hate that." Each time, her aunts, uncle, and cousins moved along with them. Late in her middle school years, Graciela parents welcomed a third daughter.

Outside school, Graciela continued to enjoy spending time with her family, but she also began to take an interest in structured activities. She attended Adams's afterschool program, where she got help with her homework. Starting in seventh grade, she joined the volleyball team "because I always liked sports." Graciela primarily enjoyed the social aspects of the team and had a lot of fun meeting girls who became her lifelong friends and traveling to different schools to compete.

As an eighth grader, Graciela joined Students Together. At the time, she reported, "I decided to join so I can at least try to do something for the community." One issue that sparked her interest was that her mother was having trouble finding affordable daycare for her younger sisters. While the service-oriented focus of Students Together fit with her interests at the time, looking back as a young adult Graciela admits that she actually decided to participate largely at the urging of her friends. Although she joined in part because of her preexisting peers, Students Together gave Graciela the opportunity to engage with new people. The program's explicit focus on communication skills taught Graciela to voice her thoughts, even in the context of this new and diverse peer group. "In seventh grade I got shy, and in eighth grade I opened up more. [Students Together] helped me with that because I was working with more people." This experience helped her gain confidence and become more outspoken. At the end of her eighth-grade year, she reported, "I have learned how to be a leader and how to speak up a little bit more and how to say what is on my mind. I feel more confident in speaking." Overall, like other participants who experienced an auxiliary degree of influence, these concrete skills—leadership and public speaking—were Graciela's big takeaways from her time in Students Together.

In the short term Graciela benefited from participation, but over the long run the influence of the program faded. As a young adult, Graciela remembered Students Together fondly without recalling details. She remembered there were meetings—"they were actually fun, I remember laughing"—though she conceded, "I don't remember much." While Graciela had a positive experience in the program and continued to use and develop the skills she learned there in subsequent years, participation did not alter her already college-bound trajectory.

Prior to joining, Graciela had a supportive family, an academically inclined peer group, strong grades, and college ambitions. As an eighth grader she described herself as "smart" and "responsible." When asked about her future plans, she replied that after "going to a nice university, I would like to be either a lawyer or an architect. I want to be a lawyer because I like to dictate stuff, and an architect because I like to build stuff and I am good at that." She backed her lofty goals by a record of achievement and many reliable sources of support. When asked to name the most important influence during her middle school years, Graciela turned the attention to her family. "I would say, once again, my mom." After a pause, she recalled two teachers that were "really good," but other than being good teachers they did not make a lasting influence on Graciela's pathway to college.

High School

Like many of her peers, Graciela attended Ridgetop High School in Bayside. She maintained a close network of friends and felt generally supported by her teachers. During her high school years, Graciela's family moved two more times within the district. Despite the moves, her family remained a steadfast anchor as Graciela's academic and extracurricular pursuits continued to expand. Graciela's career goals evolved as she set her sights on becoming a doctor.

Graciela's high school experiences were closely tailored around her goal of attending "a nice university" and going to medical school. Her parents helped shape this ambition, and she methodically sought out extracurricular and summer activities that would bring her closer to her goal. She joined the school's lacrosse team her freshman year, cross country team her sophomore and junior years, and track team her junior and senior years. She volunteered helping young children learn to read and became president of two leadership clubs during her senior year: Latino Stars and College Bound. With such a busy schedule, she found it more difficult to spend quality time with her family, "I would get home really late from my sports, and I would help clean a little bit and then just do my homework and study. My weekends were pretty busy, too." She missed spending time with her family, but she felt secure knowing they would be behind her as she pursued her goals.

Though she played no organized sports in elementary school and only volleyball during middle school, Graciela branched out during her high school years. As a freshman, she joined the lacrosse team even though she had never played before. She joined because "I wanted to try a new sport" and really liked it. She played for only one season because the practice time was not convenient for her schedule, but the experience made an impression on her. "It was a tough sport, so I learned a lot. Sometimes my coach wouldn't put me to play, but I guess it was for the best for the team, so I understood that." From there, she moved on to cross country for two years. While it was difficult—"cross country was really hard, like so hard"—she enjoyed the challenge. Her junior year, Graciela joined the track team because "I never tried it, so I'm like, 'Oh, let me go try it.' Pretty much, I'm up to trying new things." Her athletic record reflects both her sense of adventure and her social nature. Regarding her high school sports career Graciela reflected, "I get bored with repetition. So that's why I want to try new things, you know, throw myself out there. One of the reasons why I tried different sports was because I didn't want to graduate from high school and then go back and say, 'Oh, dang, why didn't I try that sport?' I don't want to be regretting anything." Overall, joining sports teams was a fun way to try new things, spend time with friends, and stay active. Graciela never intended to become a star athlete in any particular sport; rather, she signed up simply for the delight of the experience.

Graciela joined Latino Stars and College Bound for a different reason: she knew she needed demonstrable leadership experience for her college application. "I needed to step forward on my leadership skills. Through my freshman and sophomore year, I was kind of shy. So by the time I hit my junior year, I was like, things have got to change. I thought that being in a program that promoted leadership would benefit me." But in the college admissions game one leadership activity would not be enough so Graciela sought additional leadership opportunities for the express purpose of making her college applications more competitive. "I thought Latino Stars only accounted for a certain number, and I'm like, hmm, maybe I should increase my numbers." This brought her to sign up for the College Bound program. During her senior year, she was elected president of both Latino Stars and College Bound.

Though she joined to beef up her resumé, she learned a tremendous amount from participating and holding leadership roles in both organizations. For example, from serving as president of Latino Stars, she developed a more nuanced sense of leadership and collaboration: "I learned that to be a leader, you don't have to always be a leader. A true leader learns to listen to others, and, despite me being the president, I learned that it was very important that every other member was a leader as well. They were entitled to an opinion, just like I was entitled to my own opinion." From the intense college prep curriculum offered by College Bound, "I learned that you have to pretty much manage your time very wisely." Similar to Students Together, each program proved beneficial and memorable by offering Graciela skill-building opportunities in line with the program's curriculum.

In addition, from College Bound Graciela gained an influential mentor. Her College Bound teacher "was great," and, because of this personal connection with the adult leader, College Bound had a stronger influence on Graciela than most of her other extracurricular engagements. "[My College Bound teacher] helped me out with my college applications, she was just amazing. Like, I told her, 'I need a [recommendation] letter by this time,' and it was like she had it. She was always on top of things. Her life was a complete disaster simply because she had to help out so many people, but in all of that she always made time for me. That really helped me a lot!" Her College Bound teacher not only delivered the program's curriculum but also helped Graciela navigate the ins and outs of the college application process. Though the teacher was supporting a large number of students, Graciela thrived because she received personalized attention.

Graciela also participated in Project Read—a literacy tutoring program—during her junior and senior years. Along with College Bound, Project Read was one of her favorite extracurricular activities because "I felt like I grew a lot. I opened up a lot, and my communication skills improved a lot. I learned how to work with people better and work with kids." Like many of her other extracurricular pursuits, Project Read not only taught Graciela concrete skills—communication and working with children—but it also introduced her to a newfound passion. Already knowing she wanted to be a doctor, Project Read helped Graciela discover that she wanted to specialize in pediatrics.

During her summers, Graciela worked to further prepare herself for college and medical school by taking classes at a local community college. During the summer after her freshman year, she took geometry so that she would be ready for calculus by the time she was a senior. During her sophomore summer she took chemistry, and during her junior summer she took biology. Although taking supplementary summer classes during high school to prepare for the pre-med track in college is common among more privileged students, given that Graciela's parents were Mexican immigrants who did not attend college, it is a testament to her tenacity and strong support network that she possessed the cultural capital to pursue this path. When asked how she decided to sign up for summer classes in anticipation of her college goals, she recalled, "I asked a counselor if it was possible to do that and she said, 'Yeah.' So I'm like, 'Okay, I'm going to take geometry during the summer and I want to be in Algebra II next year.' Then she said—I remember I hated her for this—she said, 'I'm going to sign you up but just to let you know, it's really hard.' I was just like, 'Yeah, that's cool. Just sign me up.' And she was like, 'Are you sure?' I'm like, 'I wouldn't be telling you to sign me up if I wasn't sure.'" As a freshman in high school, Graciela already knew which courses colleges would want to see on her transcript. She was both savvy and confident enough to approach her guidance counselor and insist upon being signed up for the appropriate summer classes, even though the guidance counselor initially resisted. This is one example of how out-of-school supports—such as parents, peers, and mentors—can help students become college-ready, even when institutional agents—such as guidance counselors—create adversity.

Graciela knew that taking extra courses would be a necessary step on her journey to becoming a doctor, but her favorite summer activity was volunteering at a local medical center after her junior and senior years. She spent time at the information desk, the health education center, and shadowing a nurse practitioner. Like some of her other extracurricular activities, Graciela initially got involved because she wanted to build her resumé and because the volunteer job was a good fit for her interests. "I thought it was necessary and it was going to really give me a preview of what it is to be a doctor. I also thought it would look good as an extra activity on my college application. And it was all something I wanted to do, as a volunteer, I wanted to help people. I've always enjoyed helping people, so it was like doing three things at once." Always mindful of her college application and her career goals, the chance to volunteer at the medical center was both beneficial and enjoyable for Graciela.

Throughout high school, Graciela continued to benefit from her family's emotional and financial support. Though her family moved frequently during her adolescent years, they were mindful to always stay within the same district in order to keep Graciela's school environment consistent. Her mother would read with her and keep a careful eye on her studies. In addition, though the family was very much working class, Graciela was not expected to care for her younger siblings or work for pay during her out-of-school time. Instead, Graciela's family encouraged her to pursue the portfolio of extracurricular activities that would help her build a competitive college application.

In addition to her family, Graciela's College Bound teacher became a very influential figure on her pathway to college. Graciela was focused on attending a top-tier school, but she did not want to travel too far from home. During her senior year, as Graciela was applying to colleges, her College Bound teacher helped select schools that would be a good fit. Within a one-hour drive of Bayside, Graciela could choose from an array of competitive public and private colleges and universities. As a first-generation college student, Graciela relied mostly on word of mouth among her peers to decide which school she would like to attend. But her College Bound teacher helped Graciela diversify her options. "I was going to go to the

University of California and my mind was set on that, and then [my College Bound teacher] told me, 'You should apply to this private college. Just apply.' Well, I applied to all those schools through the common application, so I just had to click two buttons and then, bam, my application was sent." Even after applying, Graciela did not consider that she would actually attend a small private school. In her mind, she was already set on attending a larger public university. Although earning admission to the smaller private college did not alter her vision, seeing their financial aid package did:

> I got accepted and I was like, I'm not going to go to a small private college. I don't even know anything about [it]. I didn't even research it as a school or anything, because I was going to go over to the University of California. And actually, I was also thinking of going to another nearby [private] university. But when the small private college sent me their [financial aid] award letter, I was like, "I'm going!" So I set up all the paperwork and they were postmarked that same day that they were due. They were mailed and that was me on my way to a small private school!

Even with all that she had learned about the college process from College Bound and other sources, Graciela had not considered that attending a private college could cost less than attending a public university given the availability of financial aid. Although she had initially considered the school out of her range because of the price tag, she enthusiastically accepted its offer once she discovered how generous the aid package would be.

After High School

During the summer after her senior year, the college invited Graciela to attend a special pre-orientation session for students interested in the sciences. Graciela enthusiastically accepted the invitation and was grateful for the opportunity to get a head start on campus. "I got to be at school and get a little taste of it before everybody else did." Graciela started classes in the fall and, at the time of our final interview, had successfully completed her first year.

Graciela connected with many familiar activities as she transitioned into college life. She planned to double major in biology and Spanish, still intent on completing the pre-med requirements. She followed her custom of trying new sports by signing up for the crew team, but due to the academic pressures of a double major she did not plan to continue rowing in future years. She also got involved with a campus group that matches college students up with young girls for tutoring, which reminded her of the tutoring she enjoyed in high school because she got to work with children. Thanks to her generous financial aid package, she was not required to work for pay on campus.

Although the college is only a forty-five-minute drive from Bayside, Graciela seldom had time to visit or call home during the school year due to her active involvement in campus life. Even without frequent contact, Graciela still leaned heavily on her parents' support. "They did encourage me and everything, and that was helpful. But they've always been helpful!" Throughout every phase of her life, Graciela's parents played a major role in supporting her college and career goals.

After college, Graciela plans to attend medical school and become a pediatrician. When asked why she chose that career she replied, "I like working with kids. I like helping them. I basically like everything about them. I've always liked science, and I always wanted to work in a hospital environment." Thinking more long term, she thinks back to her family and her childhood: "One day, I want to go back to Mexico and I want to open up probably a private clinic or something. I don't want to just stay [in California]. I don't want to say, 'Oh, I got my education here, I'm going to stay here and work here.' No. I want to go places, move out, and help out. I don't want my help just to remain here, I want to spread it around." Graciela seemed optimistic about her future and committed to her long-standing goals of graduating from college, becoming a doctor, and using her talents and skills to help others in need.

Overall, Graciela's home, school, and out-of-school environments worked together to support her educational trajectory. Despite her family's frequent moves, she remained in safe neighborhoods that allowed her to continue attending the same schools. Though Graciela did not cite any of her teachers as particularly influential after her initial transition to the United States, she experienced a generally positive academic environment, never struggled in school, and maintained a prosocial peer group. In addition, Graciela's perseverance, academic aptitude, and social nature helped her along the way.

Like many college-bound students, Graciela's family provided unconditional love and support and prioritized resources to give Graciela the latitude to pursue application-boosting extracurricular pursuits. None of the activities that Graciela participated in had a life-changing influence, primarily because Graciela's educational trajectory had been carved out and protected by her parents at an early age. Each activity she joined in middle school and high school offered a generally positive experience, in part at least because it was a good fit for Graciela's goals and interests. Some teams and organizations further offered skill-building experiences that helped Graciela develop her talents and her resumé. Others offered fellowship, exercise, and enjoyment. Only College Bound set itself apart as particularly influential, given Graciela's close personal relationship with the teacher and the timing of her participation relative to the college application process.

Julio

Childhood and Elementary School

Julio was born in Bayside and lived there for the first few years of his life with his father, mother, and her three sons from a previous relationship. Before long, the family decided to relocate from their cramped apartment. Julio's father bought a house in a nearby city because "there were cheaper houses" there than in Bayside, but Julio remembers it as a dangerous town: "[In] the '90s, when we moved over, it was still hectic over here. It was still a lot of shootings [and] people dying. I believe it was the murder capital [of the United States] in those years." As a result, Julio and his half-brothers were required to play close to home. "We would just stay up in the front of the lawn, because it was bad outside. We couldn't really go out that much." Julio's parents were so concerned about the boys' safety that when Julio reached school age, they opted to send him out of the local neighborhood for a safer school environment.

From kindergarten through fifth grade, Julio's father would drive the children to school every day. "In the morning, he would drive and drop us off and pick us up after work. He didn't really want us to go to school [where we lived]." Because their parents were working, the boys needed a place to hang out after school until the end of the workday. Julio remembered, "Our aunt lived right across the street [from our school], so we would just walk over there and wait for [our parents]. We wouldn't have no [daily] afterschool programs." Julio and his brothers were rarely engaged in organized activities and spent most of their nonschool hours hanging out together and with other family members.

Julio attended one extracurricular program as a child. On a monthly basis, a group of elementary children traveled to the local university to meet with mentors who were undergraduate students. "We would go up to the university and would talk to some school students over there. We would just join up to them, see how they're doing in school. They would ask us the same thing. We would have meetings." Although Julio remembered little else about the program, it was influential in his life because it helped keep him out of trouble. "The university program helped me out, just being off of problems there." This attribution is common to all the extracurricular programs Julio joined; each one helped him by giving him something positive to do after school.

Middle School

Julio continued to attend Bayside schools instead of his neighborhood schools throughout his educational career, and his father continued to drive him to school every day after he transitioned to middle school at Adams. His mother gave birth to twins while he was in middle school so the house became more crowded. "Everything was good at school," and his studies were not too difficult. Throughout these years, Julio remained close to his father.

As an eighth grader, Julio became involved in the Students Together program. At the time, Julio reported that he got involved because he "didn't want to really stay at home. I just wanted to stay after school." As a young adult, he gave more detail as to why he became involved. He learned of the program from a friend and was drawn in by the opportunity to have something to do after school, the program content, and the stipend check. "I had another friend that was joining, and that's what got me into it. I remember they said, 'You're getting paid for it,' so it was like work. It was probably the pay and just having the program after school and learning more stuff about the community [that got me interested]." At the time of his eighth grade interview, Julio kept returning to the fact that Students Together gave him a reason to not go home after school.

Similar to others in the auxiliary influence category, Julio remembered little of the actual program. "We had a really big group of people. We would have meetings. We were trying to do a video to see how bad the

city was, what we needed to get changed. That's the only stuff I remember."
And like others in this category, when asked if there were any people from
the program he remembered, Julio replied: "I remember our advisor, the
main advisor that we had. I forgot her name, and I forgot the people that
were in our group. Probably if I would see them again, I would remember."
Julio credits Students Together with making him more outgoing and comfortable talking to new people: "[Students Together helped me become] a
people's person, because I would speak to other people. We would go out
there, talk to people, [and] get interviews like this. I speak to people more
because of the interviews, they helped me out a lot, talk to more people,
learn from what other people have experienced." Overall, Julio remembered participating mostly because the program provided a positive experience that not only kept him off the streets after school but also helped him
acquire better communication and public speaking skills.

In addition, like the university program he had participated in during
elementary school, Julio credits Students Together with helping him stay
out of trouble. In eighth grade he said his favorite part of the program was
"that it keeps me away from home after classes. Afterward when I'm home,
I don't want to do nothing. I just go outside. So it's good, because it keeps
you away from gangs and drugs." If he had not been involved in Students
Together, Julio felt as though he probably would have been involved with
gangs during this period of his life because "I know a lot of friends and I
have a lot of my friends that after school, they just go to their houses and go
in the backyard and start smoking. I guess they don't have enough things
to do." Julio's photo-collage of his neighborhood that he completed as
part of the Students Together curriculum showcased gang sign graffiti. He
included graffiti in public places where he believed the police should have
a stronger presence as well as graffiti that had been painted on the front
fence of his friend's house. He credits gang activity as one reason he was
happy to spend less time at home after school.

In his young adult interview, Julio reflected a similar sentiment. For
him, the main benefit of participation was getting to stay after school and
thus not associate with gang-affiliated peers.

> With Students Together we would have after school meetings, so that helped
> me out being [involved] outside [of school]. Probably the experience of just
> keeping going to school, because they would keep me in there after class, and
> they would keep saying how we have to keep our grades up good in school so

we could keep going to the program. [Because I was in Students Together]
I wouldn't really be involved with other people [or] gangs [or in] trouble. It
helped me out in that way a lot. I mean, it probably kept me going until I went
to [high school] and then fell over. Fell down on that one.

Overall, Julio puts Students Together in the same category with the other
two extracurricular programs in which he participated, one in elementary
school and one in high school. At the end of his eighth-grade year, when
asked how he had changed as a result of participation, he said, "That I
stay [at school] and I don't stay with my friends in the streets." During his
young adult interview he agreed, "All those programs that I'd say they do
help you out after being after class, probably. They just help you out stay off
of problems, because you're out and active. You're doing something after
school. You're doing homework and doing programs outside. I think you
could say that it did help me out. I can't say that much, but it helped me
out." Students Together gave Julio something to do and helped him learn
to communicate with diverse groups of people, but it did not profoundly
impact his educational trajectory. Julio did not remain involved with Students
Together after he transitioned to high school.

High School

The transition to high school presented new challenges for Julio. His father
no longer drove him to and from school every day because his high school
was on a public bus line. His mother gave birth to another boy, and two of
his half-brothers moved out of the family home and into apartments, each
with a pregnant girlfriend.

During his first two years of high school, Julio became involved with
the local Police Activities League (PAL) boxing program. "It was a good
experience for boxing." Like Students Together, he learned about it from
a friend. He had grown up watching boxing and learning about the sport
from his father. His father supported Julio's involvement by helping him
buy the required gear.

I had a friend from school that was going to PAL. He told me about it. I went
in there and I liked it. I liked their workout and their boxing abilities. My dad
did a lot of boxing; he'd watch it on TV all the time. So I was watching boxing, used to seeing it, so I kinda got that little interest on it that way. My dad

started buying me a boxing bag, some gloves, face sets, and, I don't know, I just kept going for it. I was going in for my Golden Gloves, but then I stopped. You needed to put extra time into it, so they can see how you're boxing. You'd have to go at least once every day, at least five days a week, and I didn't have that time. To be honest with you I never really got to rig a real fight. I would only box with the other guys.

PAL boxing taught Julio concrete skills—in this case, boxing skills—and brought him closer to his father. While he enjoyed the activity, it did not have a meaningful influence on his educational trajectory.

Other than boxing, Julio stayed fairly close to home during nonschool hours. "I had strict parents, so I just stayed home most of the time. I would go out only sometimes. It would be with my brother's girlfriend, my sister-in-law." His parents and family were mindful of the dangers of their neighborhood and wanted Julio to stay on the right track. They enforced a strict curfew and kept him involved in family life. Yet he began to fall in with the wrong crowd at school.

Around Julio's sophomore year, school started to feel harder, and his friends were becoming a negative influence. He admitted he was "kicking it with the wrong crowd" but was "pretty sure it happens to everybody" as they transition to high school.

It was just probably kicking it with the wrong crowd and it just started me. I had less interest in school. I guess when you start a high school, I don't know if it happens to everybody, but I know that when I went to [high school], you want to get to meet the right people and you think you're meeting the right people. You want to be cool around the crowd. I'm pretty sure that probably happens to everybody. So, I guess I was just hanging around the wrong crowd, and it was just because of the people I knew. It changed me over.

Though his family was supportive and worked to keep him on the right track, his peers did not.

By the beginning of his junior year, Julio was not earning enough credits to keep up with his class cohort and was failing multiple courses. "I was having problems with school. I wasn't getting enough credits. I was [in high school] for three years, but I had sophomore credits. It was going well the first year. The second year, it was about there. But then, I got to junior year and started messing up. I was doing bad through the year." In addition to his academic struggles, Julio learned he was about to become a father. He knew that he needed to work to support his new family and that he needed a school schedule that could accommodate his work. He did not mention the possibility that he would stay home to care for the child—to Julio his role was without question that of the provider. "I was going out with a girl, and I had a baby with her. I think it was junior [year] when my son was born. So I had to start working. I was working for a grocery store. I left there and went to a hardware store. I was good at the hardware store. It wasn't that much of an intense job, but it was all right. Their pay scale was all right." During his junior year, Julio transferred to a continuation high school within the district. Although Julio does not remember the process of how he got transferred to the continuation school, the move proved beneficial for his high school career. "Before the end of [junior] year, I got transferred [to a continuation school]. It was better scheduling. I would go there at 8:00 until 11:30. [I] would take home packages and do them. It was going great for me, so better for my schedule. I finished one hundred credits in that first year. I graduated the same year I was supposed to gradu-ate, but I graduated in December. I got my diploma from the continuation school. I was really happy for that. I really liked that school, just because they helped me out a lot [to] finish high school." Julio attended continua-tion high school in the mornings, worked nearly full-time during the day, and completed his homework packets each night. Although he had fallen nearly a year behind in credits, his perseverance at the continuation school allowed him to graduate with his high school diploma nearly on time. His girlfriend, however, dropped out of school altogether because she stayed at home with their child.

Julio took his parenting duties seriously. Soon after the birth of his son, Julio moved out of his father's house and into an apartment with his girl-friend and their son. While Julio's father supported his move, he "didn't really like it that much. But he knew I had to move out 'cause my girlfriend needed her own space." Julio committed to supporting his new family, spending as much time as possible with his girlfriend and son. He worked the jobs and hours necessary to support their family financially and left the household chores and daily childcare to his girlfriend.

Becoming a parent caused Julio to realize that he wanted to become someone his son would look up to. For Julio this meant going on to col-lege: "The most influential part of my life, I could say and really flipped me around, was when my son was born. That helped me be more responsible, more organized, be myself now. I didn't want him to see that I just went to high school and that's it. I wanted him to see that I kept going. I think that's the thing that flipped [me around], that influenced me the most." Julio felt proud of himself for completing his high school education in spite of his academic and personal setbacks. He also felt strongly that he wanted to continue his education in order to be a good role model for his son.

After High School

After completing his high school degree, Julio's schedule and qualifications allowed him to pursue other job opportunities. Julio soon accepted a position in delivery and merchandising. While the work was slightly tiring, he liked being physically active, the pay was good, and the schedule was consistent. He continued to live in an apartment with his girlfriend and son.

In addition, Julio began taking community college classes in pursuit of a career in firefighting. Julio's interest in firefighting was relatively recent and stemmed from a conversation with a friend shortly after Julio graduated from high school. "I have a friend, his brother is a volunteer firefighter. I was cool with him and one time I just saw him all dressed up. I talked to him, he's like, 'I'll take you in and see if you like it or not.' So I went up there and saw the experience, the work you put in, the intense workout they make you do. I liked it. It's great." Currently Julio volunteers as a firefighter and takes classes in fire science. While some of the classes are at the local community college campus, others are field school sessions in a rural area that is a six-hour drive from his home. "I got three certificates from [field school]: a wild land firefighter certification, a first responder for HAZMAT materials, [and] first responder for medical. [Field school] was just Saturdays and Sundays, so I work the week and then on Friday I drive up there and take my classes and then come back and work the next day. [One] class for HAZMAT materials was just three days. The first responder was a whole week, so I took off work a whole week and took the HAZ certificate. Right now, I'm taking [classes] for my EMT [at the local campus]." Julio attended the field school on his days off from his weekday job and attended the local campus for evening classes. Eventually he hoped to complete the final year of his training at the field school full-time because he prefers the field school's more "hands on" approach where he "gets to see more fires." He hopes to one day secure a full-time firefighting position at a local station.

To earn his associate's degree from the community college, he must also complete a number of general education (GE) courses.

> All I'm trying to get through right now, it's just go through all the [fire science] classes. I know that I have to go through, get my general ed. so I can get my AA. But right now, I haven't taken no GE classes. I don't know, it's just one of those classes that I don't know if I still want to take, you know, 'cause it's going back to high school. Like, I know I have to, 'cause I know I've slowed down in a couple of those [subjects]: math, English. But, I'm definitely trying to go for my AA on fire science.

At the time of our final interview, Julio was putting off taking any general education courses that would be required for his AA degree. He realized that he will eventually have to take those courses to receive a diploma but had no concrete plans to do so.

When Julio finishes his fire certifications—the AA is not required to become a firefighter—he hopes to become a firefighter at a city fire station. In the meantime, however, he was applying for seasonal fire work to gain experience. "I just finished applying for the seasonal job I wanted just to get more experience. The more experience you get, the better it looks on your resumé. I applied, but I got my first responder late and my certificate hasn't even got here yet, so I don't have proof to show that I have finished my classes. So right now I'm one of the last ones to get called out. I don't give it the best hopes, but if I do [get called], then it's great. But if it doesn't, there's still next year." Although Julio does not have a timeline for his academic and professional goals, he has a clear picture of where he would like to end up in the future. Above all, he will keep working, "Work's never going to finish. Work keeps going." In addition, Julio sees himself finishing school so he can transition to firefighting full-time. "Hopefully, I finish my AA, finish my [field school] academy. Start applying for a city [fire department]. You can't just apply anywhere, you know, you also have to look at their benefit plans. Nowadays, you have to look at your retirement plan. A lot of people do tell me, 'What are you talking about, your retirement plan, you're still young?' But trust me, you do need to look at your retirement plan. I do want to stay local, but if there is a city out there [with good benefits] that's not local . . . right on it." Julio sees no reason to pursue a bachelor's degree; instead, he sees higher education as a means to a vocation: firefighting.

He hopes his education leads him to a stable career with good benefits and the ability to provide well for his family. In addition, he looks forward to firefighting as a way to be recognized for helping others. "That's pretty much what I liked about firefighting: you can help other people, as far as medical[ly] saving somebody's life [or] going in a house [and] saving somebody. I know the city posts your name up if something were to happen to you. You do get known around the city." Julio looks forward to firefighting for not only the compensation but also the service he can offer to others through his work.

At the time of the final interview Julio's son was nearly four years old, and his girlfriend had started going back to school. She was working toward her GED at the local Adult School and planning to attend the same community college that Julio attended, with the hopes of completing a nursing degree. She dreamed of becoming a cosmetologist, and Julio was supportive of her professional goals; however, his work and school schedule meant that she remained their son's primary caregiver.

Meanwhile, Julio and his family had moved back into his childhood home with his parents. With the recent fall in the housing market, Julio's father was struggling to make the mortgage. "We moved back because my dad needed help with the house, paying the bills, [and] paying on the house. My mom spoke to me about how my dad was struggling. My mom talked to me to move back. I'm helping them out with the house right now, so we're doing fine with that." Julio does not mind helping out his family in any way that he can because he holds his father in such high esteem. "My father helped to be my influence to everything. He's the one that guided me through everything, tell me what's right to wrong, helped me go through when I had [my son]. Mostly the big guy there that I know, he influenced me the most, because he was the one that guided me through everything." Julio's strong family support, especially from his father, has helped guide him through the many trials of his life.

Overall, Julio's home, school, and out-of-school environments provided different influences on his educational trajectory. Although he experienced relative stability in his home life—for example, remaining in the same house and school system throughout his childhood—he was surrounded by a violent neighborhood, rife with gang activity. Julio's family prioritized his education, even driving him daily to out-of-district schools to provide him with a richer academic experience. Julio was close with his father and enjoyed spending time with his extended family that lived nearby. In addition, Julio's own determination and academic aptitude helped propel him toward college.

Each of the out-of-school time programs in which Julio participated during elementary, middle, and early high school provided a positive experience and an opportunity for skill building. In addition, for Julio, spending time in organized activities became a welcome reprieve from the stresses and temptations of his neighborhood. From Students Together, Julio learned communication skills. From PAL, Julio learned boxing techniques. While the programs did not prove life changing, they successfully kept him out of trouble during the time he was actively participating.

Although Julio had strong family support and was given the opportunity to participate in organized activities, rather than care for younger siblings or take on paid work, the transition to high school proved precarious. He started taking public transportation to school each day and fell in with a new peer group. His parents maintained strict control of his out-of-school time, yet the draw of the "cool" crowd pulled him off track while he was at school. Without significant teachers or other adult mentors intervening to mediate the influence of gang-affiliated peers, Julio's trajectory changed. Transferring to continuation school upon the birth of his son proved beneficial because it not only granted Julio a schedule that was conducive to work and family life but also helped sever his ties with the crowd that had steered him astray. With this change, Julio rededicated himself to his studies, his family, and a life of helping others. It remains unclear whether Julio will attain a college degree, but his commitment to both higher education and his concrete career goals are likely to pay off in the years ahead.

Relationships, Structures, and Agency

Graciela's and Julio's pathways to college reveal the overlapping influences of home, school, and out-of-school time contexts over time. In Graciela's case, those contexts provided consistent tactical and emotional support for her college ambitions, which began at a young age. Participating in Students Together was a good experience, but more influential were her parents' unwavering support and involvement in College Bound during the college search and application process. For Julio, neighborhood forces were perpetually at odds with his home and school lives. While his father sought to protect him from those influences by enrolling him in Bayside schools, a number of factors coalesced during Julio's high school years that ultimately impacted his educational trajectory. Because he was well supported during his time in Students Together by his family and his peers, he did not maintain any of his connections to the program during the transition to high school. When he started to struggle a few years later he was not involved in any extracurricular programs. This experience illustrates how the timing of participation in relation to the student's need for support matters for the degree of influence an extracurricular program might have on an adolescent's pathway to college.

Relationships

Positive relationships at the time of program participation offer one hallmark of students who experience an auxiliary degree influence. All of the Students Together participants in the auxiliary influence category had at least one significant positive relationship with an adult outside the program. For Ana and Julio, their parents—but especially their fathers—provided support and counsel. For Miguel and Graciela, both of their parents were equally important. Rosa relied on a mentor from church. Each respondent was supported by a loving adult who encouraged them to continue their education. For two of the three women in this group, however, this message came with the caveat that caring for their family—including siblings, parents, and children—should assume higher priority than continuing with school. This cultural emphasis on family loyalty, particularly for girls, adds another dimension to the consideration of the role of out-of-school time programs might play in the educational trajectories of Mexican American students.

Extended kin networks also played a role, and each former participant in this group was part of a large extended family. For some, this extended family was a positive influence. Graciela's aunts and uncles helped care for her younger sisters, which left Graciela free to participate in extracurricular activities during middle and high school. As a child, Miguel looked forward to attending large family gatherings. For others, extended family provided both positive and negative enticements. Julio's cousins were active in a gang and became some of the very peers who helped pull him off track academically in high school. As the oldest daughters, during the high school years Rosa and Ana were expected to spend a significant amount of after-school time caring for younger siblings and relatives, sometimes at the expense of their academic work. Extended family members tended to influence respondents more if contact was more frequent, and it was common for the nature of their influence to fluctuate over time.

All of the youth in this category also reported positive relationships with peers during middle school. Rosa and Graciela were close friends, and each had a number of other friends as well. The girls teased each other playfully about being "nerds" in order to encourage each other to keep up their grades. Ana, Julio, and Miguel also each had a close friend who participated in Students Together and pursued similar educational goals. At the time of program participation, these peers influenced respondents positively.

During high school, however, peer influences evolved. Both Julio and Rosa fell in with peers who encouraged them to skip classes, and as a result they fell behind in their schoolwork. Miguel struggled at first with the predominantly wealthy and white peer culture of his private school, but he found his footing after a couple of years. Graciela and Ana maintained a close cohort of positively engaged friends throughout high school. Though variable over time, peer influences proved powerful in respondents' academic trajectories. In fact, a supportive peer group at the time of program participation is a key relationship factor that differentiated the auxiliary influence group from the distinguishable influence group described in chapter 4.

Structures

While relationships play a part in shaping students' pathways to college, participants are simultaneously embedded within social structures that constrain and enable their available choices. Overall, students who experience an auxiliary degree of influence are either embedded in structures that exert a positive influence on their academic trajectories at the time of program participation or are buffered from the negative influences of these structures by supportive relationships and compensatory resources.

The Students Together program is one structure within which all the young people profiled in this book were embedded, yet students' level of engagement varied. In the auxiliary category, some participants, reporting that Students Together provided a place to go after school, noted that otherwise they would have spent time on the streets and been more closely involved with gang-affiliated peers. Yet all the respondents in the auxiliary category were involved with Students Together for only one year and did not extend their ties to the program or its staff members after the end of that year. Furthermore, though respondents in the auxiliary group all participated in at least one other extracurricular activity before graduating from high school, none of those activities was linked to Students Together or recommended by its staff members.

Although Students Together did not have a distinguishable or transformative influence for the respondents in this group, other out-of-school time organizations did. For example, being embedded in a strong religious organization was critical for some respondents. Rosa met a mentor at church, and religious involvement changed her life. Miguel described the formidable role of religion in his family and how it pulled them closer together. Benjamin became deeply embedded in his church's skateboarding ministry, which counterbalanced negative peer influences during his high school years. These experiences, along with Graciela's involvement in College Bound and Ana's involvement in a Latina support group, suggest the importance of making an array of organized activities available to adolescents. Students Together had a small influence—due to the timing of participation, fit with program content, or other factors—but continued and varied out-of-school time involvement helped buoy these young people through challenging times.

Other prominent structural factors included schools, employers, and political systems. During middle school, respondents were actively participating in Students Together, yet no student in this group reported struggling with academics or being in trouble at school. For some respondents, teachers were an important influence on their college pathway. For example, a teacher at Adams encouraged Miguel to apply to private high schools. For others, teachers were a positive but unremarkable presence. Although some students in this category of influence struggled later in their academic careers, they were no longer connected to Students Together in a way that would have enabled it to provide support.

All the former participants in this degree of influence were employed at some point along their pathway to college. Rosa and Ana worked during their high school years outside the home, and Julio got a full-time job when he transferred to continuation school. Employment experiences were only influential if the experience was directly related to the student's long-term career goals. Miguel loved his job as an EMT, and Graciela vividly recalled her summer position as a hospital intern; both want to eventually become doctors. Julio loved getting called as a volunteer firefighter. Rosa and Ana had no influential work experiences and were still unsure of their career goals at the time of the final interview.

For some respondents in this group, the immigration system was a profound structural force in their lives. I did not solicit data on citizenship status due to the political climate in California in 2008, wherein frequent Immigration and Customs Enforcement (ICE) raids created a climate of intense fear of deportation among those in the Mexican American community with close ties to undocumented immigrants. Yet some respondents alluded to the ways their own or their parents' struggles to obtain legal residency in the United States drew financial resources, wreaked emotional havoc, and inflicted profound instability on their home lives. Undocumented students also dealt with enormous hurdles in their pursuit of higher education, given their ineligibility for federal financial aid. Because this study did not focus explicitly on the role of immigration, it was unclear whether immigration status played a role in the degree of influence extracurricular participation had on students' pathways to college.

Personal Agency

Along with the relationships and structures participants were embedded within, their personalities, interests, and aptitudes also mattered for the degree of influence an extracurricular activity might have on their educational trajectory. While the students in the auxiliary influence group were drawn to the opportunity to "make a difference in their community" by joining the Students Together program, none of them felt particularly compelled to seek long-term involvement in local change-making efforts. Even though many students in this group ultimately hoped to pursue careers that would allow them to help others, such as firefighting or medicine, the community activist nature of the program did not resonate with their specific interests or goals. They did not feel the same kind of "click" with the curriculum that other respondents felt; that is, the activities were fun but not memorable, meaningful, or inspiring.

As noted previously, other out-of-school time experiences that were more closely tied to students' interests had a greater degree of influence. For example, for Graciela the College Bound program had a distinguishable influence, and for Benjamin the skateboarding ministry was transformative. In out-of-school time, like most other educational arenas, no intervention can be expected to meet the needs, tastes, and timelines of all students. Rather, a diverse continuum of accessible opportunities across each community offers greater promise of providing a safety net for adolescents in times of need.

In sum, at the time of participation students who experience an auxiliary degree of influence from an out-of-school time program tend to be already supported by healthy relationships across multiple contexts and embedded in structures that either view them positively or buffer them from the influences of harmful structures. Furthermore, students in this category identify with the program's content enough to sustain regular interest and attendance but not to the point of continuing with the program for an extended duration. Learning institutionally valued knowledge and skills—that is, cultural capital that they can employ in other settings to gain advantages—is the primary process through which these students benefit from extracurricular participation.

4

Distinguishable Influence

"It Helped Me
Find My Way . . ."

Selena, Molly, and Teresa grew up in supportive families and did well in school, yet by the time they were sixth graders at Adams they did not feel as if they fit in socially. Although Selena had been elected to student council and enjoyed her time on the cheerleading squad, she saw herself as too outspoken and progressive for her peers. Molly transferred to Adams midyear from a predominantly white charter school and, while she appreciated being part of a more diverse student body at Adams, had to work hard to find her footing. Teresa, however, viewed the Adams social scene as hostile and coped by spending as little time at school as possible. The supportive environment in Students Together gave these participants a haven where they felt welcomed and valued, and it also provided a like-minded network of peers. The program's curriculum fit well with their predilections for public service, and they relished the opportunity to develop their skills and identities as college-bound community leaders.

This chapter introduces the concept of distinguishable influence of an out-of-school time program. Students who experience a distinguishable degree of influence are already on a trajectory toward higher education prior to program participation, yet the program has a positive impact on their pathway to college that is distinct from all other factors. Out-of-school time programs influence students in this category through two primary processes: the acquisition of skills that act as institutionally valued cultural capital and the development of a role-identity or sense of self that is positively received across school, home, and community contexts.

Participants in the distinguishable influence category tend to have strong supports from many, but not all, of the contexts they inhabit. Selena, Molly, and Teresa were supported by family and teachers, but they lacked positive peer ties and did not feel a sense of belonging at school. Other students may be enmeshed in different constellations of support. For example, a student may have robust peer and family connections but negative relationships with teachers, or strong school and neighborhood contexts but difficulties at home. For students in the distinguishable degree of influence group, program participation meets an unfilled need. Because those who experience a distinguishable degree of influence have fewer preexisting supports, the potential for a program to influence them is greater than for students in the auxiliary influence category yet less than for those to whom the program offers a transformative degree of influence.

Of course, all students with a gap in their support networks do not inevitably experience a distinguishable degree of influence. Rather youth must find a good fit with regard to the goals and activities of the program as well as in regard to their relationships with staff members and fellow participants. For example, as a person with strong opinions, Selena reveled in the ways Students Together employed young people's voices for authentic action. As a more withdrawn person, Teresa felt empowered by the ways the program provided instructional scaffolding that enabled her to gradually build confidence and become more socially adept. Both former participants felt genuinely cared about and inspired by staff members. And, although neither girl embarked on a lasting friendship with anyone from their Students Together cohort, both appreciated that peer interactions were structured such that participants could collaborate and learn from one another, even across profound social differences.

Like students in the auxiliary degree of influence category, participants in the distinguishable influence category gain institutionally valued cultural capital from their time in an extracurricular program. Yet students in the distinguishable category also develop a stronger sense of self. Role-identity theory posits that Latina/o students become success-ful by adopting an all-encompassing "school kid" persona that is positively received across divergent school, home, and community contexts (Flores-González 2002). This "school kid" identity allows them to travel between multiple settings while maintaining a commitment to attaining academic success. In the most general sense, the "school kid" identity is what most Americans think of as a "good kid." The adolescent's status as a student—young people's primary role in contemporary society—anchors the iden-tity, but it is cumulative across school, home, and community contexts, such that it encompasses other aspects of being a "good kid," like being a well-mannered son or a responsible employee.

Emergence of this identity is contingent upon the presence of multiple factors, and some out-of-school time activities may provide key supports for the identity development process among some adolescents. But because maintaining a "school kid" identity requires convergence across several contexts, not all students will be embedded in ecologies that leave room for extracurricular activities to play an active part. Development of the "school kid" identity is dependent upon the role being socially appropriate and socially supported, such that it garners prestige or rewards; it also requires extensive and intensive relationships, the presence of identity-enhancing events, and links to favorable visions of possible future selves. In addition to these structural factors, personal agency is paramount; the student must perform the role appropriately in order to trigger the expected reaction from other social actors. For adolescents who already experience some of these conditions, an out-of-school time program may offer a crucial com-plement. Specifically, for either participants whose identity is consistent but not positively received across all contexts or participants who struggle to maintain different role-identities in disparate settings, an out-of-school time program might help develop and reinforce a transferable and affirmed sense of self linked to tangible educational goals.

For example, many aspects of the Students Together program worked to create an environment where participants who struggled to develop a posi-tive role-identity, like Teresa and Selena, could be supported in this pro-cess. First, applicants were only admitted to the program if their transcript showed they had maintained at least a C average. This requirement not only rewarded students who were getting good grades but also produced a peer environment in which academic success was the norm. Second, each cohort was limited to about fifteen students. The relatively small size of the program made it possible for staff members to know each participant personally and offer targeted advice and caring affirmations. The low youth-to-adult ratio also enabled staff members to monitor and guide peer-to-peer interactions within the program such that participants could learn to support and value one another for their unique contributions to the group. Third, staff members trained participants to become engaged local citizens. Thus, participants developed competencies that were not only useful at school but also well received within the community. Finally, because staff members were fluent in Spanish and resided locally, they were able to coach students in a culturally responsive manner to advocate for themselves in dissimilar and evolving home and school contexts. Overall, the Students Together program provided a supportive context where identity-enhancing events, looked upon favorably by family members, school personnel, and like-minded peers, could occur—such as public-speaking opportunities at a nearby university or town council meeting.

To situate the ways that cultural capital and identity development stemming from extracurricular participation influence students' educational trajectories to a distinguishable degree within the broader context of family, school, and out-of-school time, chapter 4 profiles Teresa and Selena. Like the case studies presented in chapter 3, these profiles draw on interviews that were conducted starting when each student was an eighth grader at Adams Middle School and new to the Students Together program and continue until their young adult years. Teresa and Selena were both born in the United States to US-born Mexican American parents. They arrived at elementary school fluent English speakers and resided in the same home throughout their childhoods. Despite their starkly contrasting personality types, both felt inspired by Students Together staff members, reported a high level of engagement with the program, and used it as a gateway to become involved with other out-of-school activities. After their time in the program, however, the girls' paths diverged. Teresa attended a local public high school and volunteered for myriad service groups, all while working part-time as a grocery cashier. After graduation, she enrolled in full-time community college, with the hopes of eventually transferring to a four-year program for a nursing degree. Selena enrolled at an elite private day school and channeled her energies into combating the racism rampant within the school's culture and structure. She set her sights on becoming a lawyer and pursued multiple out-of-school time programs relevant to that goal. At the time of our final interview, she was preparing to graduate one semester ahead of schedule from a selective private university. By taking a closer look at the structures and relationships in which each was embedded before, during, and after their time in Students Together, as well as each girl's personal agency, these profiles illustrate how a high-quality out-of-school time program can have a distinguishable influence on the educational attainment of diverse participants.

Teresa

Childhood and Elementary School

Teresa grew up in a mobile home park in an industrial area of Bayside with her mother, father, and two siblings. A self-described "shy and nerdy" child, Teresa remembers "just spending time with my friends and my family doing random things like playing. I had a good time in childhood." She described her younger years as uneventful and happy, with both school and home feeling supportive and enriching.

Teresa attended Harrison Elementary School from kindergarten through fifth grade and had "a good experience there." She had "a lot of good teachers," and the relationships she developed during this time helped her begin to overcome her shyness. "I learned so much [at Harrison]—not only about regular school but just being with the people." She was studious—"I did all the work"—and relished getting to try new things.

At the end of the day, Teresa enjoyed participating in a variety of school-sponsored extracurricular activities. These activities afforded her opportunities to expand her horizons and gain confidence in social interactions. "I did all those afterschool programs. I would say they were fun. All the people in there, they were really nice and they seemed like they really cared about kids. I got a lot of experiences, learning new things, and becoming more outgoing, too, because [when] you spend time with a lot of people, you're talking and [gaining] confidence." Because she was well supported by her family and teachers, these out-of-school time programs had an auxiliary influence, providing a pleasant experience and helping instill new skills and experiences. Overall, Teresa excelled academically and began to branch out socially during her elementary school years.

Middle School

When Teresa transitioned to Adams Middle School as a sixth grader, things began to go downhill. Her academics remained strong, and the easiest parts of middle school were "the schoolwork because that was pretty much all I did." Meanwhile, the social aspects became more and more unbearable each day. "[In] middle school, kids are annoying. People are mean. In sixth grade and seventh grade, I never really went to school that much because I didn't really like it, so I just left. I would just pretend I was sick so I wouldn't have to go." Teresa, disengaging from the middle school social scene almost entirely, chose instead the comfort of her home, neighborhood, and family as often as her parents would allow.

After two years of avoiding school, the opportunity to join Students Together presented a beacon of hope. Teresa decided to join because she missed having a constructive peer group, and "it just seemed like a really cool program and a really positive place to be." As a young adult, she credited the program with turning her middle school career around. "Eighth grade was okay because I had Students Together. Students Together was a good program." After enduring the negativity and meanness of her classmates for too long, participating in Students Together helped Teresa feel valued and capable, and gave her the chance to redevelop her confidence.

Teresa credited the adult leaders—Jennifer, Amy, and Carolina—with creating an environment where she felt cared about, learned concrete skills, and was encouraged to see herself in a new light. The adult leaders created an environment that felt safe enough for Teresa to challenge herself as she tried out new skills, like public speaking. Within this nurturing environment, Teresa began to develop a better sense of herself and her potential.

> I've been shy, like in front of kids and stuff, but because we did so many things in front of people [Students Together] just helped with [my] confidence and stuff. We worked with so many people. We'd go to [a nearby university] and do all these presentations and it was stuff that I was not used to. But Jennifer always made us prepare for it and it was really good. It brought me out of my shell. Like, I was kind of forced to talk to people, it was good. We did a lot of retreats and stuff, too—like we would go and have a lot of bonding with the group, which is good. It helped me meet a lot of people. All this Students Together stuff helped me in going through middle school and high school. It definitely changes you. I became more outgoing and everything.

Through well-scaffolded and repeated opportunities to present to groups and interact with peers and adults outside the school day, participating in the program not only taught Teresa concrete skills for public speaking and impromptu interactions but also helped her become more confident and outgoing, a change that lasted long after her time in the program had ended.

In addition, Students Together helped cement Teresa's college plans. Although Teresa possessed aspirations to attain a four-year degree prior to joining the program, she did not have a concrete sense of how to attain this goal. Coaching from Students Together staff members made a lasting impression on Teresa: "I knew I was going to go to college, I just wasn't sure if I was going to go right after high school. But [in] Students Together, they're always like, 'Apply for this college.' I mean, they're even saying, 'Apply to Harvard.' I'm like, 'Okay, no, I won't get in.' But they were just like always, 'Go to college. Do this. Get yourself educated. Education is good.' And that helped pushing me and it's really good." Being encouraged to begin making strides toward attending college as an eighth grader helped put Teresa on track toward developing tangible educational and career goals.

Though she was well supported at home and academically successful, Teresa did not have a positive peer group at the time she joined Students Together. Students Together had a distinguishable influence on Teresa's academic trajectory because the program's supportive environment helped her leave behind her shy, disengaged persona and reenvision herself as a confident, college-bound young woman.

High School

For Teresa, high school was "a lot better than middle school." Teresa intentionally attended a different in-district high school from her middle school peers in order to meet new people. This strategy proved successful: Teresa met her best friend, Angie, on the bus to school during her freshman year, and that friendship continued to blossom throughout high school and into college. Teresa felt supported by her parents, teachers, and peers and remembered having "a lot of good experiences."

Outside school, Teresa spent most of her time volunteering. She volunteered as a mentor in Students Together, acted as a board member for Bayside Parks and Recreation Department's Youth Council, performed various duties at the Bayside Senior Center, and helped out at the public library during children's story time. "I met a lot of people and I felt like I was helping a lot of people with the volunteer work I did. So, it was pretty rewarding." Starting her sophomore year, Teresa was also expected to get a job and contribute to the family's earnings. Initially she worked retail at the local shopping mall, but during her junior year she switched to a nearby grocery store, where she met her long-term boyfriend, Danny. Teresa enjoyed her extracurricular activities and acquired new skills and experiences from each.

As a freshman and sophomore, Teresa decided to continue with Students Together as a mentor because "I really like Students Together. Just spending time with the kids, I feel like you really make a difference, the kids really remember you." Teresa felt as though she had gained a lot from participating and took pride in the opportunity to give back to a program she cared so much about.

Students Together also started Teresa into a progression of other local activities, one example of how out-of-school time programs can exact a longitudinal influence. Teresa learned about Bayside's Youth Council from Jennifer, one of the Students Together staff members. "Jennifer's like, 'Oh, this is a really good program.' And I trust Jennifer, so I didn't want to do it at first, but it's good. I'm glad I did it." From Youth Council, Teresa learned "dedication" and "perseverance because we always had to do presentations and all that kind of stuff." Because she was now well supported outside the program, her primary take-away was institutionally valued cultural capital. Teresa stayed involved with Youth Council throughout all four years of high school.

Although Teresa's connections to the Senior Center and the library did not stem from Students Together, her increased confidence and inclination toward helping others pushed her to take advantage of new opportunities. For example, she got involved with the Senior Center because of her grandmother. "My grandma, she volunteered like hella there. There's a program where you shop for older people that couldn't go outside their house. And then I did Bingo with old people, so that was pretty fun." Teresa did the shopping program once every week and played Bingo twice a week. When asked what she took away from the experience, she replied: "I learned just dealing with the public and dealing with old people. You know how some people can be hella rude to old people, so abusive and stuff, so I learned how to have different points of view. Because I like old people, they're nice." Teresa's affinity for helping others is a common theme throughout her extracurricular experiences that carried into her longer-term career goals.

As a senior, Teresa got involved with story time through the public library owing to a school graduation requirement to volunteer twenty hours, for an organization with which she was not already involved. She saw a flier at the library and remembered story time fondly from when she was a kid. "I like to read and little kids." Though she began reading because of the school requirement, she continued with the program into her college years.

The most influential forces for Teresa during high school were her parents, teachers, and friends, along with the Students Together and Youth Council leaders, Jennifer and Tim, respectively. Teresa notes that the adult leaders of each out-of-school time activity were most influential during the time she was active in the program, but she did not continue those relationships after she concluded her time in each program.

After High School

After graduating from high school, Teresa moved into an apartment in Bayside with her boyfriend, Danny, and her best friend, Angie. All three attended the same local community college. Although Teresa's older brother fathered a baby soon after high school and did not go to college, her sister also enrolled at the same local community college.

Teresa saw herself as college-bound ever since participating in Students Together as an eighth grader. She was motivated to go to college because "I just wanted to continue [school]. I decided I need to get it done, so I'll go to school right after high school and finish sooner. I don't want to end up at a dead-end job. I want to do something with my life." Her friends and family were very supportive, though they let Teresa guide her own career choices. "My parents, they're like, 'You know you need to get an education. You need to go to college and make something of yourself.'" Given the freedom to choose her own career, her ambitions developed slowly over time: "I wasn't sure exactly what I wanted to do. I kind of wanted to be a pediatrician first because I like kids, but then it was too much school so I just decided to become a nurse." Ultimately, she was happy with her choice. "I like nursing, too. It's really rewarding—you help people." Teresa developed high educational aspirations thanks to her parents and her time in Students Together, and then she drew on various available resources to follow through on her plan.

Two years out of high school, Teresa had nearly completed the two-year program in nursing and was preparing to transfer to a four-year university to complete her degree. She continued to excel academically and relish the challenge of learning new things. "This is going to kind of sound lame, but I like school. I'm taking a lot of interesting classes for nursing and stuff. I like it, but it's really challenging too, sometimes." She was confident she would complete her bachelor's degree in the near future, even if it required applying to four-year programs more than once. "It just sucks because the program's really competitive, so hopefully I get accepted the first time I apply." Teresa had researched the schools to know the nursing programs to which she was interested in applying and hoped to continue residing in Bayside while she completed her education.

While Teresa attended community college, she also worked full-time, but she saw her job as a means to an end. "I just applied anywhere, and then I was like, 'Okay, I'll work at the grocery store.' You know, like whatever." She admitted her job "could suck sometimes, but it's good. I don't mind. I'm just doing it through school. So after I'm done with school I'll find a better job." Being a checker at the supermarket paid enough for Teresa to cover rent, bills, and tuition, and, though her work there was not directly related to her career goals, she saw it as a way of getting to where she ultimately hoped to be.

Outside school and work, Teresa continued volunteering. For example, she still helped out with library story time because "I think it helps a lot with kids, especially ESL, it helps a lot with English and stuff. I feel like I'm helping them out, which is good." Teresa is "pretty fluent" in Spanish though she concedes, "I'm not full[y] bilingual. I'm taking it again in college, too, so that helps a lot." She credited Students Together with her interest in volunteering: "Students Together got me turned onto Youth Council and then Senior Center and then just a lot." Though she did not stay in touch with Students Together staff members after her years as a mentor, she still felt the domino effect of participation in her young adult life.

In addition to volunteering, Teresa also enjoyed "hanging out with my friends, my boyfriend, going out to places when I have time on the weekends and stuff." Although at the time of the final interview she conceded that her life was "mainly just at school and work," she believed that her diligence will be worth it in the long run. "I don't really have that much of a life. It sucks, but it'll pay off so it's all right." Support from her family remained strong, and she received encouragement from her friend Angie, her sister, and her boyfriend. "Just a small group of people has helped me with a lot of stuff."

Overall, Teresa's home, school, and out-of-school environments worked together to support her pathway to college. Her family lived in the same mobile home park throughout her childhood, and, even when the social scene at school got rough, Teresa enjoyed the company of her neighborhood friends. Teresa did well in school and had caring relationships with her teachers. She enjoyed positive peer interactions throughout elementary school and developed a small group of good friends in high school. In addition, Teresa's studious nature and academic aptitude helped her along the way.

Like many college-bound students, Teresa's family provided unconditional love and support and gave Teresa the latitude to pursue volunteer opportunities along with her paid employment. Because she was well supported by her family and her teachers, most of Teresa's extracurricular pursuits had an auxiliary influence on her educational trajectory. From her elementary afterschool program to grocery shopping for senior citizens to reading aloud to young children, each activity offered fun and fulfillment. As Teresa grew older, her out-of-school time activities also helped her hone in on her passion for helping others, which ultimately led her to pursue a career in nursing.

Students Together stands apart as the one extracurricular activity that had a distinguishable influence on Teresa's college pathway. The timing of participation was key; because of the social struggles Teresa endured during her middle school years, the program offered refuge at a critical point in her life. In addition, the content of the program provided a good fit with Teresa's particular needs. While Teresa struggled with mean peers and feelings of shyness, Students Together taught teamwork, collaboration, and public speaking. Furthermore, staff members connected Teresa with continuing opportunities to engage in the community; even after her time in Students Together had ended she remained engaged and supported. Overall, Students Together's central contribution to Teresa's college pathway was in supporting her to develop confidence and in bringing to light her sincere interest in helping others, a positively received identity that carried her from eighth grade into young adulthood.

Selena

Childhood and Elementary School

Throughout her entire life, Selena has lived with her mother in the same house in a Bayside neighborhood where "we would keep our yard clean and people would throw soda cans or leave shopping carts in it. Every day my mom goes out and picks up out in front of our house." Although her father lived with the family when she was very young, her parents divorced when Selena was still a toddler. Her father then moved to a town about thirty miles away. He picked up Selena for a visit every other weekend and for a few weeks each summer. Selena, referring to him affectionately as her "weekend dad," admitted that their schedule was a bit cliché but that her visits with her dad were "good" and she "had fun." When Selena was in sixth grade, her father moved abroad. While he still occasionally visits and "I still talk to him a little bit," she is quick to add that their relationship is "definitely not like I am with my mother." Selena's relationship with her mother has influenced Selena in overwhelmingly positive ways.

Thanks to all of their one-on-one time, Selena and her mother are very close. Describing their relationship as "pretty great," Selena noted that she enjoyed spending lots of time with her mom: "Me and my mom, we really have each other. We were like friends. I mean, of course once you hit high school, it starts getting weird, but most of the time it was really good. I was the kid [who] liked to go places with my mom when I was little." Due to her mother's work as an office manager at a local school, her mother was able to be intimately involved in Selena's schooling and extracurricular pursuits.

Selena also had three sisters who were more than ten years her senior. Her family was "very close," and growing up her sisters were stricter with her than her mom: "My oldest sister is more like a mom than my own mom. She's like, 'Where are you going? Who are you going with? Did you ask mom?' My mom's like, 'Okay, when will you be back? Come back later. Well, where did you go?' It's like I have sisters as well as three mothers." As her sisters went off to college during Selena's elementary school years, Selena spent the majority of her childhood and adolescence "just me and my mom."

Selena started her elementary school years at a public magnet school where her family had a strong history. Her mother had been one of the founding parents, her uncle taught there, and all of her older sisters had attended through fifth grade. She described it as "the kind of school where the parents come volunteer a lot" and recalled the emphasis on individual students. "We did focus on grammar and things like that, but a lot of it was just bringing out your individualism through creativity in different arts, different games." As "a very opinionated child," the character of the school was a good fit for Selena's personality. "I liked [school] because it really did foster creativity." Selena was adept at language arts and social studies but less of a fan of math and science. Overall, she felt successful and enjoyed the "unique" aspects of her elementary school.

During her third grade year, however, Selena's inclination toward independent thinking tested the limits of the school's emphasis on individuality. She had "some differences with their teaching styles and their mission," and one particular incident proved "the tipping point" in why her mother ultimately decided to move Selena to a different school.

> I was never one to just be told something and just take it as that—so my teacher and me, you can only imagine! I remember we had this Oregon Trail project and there was this whole pioneer project. The teacher assigned each one of us to be a pioneer. We were supposed to learn how you track, your supplies, the food, the life of a pioneer. I started to have problems and I told her that I didn't think that this game or simulation was a fair representation because I was like: What about the Indians? And that was not part of her happy pioneer project. I was totally defiant. I said I didn't want to participate and I didn't want to be a pioneer because they killed the Indians and they exploited them, and I didn't think it was doing justice and we weren't representing all parties involved and representing it historically accurately. So in the end, we had nineteen pioneers and one little Indian. It was a big fight. From then on, me and my teacher just . . . it was time I went to a different school.

Even as a third grader, Selena could not tolerate a classroom reenactment of the pioneer experience without acknowledgment of the cruelty settlers inflicted upon Native Americans. She stood by her convictions until her teacher finally acquiesced to her demands. While Selena recalled "we had a lot of events like that," her showdown with the teacher over the Indians was ultimately the straw that broke their relationship beyond repair. Selena's mother decided to have Selena change schools, and Selena agreed with the choice.

Selena switched, starting in fourth grade, to another public school. Selena's mother selected the school based on her intimate knowledge of the district and the location of her own work. Selena "really liked" her new school for multiple reasons. First, its proximity to her mom's office allowed her to see her mom during lunch and after school more easily. Selena also appreciated the diversity of her new school. Her new school was predominantly Latino/a, complemented by a mix of other ethnicities. Selena had never realized that her first school was predominantly white and lacked the diversity of Bayside's general population. She had never considered how it would make her feel to go to school with other children who looked like her. "That's always better, you know, when you see kids that look like you [at school]. That was good."

Outside school, Selena participated in cheerleading, starting in third grade and continuing throughout her middle school years. Fitting with Selena's tendency to go against the grain, she had intended to sign up for the football team, but girls were not allowed to play football. "I wanted to be a wide receiver on the football team. They were just like, 'No.' I'm sure now I could be on it, but then it wasn't allowed. I wanted to drag that one out into a huge battle, but then the cheerleading was interesting to me, too." Although she intended to play football and was prohibited, cheerleading turned out to be a good choice. Selena knew older girls in the group and enjoyed the sport. "I think it all worked out. [Cheerleading was] an activity for me that was something my family came to watch. Really, my mom and my sister came to all my competitions, so it was fun." In the end Selena embraced cheerleading, its social scene, and the positive encouragement she got from her family for participating.

Over the years, Selena spent a lot of time at cheerleading practice—anywhere from three to ten hours per week, depending on whether it was football season and if there was a competition coming—in addition to the time it took to memorize all the routines. "Sometimes we'd be out there at night and they'd actually bring the football lights out onto the field because our coach was like, 'You need to know these [routines].'" There were also many fun times, like snack breaks at practice and trips to competitions. As the cheerleading world was new to Selena and her mom, Selena occasionally found herself befuddled at the intricacies of cheer-culture. "It was weird, your curls had to be perfect. You couldn't have a droopy end." Although she sometimes rolled her eyes at aspects of cheerleading, Selena enjoyed the sport and the fellowship and learned many lessons that stayed with her over the years. "You had to work together and you had to help everyone else. Because the thing was, you wanted to do well. You didn't do well if everyone else didn't do well, so it was a team effort. After practice we'd go to other girls' houses, go over the routines, and just hang out with each other. But there really was a sense of solidarity in needing each other to do well. I think those are good transferable skills: working well with others." Although she does not still keep in touch with any of her cheerleading teammates or remember any of them individually, Selena learned how to work with others toward a common goal through her continued participation in the sport.

Middle School

Starting in sixth grade, Selena attended Adams Middle School, and, like Teresa, she struggled with the social scene. "Coming in as a sixth grader, I think middle school's really hard! I mean, just all the pressures in every way. You don't know who you are, you don't know friends, you get dropped in there and it's sink-or-swim." Selena detested the pressures she and her peers were experiencing, noting that the "cliquey" nature of social interactions could be hurtful. "It was that whole mentality of if so-and-so's friend doesn't like her but you're her friend and you have nothing against her friend, you can't be her friend because, by default, your friend doesn't like her." Above all, the pressure to conform was hard for Selena. "There's this sense like everyone needs to conform to the same standard. Everyone had to have the same Nike shoes, the same hooded sweatshirt. If you didn't, people were really mean to each other sometimes." Selena tried to stay above the fray by being friendly and encouraging others to follow their own tastes rather than feel pressured into conformity. While her close relationship with her mom helped her retain her independent spirit, extracurricular programs also provided an outlet where she could be herself.

During middle school, Selena participated in a variety of out-of-school time programs. Selena ran for and was elected to student council at Adams. Selena joined Students Together and participated in Bayside Youth Council. Throughout middle school, Selena continued to participate in cheerleading. Across each of these activities, she gained various skills and experiences.

Selena ran and was elected to her school's student council for two years. Campaigning for office taught her the realities of politics. "I was running, and another friend was running, and people kept [giving away] candy and spreading rumors. It's like you're running for the president! [Laughing.] Politics is mean and messy, even in middle school." Reflecting on her time on student council, Selena was split. While she enjoyed getting to talk to her classmates and getting out of class for meetings, she also felt the matters the council tackled were somewhat trivial. "It wasn't like you were making huge decisions. We were wanting to petition to have pizza on Fridays. Or everyone wanted to have a water fun day because normally we're not allowed to play with water, but some days it's really hot. I don't know how much power we really had or anything. But it was cool to kind of participate, even if it was lip service a little bit. It was cool just to have that position and talk to your classmates." Selena liked being on student council enough that she ran and was elected two years in a row; however, she recognized that the highlight of the experience was interacting with her peers rather than having a say in meaningful decisions.

During eighth grade, Selena also participated in Students Together. Selena felt drawn to Students Together's mission from the first moment she heard about the program. When asked in her eighth-grade interview what she hoped she would get out of the project, she replied, "Knowing that we helped make a difference." As a young adult, she recognized other benefits of the program: "When I was little, people were like, 'Shh, your opinions, keep those away.' I remember when Jennifer came in and made a presentation to our class and told us about Students Together, it seemed really cool because it was someone saying someone would hear my opinions. Someone would be like, 'We are asking, we really want you to come and give us your opinions.' It's like, wow, that's not a bad way to start for a kid that feels like you're always wanting to say something and no one's listening." Selena felt relief and excitement to finally have the opportunity to participate in a program where the opinionated parts of her personality were welcomed and encouraged. To Selena, "It was a really empowering experience." Until this point, her opinionated nature had only gotten her into trouble, such as when she insisted on being an Indian in her elementary school reenactment. In Students Together, she had opportunities to grow and develop her more outspoken side.

For example, when Selena, as an eighth grader, explained pictures of her neighborhood that she had taken for a Students Together research project she already had a keen eye toward the injustices around her. "This is the picture of my park, and this is supposed to be a place where youth can go and play and then it says, 'No.' It has like all this grass, yet it says 'No soccer.' Maybe they're saying it's for safety, I don't know. But it's a park, it has grass. Where are people going to play soccer? In the street? I think it's being prejudiced, I really do. I think they're trying to keep Hispanics out of the park." Another photo in the collage showed a cigarette advertisement. Selena explained, "I noticed that cigarette ads and alcohol ads are always in the poorer neighborhoods. Like if I go up to Fir Point, which is a wealthy neighborhood, I'm not going to see 'Newport and Pall Mall on sale.' People want some kids to ruin their lives early." When asked why she thought cigarettes were not being advertised in wealthy neighborhoods, eighth-grade Selena replied, "Because they're predominantly, rich, white neighborhoods. And they have louder voices, you know? Their voices are heard." Even though Selena reported feeling "safe in her neighborhood" because she "knows people," she was keenly aware of the inequalities surrounding her.

One aspect of Students Together that made Selena feel important and mature was the way staff members treated participants. The process by which the program leaders generated ideas from the students made her feel not only listened to but also respected as a citizen with valid opinions.

> I liked it because it was never necessarily like: here's an agenda we're setting out for you. What's a problem in your community, A or B? It was always more discussion-oriented, not like being fed things, but more like helping you bring them out and identifying them. So often you feel rendered voiceless when you're in middle school. You get in trouble for being tardy at school, but you can't even drive yourself there, you can't control the bus, you can't control your parents to take you. I feel like in that time period you feel like you lack authority, and to have an outlet where you feel that the people there are sincere and you feel that you're not being babied mattered. I remember one thing I always liked about Students Together staff members: they never talked to you like you were a child, or even in that same way as your teacher. It was always professional, but it felt like you were meeting on the same playing ground. Because of that, you felt more comfortable and more empowered to say what you felt.

This sense of empowerment had a profound impact on Selena's sense of self.

Students Together's curriculum also piqued Selena's interest in public policy. As an eighth grader, she reported that getting to help make decisions was one of the most important parts of the program. "Let's say all these adults are like, 'We think youth need a place where they can learn how to play golf.' And we're like, 'Wait, all the kids don't want to play golf, maybe kids want basketball more?' We make the decisions to build things that kids want. When it comes to decisions about us, we're the best ones to make 'em." She felt grown up and useful in the contributions she and her peers made to the city planning process. As a young adult she expressed similar sentiments: "I can remember specific meetings and having recommendations and speaking of policy. Through Students Together we got to sit on part of the [citywide] Housing and Human Concerns committee and we were reading through all these proposals. I remember reading [the proposals] and just having so much fun. And [I remember] actually— like every other resident of Bayside who could take their two minutes— actually giving a presentation and seeing that your city council—even though I can't even vote to elect them—that they are listening to you." The content of the Students Together program and the real-life opportunities to interact with the political system gave Selena a peek at what the years ahead would hold for her.

In addition to feeling empowered and being exposed to a field that sparked her passion, Students Together taught Selena skills for collaboration across differences. Conversations with peers from different neighborhoods helped her realize the diversity of experiences youth were having within her community. "I remember someone would think of some issue and then another kid wouldn't [think it was an issue]. Then you'd talk about it and [realize], I don't live [where they live], I didn't know this is how it was over there. We did a video project where we each had a camera, and we each went to our respective neighborhoods and videotaped it. When you go to someone's neighborhood and it is totally different than yours, you know you didn't know them as well as you thought you did." By making connections with fellow students from other parts of town, Selena was exposed to how their lives outside of school varied widely. This eye-opening experience helped cultivate Selena's questioning nature. Students Together not only embraced Selena's opinionated temperament but also allowed her to be part of the policy-making process and introduced her to new people within her school community. Overall, the Students Together program was a good match for Selena.

In addition, Selena gained inspiration and practical advice that helped bring her educational aspirations to life. Selena found it particularly inspiring to hear tales of what college courses and campus life would be like from

Carolina, a staff member who was Latina and had attended public schools before going to an elite college. Although all of Selena's older sisters had graduated from college by this point, having a college-educated Latina role model outside her family was particularly impactful.

As an eighth grader, Selena also participated in Bayside's Youth Council, sponsored by the city's Parks and Recreation Department. Selena enjoyed getting to be active in the community: "We did a lot stuff with the community, like organized a Halloween maze at the Recreation Center, and I really loved those events because I'd tell my family to come and you'd see your friends' little sisters and brothers and people coming. It was something that was fun for everyone." Selena also enjoyed being able to give advice to the city council, although she recognized quickly that their input did not carry decision-making authority.

> I remember a big thing we talked about was how they wanted to put in this skate park, actually where it is now. But [the location] wasn't accessible to people who live on the other side of Bayside, with transportation costs. It was in a more affluent area where people already had lots of facilities. They claimed, "Oh, it's going to be great, everyone can come and skate," but if you have to take two buses and you're paying [bus fare] and you're a kid and your parents are working and no one can drive you to the skate park, it's really not accessible. They were like, "Oh, we never thought about those kids over there."

Although Selena and her fellow board members gave well-reasoned advice, ultimately their opinions did not influence local policy. Even in light of not having significant authority, however, the experience opened Selena's eyes even more to her peers' experiences.

Over time Selena came to question the underlying assumption that there was a monolithic "youth opinion." Her experiences on the board instead helped her realize how diverse teenagers' points of view can be. "It wasn't just about us all being kids and thinking the same, because there were kids who totally disagreed with what I thought about things. I think that was the best thing from Youth Council, just to see that everyone—regardless of your age or whatever—we all have different opinions." From Youth Council, Selena experienced another setting where teamwork across differences was vital to success. She learned the value of speaking your opinion, listening to others, and working to find a middle ground. "[I learned] some of the same things like we were talking about cheerleading. Just that same working together, and as much as you want to be heard, understanding that it's important for you to hear others, as well. And coming to a common ground where even if you don't agree with someone, you can find some sort of compromise or understanding." Youth Council comprised her first sustained experience with policymaking, a topic that continued to interest her acutely.

Overall, Selena's interest in civic engagement was obvious from her extracurricular activities during her middle school years. She enjoyed engaging with her peers as well as with adult leaders across her various activities. She noted which experiences felt like more than "lip service" and heartily preferred them over others. Across cheerleading, Students Together, Youth Council, and student council, Students Together was the most influential force during Selena's middle school years. Students Together created a haven for her opinionated nature and allowed her to channel those tendencies into real action. As an eighth grader she reported that Students Together had helped her "respect people's opinions more." As a young adult she explained in more depth how Students Together had benefited her through both cultural capital and identity development:

> I always like to question things, but I think Students Together really made me feel like I could. It gave you those tools. All the things within Students Together weren't just making statement, but it was making a statement and backing it up. I think that's what Students Together equipped me with— not the evidence, but the tools to find that [evidence], to find your way and maneuver your way through things. I've always been too passionate either in the positive or in the negative way. I think what Students Together did too, is help me in articulating a statement and still having that passion but not repre-senting it in a way where it puts other people off or makes them feel uncom-fortable and not want to hear that. In that sense, it was very helpful to me.

While Selena learned from each of her activities, Students Together was most memorable because it taught her meaningful skills that matched her interests in an engaging and empowering manner, which also contributed to her developing sense of self.

In addition to extracurricular activities, Selena's summer pursuits had a distinguishable impact on her college trajectory. During the summers after sixth and seventh grade, Selena attended tuition-paid enrichment summer programs for high-achieving minority youth at nearby private high schools.

"I just loved it. It was all day, and there were dance classes, an art class, creative writing classes. It was all girls, and I really enjoyed that. It took away all those pressures and unnecessary things, and it was just a whole bunch of girls who wanted to be there and wanted to be learning all these great things." The content and the company of the program were invigorating to Selena, but the exposure to the world of private high schools proved to be the most lasting effect. Although she did not end up attending either school where she had spent time over the summers, she ultimately applied to and was accepted at a similar institution.

When asked how she ended up applying to and attending Oak Park Prep, Selena jokingly replied, "my mother!" Her mother played a leading role in piquing Selena's interest in a particular private school, but Selena also had agency in the process.

> [The summer program] introduced me to that they had private schools
> and you could apply to them, if you liked them. Then, I was back in middle
> school and a teacher at Adams was a former teacher at Oak Park Prep, and she
> thought I was really smart. She would tell my mom, "Your daughter should
> apply." She got my mom interested in Oak Park, and then somehow that made
> me interested in Oak Park. I was interested, but all my friends were going to
> Ridgetop High and that was it. So applying to Oak Park Prep was kind of
> scary. I was excited but at the same time I was hesitant because it was different.

Two of Selena's sisters had attended public high schools, and one had attended private high school. Selena felt somewhat conflicted over her choice to apply to the private school because it would mean leaving her friends. Over time her fears were realized. When she ultimately decided to attend Oak Park Prep, many of her friends chastised her for "selling out." According to Selena, "When I went to private school, some of my friends were not really happy that I was going. Everyone was like, 'You're selling out. You think you're better than us, you're going to private school.'" Over time, Selena remained close with some of her middle school friends and severed ties with others.

High School

Selena attended Oak Park Prep, a small predominantly white private high school, from ninth through twelfth grade. She described the school as "a beige utopian world where flip-flops are worn year-round and boys wear pink shirts." As one of the few minority students at the school, the wealth and the whiteness of the student body heavily impacted her experiences there. "I could count the number of people of color on one hand, myself included. It was just a total culture clash. I mean, there were people in my school whose fathers were, you know, CEOs. It was just a totally different place and I did definitely struggle." Even though Selena had attended a predominantly white magnet elementary school and participated in extracurricular activities, like cheerleading, that required parent involvement, she had never been exposed to an environment so rife with wealth.

Students' and teachers' attitudes regarding race and class differences made the experience difficult for Selena. Selena experienced rampant racism and often felt pressured to speak on behalf of all people of color.

> Whether it was overt or not, there was a lot of racism at my school. There was a lot of prejudice and there's a lot of misunderstandings. It was hard to be a person of color in that school in so many senses. Like, we can be talking about Martin Luther King and it would be like, "So, Selena, what do you think about that?" And I'm like, "Oh, well, I'm speaking on behalf of every African American, Asian American, Latino American. Let me speak for my people." Just that pressure. At the same time, the feeling like if I didn't speak up to someone who said something horrible, like just that sense of obligation. It became really tiresome.

Even though the city of Bayside was reasonably diverse, many students at Selena's school had not attended schools or lived in neighborhoods where they would interact with people of color. She felt immense pressure to speak up in the face of racist remarks; likewise, she resented that she had to always be the one who would speak up. "The truth was the school wanted to bring in students of color, and they just didn't have the means or even know how to deal with the issues that would come with that. Most of the kids in the school went to the same preschools, went to the same elementary schools, they've gone to middle school, and to high school. Their parents go to the same parties. You know, they're the same country club. People just didn't know what happened outside of [their neighborhoods]." Selena channeled her frustration into her involvement with a club for Latino/a students at her school. She also became involved with the club for African American students due to the fact that "that's how few people of color are at my school."

Selena's struggles surrounding the Columbus Day holiday epitomize many of her experiences in high school. Her account comes from her young adult interview, although she gives a nearly identical account of the experience in an interview conducted during her high school years.

> I remember being like "[Our school] celebrates Columbus Day? What?" So, I remember bringing that [up]. I wanted to change it to "Indigenous People's Day." I never thought that issue would divide my school, but it was like you could cut the tension with a knife. [According to my opponents,] I was reverse-racist. I was taking away their holiday. I had to get signatures and ultimately we formed a committee and we had to discuss. Then people said, "Indigenous People's Day, that's not going to be fair, either." Ultimately, it ended up being "Rediscovering History Day," which would then be a day used in our school to have workshops all day, and you could choose to go to what you wanted. So, whether you wanted to learn something about [Columbus's] actual passage and things like that you could. But if you wanted to learn about indigenous people, you had different speakers and you could choose where you wanted. Any racial issues at my school, they already were swept under the rug. This was the event that allowed them to all culminate and just explode. And it was painful. People said horrible things, and it was just a really bad time in my life.

Being opinionated from a young age set Selena up to confront directly many issues surrounding racism in her high school. Planning an alternative to Columbus Day gave Selena an avenue to engage her classmates in the discussions that were often ignored. Challenging the school practices she viewed as ignorant did not feel optional to Selena, yet the experience left her emotionally beaten down. For some adolescents, this degree of struggle may have turned them away from organizing or pursuing social justice, but not Selena.

Selena fought to reconcile the caliber of the education she was getting at her private school with the discrimination she faced. "It was one of the times that has made me the strong person I am, but it was definitely a very hard time for me." The quality of her education relative to her middle school and the fact that she wanted to be academically successful motivated her to continue at the school.

> The classes were really hard. I feel like I may have worked harder in high school sometimes than in college. My public middle school science was having flour babies so I wouldn't be a teen mother. Just trying not to have me get pregnant,

that was our curriculum in science. Then you go to a school where there's Bunsen burners and people are using their petri dishes and putting stuff in. You're balancing equations in physics and chemistry, and you're like, wow! It just made me aware that we live in the US and the disparities are just vast! I feel very conflicted about it. On the one hand, I know that the education I received there was remarkable, but at the same time, socially, it was like I went to school across the world. Like although I lived five minutes away from my school, it was literally like traveling. I might as well live across the world.

This "culture shock" took its toll on Selena, but ultimately her difficult high school years made her stronger and gave her critical academic skills for college success.

For Selena, her family, her extracurricular activities, and her intense determination helped sustain her through this difficult time. Most important, though, her mother provided unwavering support. "I have a really strong family, and the women in my family are all very strong. I think that, more than anything, my mother was a really big support to me." In addition, her extracurricular pursuits helped nourish her spirit. "All the extracurricular activities help me make it through the school week because those are the things that I'm really passionate about. I know if I do all my schoolwork then I can go to this, if I do all my schoolwork I can go to that. And they kind of fuel me because all the stuff I'm involved in is kind of political stuff." Selena had become very skilled at spotting injustices and used them to initiate change rather than accept defeat. The sense that she was battling adversity actually helped propel her forward. "I'm one of those people that if someone doesn't think I can do something or if I feel like it's believed that, you know, what are the odds that a person of color graduates from high school and college, and you see the comparison to other groups, and you see these huge differences, I'm not going to be that statistic. I'm going to change this. Every time something was harder, it just made me more determined to get through it." Summing up what got her through, she concluded, "My family, mostly. And just me being pissed off!"

During the summers after her ninth and tenth grade years, Selena worked as a teaching assistant and counselor at the summer program she had attended as a middle school student. She enjoyed the experience and found it rewarding to work with students she saw as similar to herself. She found meaning in demonstrating to her mentees that the older gang-affiliated youth they hung out with were not good role models and tried to connect them with the resources to get and stay on a pathway to college. To Selena, the defining aspect of this experience was the opportunity to build lasting relationships with youth.

> That was so many years ago, and I still am in contact with my mentees. Actually last year, his senior year in high school, [one of my mentees] told me that his teacher said something really racist to him. Something about [how] he was making fun of a kid in class and it was first his test score and she said, "I wouldn't talk like that, he'll be your boss one day," like "You know, it's not like you're going to succeed." He called me up and he was like, "What do I do?" I was like, "I'm so sorry. You need to go to your principal or you have an advisor at your school, you need to go through them. First of all, you need to call your parents, because if your parents don't show that you're upset, usually in schools things fall through the cracks." His mom and his dad, they don't really speak English very well, so I called the school. I said I was calling on behalf of my aunt and I was his cousin, and I was outraged. I wanted to know what was going on. I want a meeting. And then things get done. It's like who was going to call for him? It's not that his parents didn't want to or couldn't, but it's like when you work all day and you have a job at night and you don't have a great grasp of the English language because you don't even have time to learn English because you're trying to support your family, I think it does take a lot of people to help. I had that. If something was wrong, I was fortunate enough to have a mother who was in the office, who was calling, who was concerned. But not everyone is that fortunate.

This experience provided yet another example of how Selena channeled her social justice inclinations and opinionated nature.

During her ninth-grade summer, Selena also got accepted to take part in a youth activist program through a national civil rights group. For years prior to attending, Selena had heard about the experience from her cousins, but she had not been old enough to participate. "It was one of those things I always wanted to go do and I finally got a chance." For Selena, the trip was a turning point.

> If you could put [together] a trip that totally changed our lives that was definitely it. That was just a complete eye-opening experience. You think you're so progressive and you think you're so wanting to do the right thing. [For example,] I'd always been a person like, if they use sweatshop labor, then I'm

not going to patronize this place. Then when I met these women who worked in these factories like Forever 21 and they told me, "Unless the workers themselves have called a boycott, you're hurting me. Because if we haven't [and you boycott], then we're just getting paid less or we're getting fired." That was the last thing I wanted or intended to do. It was just something I had never thought of. Here I felt like I was trying to be so good and I was doing the exact opposite.

Although Selena's conceptions of how to combat unfair labor practices were shattered, she learned other ways of working toward causes she felt strongly about. "I learned to do things like cut off the tag of my shirts. I started writing Banana Republic, Gap. 'I know that you use unfair labor practices and sweatshop labor, and if you continue to do so, you will lose my business.' I didn't stop buying it, I let them know that I am a customer but I don't condone what you're doing. So, just learning little things like this were mind-blowing to me." For Selena, the influence of the trip was more than just learning strategies for activism, she also began to see the larger systemic constraints running throughout individuals' interactions with law and policy.

This trip solidified Selena's career goal of becoming a lawyer and helped her locate which kind of law she would be most interested in practicing. "That [trip] really solidified me wanting to go into immigration law. We met with lawyers who talked about how there are so many injustices and things are so hard for so many people. It inspired me into participating." Selena realized that her commitment to social justice, not the material rewards, drew her to immigration law. Following the trip, Selena and her peers remained involved with a youth activist committee that organized conferences teaching high school students to understand their legal rights. While assisting with these conferences felt meaningful to Selena, the trip imprinted her most strongly.

During the summers after her junior and senior years and occasionally during the school years, Selena took her career ambitions and put them into action by working at a law firm. She learned a lot from the experience, which began with the application process.

My brother-in-law works at the law firm. I applied for the job, and it was really intense and I was doing four rounds of interviews with different people, had to have my resumé perfect and my cover letter. In that sense it was really good because it taught me to do a cover letter when I was in high school. All my friends were filling out applications at the mall. I was like, "I've got to do my cover letter!" I would e-mail it to my brother-in-law "Can you look at this?" I think [the application process] just taught me a lot about being prepared and people's expectations and wanting to meet those expectations.

As Selena worked at the firm, she encountered a very high-stress environment. Within that environment, she ranked lowest. Often secretaries and legal assistants gave her undesirable and difficult tasks to complete. "That taught me a lot about the real world. It was just really demanding. But it was really good to teach me that people have really high expectations." She felt frustrated that her superiors rarely gave her credit for the work she had done, but she also learned to pick which battles were worth fighting. "The legal secretaries would pass stuff off to me that was really their work to do. And, of course, I do it. Then, I'd see her handing it to the attorney, and he's like, 'You did such a wonderful job!' I'm like, 'I did that!' Sometimes you think speaking up would be good, but there could be negative ramifications where it wasn't even worth getting that, 'Thanks for helping with this.' All these other [programs] taught me how to speak my mind, [the law firm is] the place where I learned how to pick my battle." Selena also learned concrete skills, like how to put together legal briefs, and gleaned insights into the legal profession. When asked how she knew she wanted to be a lawyer, Selena replied, laughing, "Probably when I was the only Indian," reaching back to her confrontation with her third-grade teacher.

Although countless young people have career aspirations like Selena's from an early age, many do not encounter the experiences and relationships that help them learn exactly what they need to do to achieve those aspirations. Selena's family provided emotional support and encouragement toward attaining her goal, and her sisters provided tactical advice. Her competitive private high school gave her outstanding academic training. In addition, her varied experiences outside school and family helped her figure out how to make her dream a reality. In Selena's case, unlike many of her peers, her family network connected her to many of these opportunities. For example, her mother pushed her to attend a private high school, her cousin told her about the trip where she learned more about immigration, and her brother-in-law told her about the law firm job.

After High School

Selena attended a private four-year university about thirty miles from Bayside. At the time of our final interview, she was preparing to graduate with a bachelor's degree after only three and a half years in school. She chose this particular university due to its location in a diverse urban area, proximity to her family, and the small class sizes.

> After going to Oak Park Prep, [moving to the city] is very attractive, for clear reasons. I wanted to go to a school that was more diverse and it's pretty diverse here. The one thing I did love about Oak Park is we had really small classes. I liked the fact that my teacher knows my name. The thought of being in this huge lecture hall with three hundred students wasn't appealing to me. My family is really important and we're really a close family, so I wanted to be far enough away where I wasn't living at home or going home every day, but if I needed my family or they needed me, it wasn't an expensive plane ticket or wait until Thanksgiving.

Selena enjoyed her college experience. She liked picking her own classes and studying topics that interested her. She also enjoyed city life, such as visiting galleries and exhibits in the evenings.

While Selena was involved in extracurricular activities at her high school, she decided not to become involved on campus during college. "I feel like I was over-involved in high school, and a lot of the campaigns, changing stuff within my school. I kind of took some 'me' time in college." Instead she was involved off campus working part-time for a labor union. This "great experience" taught her "so much about organizing." By seeing hotel organizing campaigns from underground to public, Selena got to see both the difficulties and rewards in the work of an organizer. On top of organizing skills, Selena also felt as though she gained a better understanding of people from this position. "As much as you want to convince people to organize, you have to understand that they have families. So, you understand they're like, maybe it's not so great here but this pays my rent, feeds my family. Are you going to pay my rent and feed my family if there's a strike and I'm locked out? And it's just coming to terms with wishing better for people but at the same time respecting that they are an autonomous person and they have to make their own choices." Selena came to understand that although she could try to help others, ultimately the risk was not hers. This work complemented not only Selena's long-term goal of becoming a lawyer but also her previous experiences, including her high school summer work focusing on relationship building with young people.

Selena graduated from college about one week after our final interview. While she was unsure of her immediate plans, her long-term agenda stayed true to her lifelong ambition. "I kind of want to work for a little while and gain some experience, and then head to law school." She had not ruled out moving home with her mom where "rent is free," but she hoped to find a job in the city instead.

Thinking back on her life, Selena felt like the diversity of her experiences had been key to her growth and development. "I've gained things from all of my experiences. I like to always have different perspectives." Some people and experiences across different periods of her life were, however, more influential than others. In middle school, Students Together was a driving force, while in high school a select few teachers and tutors mattered most. The common thread among all of her biggest influencers? They have all been "strong women." Of course, Selena's list of strong women would be replete without marquee mention of her mother and older sisters. Across the years, Selena's family was the most influential support in her life: "I feel like a lot of my values and things that I have are from them. I feel like they are the ones who truly understand me. They can also be the ones who can truly call me out on things when I'm wrong, too. My family has been there for me." Throughout her coming of age trials and triumphs—much like Julio, Graciela, and Teresa—Selena's family played a significant role.

Relationships, Structures, and Agency

Teresa's and Selena's educational journeys reveal the overlapping influences of family, school, and out-of-school time contexts for students who experience a distinguishable degree of influence. Namely, both benefited from stable home lives and strong family support throughout their academic careers. Selena's mother played a pivotal role by actively jockeying for her daughter to attend a private high school, while Teresa's parents allowed her to escape toxic peer influences by enrolling at a different public school. Academically, both girls boasted strong scholastic records, enjoyed placid relationships with teachers, and stayed out of trouble at school. Yet both struggled to fit in socially and relied on an array of out-of-school time programs over the years to help them develop and sustain a positive and consistent sense of self across multiple contexts. Their case studies illustrate how extracurricular activities can influence students' pathways to college by compensating for gaps in participants' networks of support.

In addition, their experiences highlight the importance of finding a "fit" with regard to program content, peers, and personnel. For Teresa and Selena, the curriculum of Students Together appealed to their interests, the progression of activities built confidence and competence in an engaging way, and the caring environment empowered them to become more effective speakers and listeners. While each had already set her sights on college prior to joining Students Together, the program not only taught valuable skills but also instilled a sense of confidence and purpose that carried over into their high school and college years. Because participation in Students Together sparked involvement in similar activities, the influence of the program lasted even as the girls began the transition into adulthood. In the final pages of chapter 4, I highlight how relationships, structures, and personal agency intersect and overlap to mold the distinguishable degree of influence.

Relationships

The distinguishable degree of influence is characterized by strong relationships in most, but not all, contexts a student inhabits. The respondents in this study who experienced a distinguishable influence had a supportive and positive relationship with at least one parent who encouraged them to go to college. In addition, no respondent had a significant negative relationship with an adult. Each respondent was surrounded by an extended family of siblings, aunts, and others who exercised a largely positive influence. In Selena's case, extended family relationships helped her learn about many of the extracurricular experiences that had a profound impact on her career pathway, such as the law firm job and activism trip.

Family members did not impose expectations of care-taking on the young women in this group in the same way as they did for most of the other Latinas in this study. This could be due to the fact that all the students in this groups were, by chance, the youngest child in their families. It could alternately be attributed to the fact that none of the women in this group was a first- or second-generation immigrant, and thus each was privy to more Americanized gender expectations.

Although both Selena and Teresa reported having friends during middle school, both strongly disliked the peer culture at Adams. While Selena was outgoing and combated this culture by maintaining an affirming stance toward others, Teresa was shy and responded by socially withdrawing. At the time of program participation, these peers influenced Selena and Teresa negatively. The positive peer culture within Students Together counteracted the less welcoming school culture and provided a place for both shy and outgoing youth to experience a sense of belonging. Building on this experience, both girls sustained healthy friendships during high school.

While the respondents who experienced a distinguishable influence did not have deep relationships with staff members at Students Together, they cited the adult leaders as important and inspiring. Selena, Teresa, and Molly remember talking with adult staff members about the process of getting into college and what college would be like. This practical knowledge comprised one way that Students Together benefitted respondents' educational trajectories. Whereas the gender of Students Together leaders was important for some young women in the program, in this category of embedded influence only Selena specifically mentioned the beneficial aspects of the Students Together leaders being women.

Structures

Like participants who experienced an auxiliary degree of influence, youth in the distinguishable influence category were positively seen within the major structures in their lives at the time they joined the program. No respondent in this group struggled academically or got in trouble at school, and teachers were noted as positive mentors. These students cited employment experiences starting in high school, though those experiences were most influential if the job was related to the individual's long-term career goals. For instance, Selena remembered her work at the law firm, while Teresa remembered her work at a nursing home. None of the youth in this group reported meaningful religious involvement or entanglements with the immigration system.

Students Together was an important structure for respondents who experienced a distinguishable degree of influence because it not only imparted cultural capital and provided a space for identity development but also served as a gateway to other extracurricular opportunities. For example, Teresa stayed with Students Together for two years as a paid mentor, and both Teresa and Selena became involved in Bayside Youth Council at the encouragement of Students Together staff members. Students Together was the first rung on a ladder of opportunities. Unlike most other respondents, the fact that Students Together provided a refuge from the streets after school was not important to the young women in this group, as all would have likely been involved with another program had they not been involved with Students Together.

In fact, youth who experienced this degree of influence tended to be involved in other extracurricular activities both before and after participating in Students Together. For Teresa, those other activities ranged but tended to cluster around community service. Given the strong sense of self she was supported to develop during her time in Students Together and the ways that her peer networks shifted during high school, all her subsequent extracurricular pursuits yielded an auxiliary influence. For Selena, because of the hostile racial environment in her high school, many of the activities she participated in after Students Together also had a distinguishable influence on her pathway to college.

Personal Agency

For participants who experience a distinguishable degree of influence, the out-of-school time program tends to their unmet needs and fits well with their personality and interests. Despite their differences, in the case of the students profiled in this chapter, Students Together offered this match. Carolina and Jennifer inspired the students and made them feel cared about. The program structure provided both a reprieve from the banter of middle school peers and encouragement for their college ambitions. The curriculum focused on content areas that interested them: Teresa enjoyed volunteering, and Selena loved public policy. Like the auxiliary group, they gained valuable skills from participating, such as public speaking and how to work with a diverse team. Unlike the auxiliary group, they also felt a strong sense of belonging and identification with the program's goals. Students Together provided a setting where they developed a stronger sense of themselves and began to feel at home in their own skin. Because students in the distinguishable category gained more than just resume lines and concrete skills, the program had a higher degree of embedded influence on their educational trajectories.

5

Transformative Influence

"It Changed My Whole Life!"

Felicia, Maria, and Victoria participated in the Students Together program as eighth graders at Adams Middle School. Like other Students Together participants, they learned how to communicate with a diverse team and craft public presentations. They came to see themselves as competent students and engaged community members. They felt supported by caring and knowledgeable adults and connected with other extracurricular programs. For their peers in the auxiliary category, these experiences offered a rich supplement to an already robust network of support. For youth in the distinguishable category, these opportunities covered a gap left open by troublesome peers, teachers, or family members. But for the young people in the transformative category, who lacked positive supports across multiple contexts in their lives, participation in a high-quality out-of-school time program acted as a savior by reorienting their pathway from prison to college.

Maria arrived in the United States at age seven speaking no English, changed schools at least once each year during elementary school, and spent her nonschool hours in a household plagued by physical and emotional violence. By sixth grade she was getting into fights with eighth-grade boys, being introduced to the intricacies of gang life, and uninterested in keeping up with her homework. No one in her life saw her as college-bound—not her family, her friends, or her teachers. Yet as a twenty-something, she was enrolled in community college and preparing to transfer to a four-year university, working full-time in a job with upward mobility, and lovingly tending to her younger siblings every afternoon.

Felicia grew up in low-income housing with her mother, whom she described as "totally hands off." She enjoyed a peaceful childhood until the entrance of her abusive stepfather, driving away the extended family members who had been raising her. From that point on, her home life was simply "awful." In elementary school she was bullied for being overweight. In middle school, she was bullied because she thought Latinas ought to be expected to do more than "wear tight clothes and sit around." By age fifteen, she was addicted to drugs and only sporadically going to school. Yet at the time of our final interview, Felicia had been admitted with a full scholarship as a transfer student to a competitive four-year university, was deeply engaged in her job as a community organizer, and had begun to take on more responsibility with her younger siblings at home.

Victoria also grew up in a home rife with physical and emotional abuse. Though she remained in the same school throughout her elementary years, the stability only cemented her reputation as a delinquent. By sixth grade her primary sources of support were older gang-affiliated friends, and she began to envision a similar life for herself. Yet as a young adult, even after suffering the death of her mother and the deportation of her father, she had earned nearly two years of college credit, a full-time job, and a strong relationship with her sister and nephew.

What happened? How did each of these young people transform from a troubled teenager to a responsible college student? The short answer is extracurricular participation.

Chapter 5 introduces the highest degree of embedded influence from an out-of-school time program: transformative influence. Transformative influence depicts students for whom participation in an out-of-school time program triggers a drastic and positive change in their lives, significantly impacting their pathway to college. Prior to joining a program, these students are not oriented toward higher education; instead, they have started along a road toward delinquency, gang-affiliation, dropping out, or other problem behaviors. Youth who experience this degree of positive programmatic influence tend to lack positive supports across multiple contexts and often are embedded in apathetic or abusive relationships with family, peers, and school personnel.

During their time in an extracurricular program, students who experience a transformative degree of influence tend to distance themselves from damaging relationships and turn their intentions toward academic attainment, positive peer interactions, and constructive community engagement. Like other participants, they often benefit from acquiring new skills and cultural capital. They also benefit from becoming immersed in an environment that rewards prosocial behaviors and helps them to develop a "school kid" identity. Yet participants who experience a transformative degree of influence additionally benefit from developing close relationships with compassionate and knowledgeable adult staff members. These relationships have the potential to transmit valuable social capital that directly influences students' pathways to college, even after participation in the program has ended. Overall, out-of-school time participation is associated with both changing these participants' outlooks and identities and sparking a domino effect of beneficial supports and experiences that propels them toward educational attainment.

Social embeddedness theory argues that individuals are embedded within social networks that serve to limit or enable our movement within society (Furstenberg and Hughes 1995; Granovetter 1985; Stanton-Salazar 2001). Prior to program participation, youth in the transformative degree of influence category tend to be embedded in social networks that pave the way for school failure. These students, often cut off from much needed love and care by damaging relationships at home, are left to deal with schoolwork on their own. Bullying peers may leave them feeling ostracized and alone, or delinquent friends might give the impression that the only way to belong is to engage in harmful acts. Either way, peer influences may actively discourage academic achievement and healthy development. Teachers and school personnel might assign these students detrimental labels or act on discriminatory stereotypes. Neighborhood and community contexts— often linked to extended kin networks—are often either subject to constant change and instability or rich with illegal activity or both. Because of the social networks these young people find themselves embedded within, students in this category tend to have ample opportunities to engage in criminal or unhealthy behaviors, but they are offered few chances to develop nurturing relationships, few rewards for academic success, or few incentives to test new interests in developmentally appropriate settings.

For students who lack access to the kinds of relationships and experiences that open the door to higher education, an out-of-school time program has the potential to replace negative or neutral contexts with generative ones. For example, adult staff members might provide unconditional support and positive encouragement and act as role models for youth facing limited social or cultural expectations based on race, ethnicity, gender, ability, or other factors. Adult staff members might help students complete their homework, seek out tutoring, or establish connections with teachers. They can teach and reinforce constructive styles of interaction that enable positive exchanges with peers and generate a sense of safety and belonging. They may introduce engaging activities and coach students to learn new skills, which may increase competence and confidence, or offer tactical advice leading up to and during the college search and application process. In addition, adult staff members can create opportunities for young people to participate in out-of-school time programs over an extended period of time by establishing an extended network of support that spans from adolescence into adulthood. By generating relationships with adult staff members and becoming embedded in new social networks, participants who experience a transformative degree of influence have the opportunity to gain critical social capital (Coleman 1988). Because the additional benefits associated with the transformative degree of influence are decidedly dependent upon the actions and attitudes of the adult leaders, the emergence of this degree of influence is likely to pivot on both the skills and talents of individual staff members and a program structure that enables deep and lasting relationships.

In the case of the Students Together participants profiled for this book, those who experienced a transformative degree of influence shared some common traits with students who experienced an auxiliary degree of influence. Two of the three respondents in the transformative category were born in Mexico and immigrated to the United States prior to starting elementary school, and all three count themselves as native Spanish speakers initially placed in bilingual classrooms. One moved at least five times during elementary school, another remained in the same house but watched extended family members shuffle in and out, and the third did not move after her initial migration from Mexico. All attended Adams Middle School for sixth, seventh, and eighth grades. For high school, two respondents graduated from Ridgetop High, while the third received her diploma from a community college-based program. All three had large extended families in the United States and Mexico.

What set the students in the transformative category apart from their peers is not their status as Mexican American people, Spanish speakers, immigrants, or youth lower down the socioeconomic ladder. Instead, both the nature of the social networks within which they were embedded at the time of program—participation across family, school, and community contexts—and the social capital they gained from becoming active in Students Together set these students apart. Like others, their social networks were bounded by social class, ethnicity, and immigration status, yet in addition to macrolevel structural constraints, these participants' social networks were also plagued with personal trauma. Family members perpetrated abuse, peers inflicted isolation or pressure to affiliate with a gang, and teachers exhibited apathy or animosity. To illustrate how and why an out-of-school time program jump-started and reinforced personal transformation, chapter 5 profiles Maria and Victoria.

Maria

Childhood and Elementary School

Maria was born in México City and attended preschool there before immigrating to the United States with her mother, father, and younger brother. The family initially settled in a house where some of her aunts and uncles were already living, in an urban community about twenty miles from Bayside. Less than a year later, Maria's mother left her father, and Maria, her brother, and her mother moved into an apartment with her aunt in a nearby city. They stayed there only briefly before moving fifteen miles south, this time with Maria's mother's boyfriend who had joined the household. Maria settled into her third elementary school since arriving in the United States as a third grader taking English-only classes for the first time. A competent student and quick learner, at the end of third grade Maria was promoted to fifth grade. A few months into the new school year, the family moved again, this time to Bayside. At the end of her fifth-grade year, Maria's mother gave birth to a baby boy.

Throughout her elementary school years, Maria's home life was tumultuous. Each residential move was the product of family discord, an attempt to mitigate disaster that inevitably brought about more trouble. Maria described one of the moves: "My uncle had a problem with somebody else, and I guess my mom's boyfriend was involved in it as well. And before we knew, one day we got home and somebody broke into our house. Everybody was scared, so we moved. One day pretty much to another, we moved." The moves took a toll on Maria. "This was a very hard time for me because we were moving all over the place and I was switching schools all the time. Everything was so vulnerable." Although she enjoyed the liveliness of being surrounded by changing constellations of extended family, her needs were often lost in the shuffle. "It was always a lot of fun in my house. Every weekend was people coming over and dancing. Always parties, always food. It was like 1:00 a.m. and the kids were playing and just all over the place." Maria loved her family but did not feel supported academically or emotionally.

Both Maria's father and her mother's new boyfriend added layers of difficulty to her already chaotic home life. Maria's father was verbally abusive, and her mother's new boyfriend was physically abusive. The abuse was shrouded in a secrecy that further isolated Maria. "[My mother] basically suffered domestic violence whenever she got with [her boyfriend]. She never did anything about it and it was the hidden secret, like nobody's supposed to know, you're not supposed to say anything. One time I said something, and I regretted saying anything because it was really bad. That's when I learned that I was supposed to be quiet, period, about what went on at home." Her mother's physical abuse and the associated code of silence continued throughout Maria's elementary and middle school years.

Meanwhile, Maria's father tormented her in a different way. Though engaged to a new woman and visiting Maria and her brother infrequently, he became jealous of Maria's mother's new boyfriend, especially when he learned they were expecting a child together. He took his feelings out on the kids. "My dad still had feelings for my mom, so my dad's always putting this idea in my head that, 'Oh, you're going to have a brother and [your mother's] not going to love you anymore,' and blah blah blah. So, the majority of my time during this point of my life, I always wanted to sleep over my aunt's house, I always wanted to sleep over my cousin's house. I never wanted to be home. During her whole entire pregnancy I never touched her belly 'cause I was so jealous." Once the baby was born, Maria learned that her mother's affection for her had not changed and experienced a wave of relief. Her father's threats, however, had a profound negative effect on Maria. "I think not having my dad in my life was a big thing for me. There's nothing bad about not having your dad. It can be sad, but my mom has given me that and more." As a child she mourned not getting more time with her father, but as a young adult Maria saw the loss as positive.

To cope with the trauma at home, Maria sought refuge at school. She came to the United States knowing no English and worked diligently to gain proficiency. Like other parents profiled in this book, Maria's mother took pride in her progress; unlike other parents, however, no one in Maria's household provided active support for her academic work. "I was maybe in third grade when I started speaking more English than Spanish because all my classes were in English. I remember one time we had a conference and my teacher didn't speak Spanish and my mom didn't speak English, so I had to be the translator in the middle. My English wasn't that great, so it was kind of hard for me. But that was the first time my mom ever heard me speak English and actually translate it into Spanish. And my mom started crying in the middle of the conference [because she was proud of me]." Across the various elementary schools Maria attended, she constantly looked to her teachers for advice and support. "A lot of what helped me was finding those teachers who led you in the right way, who told you, 'This is what you're supposed to do. This is what you're not supposed to do.'" Her teachers helped her acclimate to the culture and customs of each new place, in addition to guiding Maria in her studies. Bright but uninterested in academics, Maria had little ambition throughout elementary school.

Middle School

When Maria started sixth grade at Adams Middle School she knew no one. Because she was new in town she was very shy, and because Maria had skipped a grade in elementary school she was a year younger than her classmates. Like other respondents have noted, the social scene at Adams was sharply divided. Maria fell in with an older crowd, many of whom were already nurturing gang ties.

> When I got to Adams, there was a really huge mix of ways and styles and it was sort of the place where you needed to find who you were. I started to hang out with the wrong people. I was a little troublemaker in school. I would always be in fights with other people—all through sixth and seventh grade. Girls, and guys too; I got in a fight with this guy, he pushed me and I slapped him across the face. I was hanging at the wrong places at the wrong times, and I was getting all these things in my life that really shouldn't have been there, at that age especially.

With each passing year, Maria crept closer to gang involvement. Her grades were poor, and she felt little connection to school. By the beginning of eighth grade she was on the verge of dropping out.

A confluence of factors pushed Maria to join Students Together. Given her family's financial struggles, the notion of getting paid for participation was very appealing. "When I hit eighth grade, that's when money came into my head. Like, where do we get money from? That's exactly when I found out about Students Together." She also remembered Carolina coming into her class to encourage students to apply and how excited she was at the prospect. Furthermore, she was ready to make a change. Her guidance counselor supported her application to the program and encouraged staff members to make an exception to the minimum C average rule on her behalf.

> I was kind of tired of what I was doing before. I needed something different. I was always hanging out with the older people, so once I was in eighth grade most of them were already gone. There is a time when all these people are influencing you in your life and there's a pause. And during that pause, if somebody else comes it kind of replaces them, right? I feel that's part of what happened. Students Together was my opportunity to expand myself in a different way—that if I was going to be at the office, it wasn't because I was in trouble. That was a big change in my life. I don't really know what would have happened if I wouldn't have been [in Students Together]. I don't think I would be where I am.

Over the course of the year, Maria's grades improved significantly. Maria, citing the opportunity the program gave her to think about the problems in her community and the role she could play in the solutions, credited Students Together for her academic turnaround. "I started to think a little bit better about who I am and what I want. Everything used to be all blank. I just acted. I didn't even know what I was doing." People around her began to notice the change. "The day when my science teacher said to the principal, 'I want to show you the star of my class.' The principal just looked at me, and then he said, 'Oh wow!'" Maria's commitment to her education prompted her teachers and peers to begin to see her differently.

Three primary factors contributed to the transformative influence Students Together had on Maria's pathway to college: concrete skills, a new sense of identity, and relationships with adult staff members. Like her peers in all three categories of influence, she benefited from acquiring new skills, such as how to work with a diverse group of people and how to speak publicly. Unlike her peers in the auxiliary influence group, those new skills led Maria to feel a strong sense of identification with the program's curriculum and gave her the foundation on which to build a new sense of herself. As a young adult, she linked each new skill with monumental personal growth and development. For example, Maria described the moment she realized how much she enjoyed public speaking and the domino effect it had on her educational trajectory:

> I realized that what I really liked doing was talking in front of people. There was one [activity] where Carolina put little things inside a bag, and we were supposed to get on top of the table and make a commercial out of it; in the moment you have to come up with something. That's when I started to realize that that's what I like doing. After that, everything changed. I started hanging out with different people. I started to behave differently, because I started to see the world very differently; it wasn't only about having fun and being a kid, I realized there was more purpose to life than just school. I think that was the perfect time for me, because if I wouldn't have gotten the right direction [in eighth grade], I don't think I would have made it all the way [to college].

Learning to work with a diverse group of people had a similar impact:

> I got to meet a lot of people who I never thought I would ever end up talking to, ever in my life. That was my opportunity to grow and show really who I was. I started to realize that you need to share everything with other people who not only are different than you, but think differently. I was so used to being with my people. This was an opportunity where I realized that it wasn't only me and it wasn't only the people that thought like me, but there was a whole bunch of people who had different ideas.

Students Together broadened Maria's horizons to include new ways of thinking and interacting. These new skills pointed Maria toward a renewed sense of who she wanted to be known as. "I was exposed to all that positive energy and positive attitude, and that's when I realized that's where I belonged, that's who I wanted to be, that's who I was proud to be, that's what defined me. I learned to be different, and I learned that being different wasn't bad, and that there was an opportunity to change, and there was an opportunity to grow and learn. Once I hit that point, it was a huge change in my life." Learning to see herself and others in new ways profoundly influenced Maria's identity and the ways she worked to be recognized within school and community contexts.

Finally, the relationships Maria formed with adult leaders in Students Together contributed to the lasting and transformative influence the program had on her trajectory. The philosophy of the program combined with hands-on support from Carolina and Jennifer made Maria feel empowered: "Students Together was different in the sense that there was a purpose of, 'What do you want to do?' Not, 'this is what we want you to do.' So, 'this is what you want to do? Now how are you going to do it? How can I help you achieve that goal you want?' That point where you have a mentor that guides you through the steps and helps you around, but is not doing it for you and is not telling you what you're supposed to do." During her time in the program, Maria grew close with Carolina, and Carolina became both a role model and a mentor. "I got to know Carolina on a very different level. It was sort of that one person that I looked up to, that I felt like you could be all these things at once; you can be nice, you can be supportive. Because of the way I grew up and where I grew up, I never really saw women take any role more than being a housewife, cleaning the house and the dishes. This was my first encounter with a Latina woman who has so much that I felt like I could learn from." Joining Students Together connected Maria with resources and relationships to point her in a new direction; moreover, the bonds she developed with staff members supported and sustained her long after her initial year in the program. In one year she had gone from gang affiliation to top student, but, given the adversity she faced at home and the pending reintroduction of her older friends, she needed ongoing support to help her stay on the pathway to college.

High School

As Maria began the new school year at Ridgetop High School, she knew she would have the chance to reunite with her older friends. While the prospect of this reunion was exciting, it was also confusing. Because she had worked to change her identity during eighth grade, Maria now faced a choice between her old trouble-making crowd and her new sense of self. "It was really hard because you're like, 'I don't know anybody else.' The other kids that went to middle school with me, they have their own thing going on. Also because [my old friends] were older I felt protected, so I started hanging out with them the first day." Even though she knew she should not associate herself with her gang-affiliated and drug-dealing friends, Maria had trouble resisting the familiarity of their company. Maria began to severe her ties with what she calls her "bad friends" only when a classmate's sister intervened:

> One day, I'm with my bad friends and [my classmate's sister] just grabs me, like, "Come with me." One of the guys that was there, he's like, "If you keep hanging out with those girls over there, you're going to end up in jail; you're going to end up beat up all the time; and most of all, you're going to wear this big banner on your head all the time that categorizes you a certain way. And that's not what you want." After that, everything changed again. I met all these [new] people who are in some sense so much like me—as far as we grew up in the same place in Mexico City, the music, all these things. I was like, this [crowd] is where I'm staying.

While this intervention kept Maria clear of a gang affiliation, it did not help her keep up with her schoolwork. "I became more about the parties. It was hard for me to keep up in school." She helped out with Students Together on occasion, but she continued to flounder.

As a sophomore, Maria recommitted herself to the identity she had worked to establish as an eighth grader. Because she had previously developed strong ties with Students Together staff members, she was able to draw on these relationships to help her get back on track. "I got in contact with Carolina and Jennifer and most of my day was at Students Together. I'd get off school, walk or take the bus to Adams, and that's where I was the whole entire day. That was my life—that was who I was. Carolina would tell us about other events going on in the community. I was always looking for opportunities to be involved here and there. I felt very important. I felt like I was playing a huge role in my community and school and I was really excited." Carolina hired Maria as a Students Together mentor and kept her up to date on other community events. Maria volunteered as a reading tutor, presented workshops at national youth development conferences, and cofounded a support group for young Latinas. She credited Students Together with creating the ladder of opportunities that made all of this possible. "It is like the trunk of the tree and all these other programs and opportunities are the branches. If I didn't keep going in Students

Together, I would be a different person right now. I have a lot of friends who are in jail, some of my friends are pregnant and they have babies, some are married already." As an eighth grader, Maria was on the path to similar outcomes, yet Students Together supported Maria to maintain a college-bound trajectory and a "school kid" identity, even as the struggles in her home life reached a breaking point.

Although Maria's mother had long been a victim of domestic violence, the threat began to escalate during Maria's sophomore year. "Literally, I felt he was going to kill her." Maria took it upon herself to intervene.

> The day that my mom's husband hit her really bad, I was calling my friends and nobody was there, and so I end up calling [my friend's uncle] and he's like, "Call the cops!" I'm sitting in the kitchen and [my mom's husband's] brother was witnessing the whole fight, and I was begging him to make his brother stop! And he was sitting in the kitchen eating! He said, "I can't do anything, it's not my business." I say, "I'm going to call the cops," he tells me, "No, don't call the cops." And we're fighting with the phone, and he throws the phone and I go and I put the battery in and I leave the house. I call the cops and then the cops come. I point them to the room, 'cause [my mom's husband has] locked the room. You could hear my mom screaming all the way outside. They're knocking, they're like, "The cops!" And the cops slammed the door and broke it in. My mom was crying, and [her husband's] like, "I didn't hit her." Then, bam, I hear a big loud noise. I heard my mom's husband screaming and I see the cops come out with him handcuffed. At this point, my mom comes out and the first thing I tell my mom is, "I'm sorry." My mom starts crying and crying. She's like, "You don't have to be sorry about anything." Her whole eye is black. And she showed me everything, and then we talked.

This incident had a weighty influence on Maria; it drove a wedge between her and her stepfather, but it brought her closer to her mother.

The incident also impacted her daily life in a significant way; because Maria's stepfather had been the primary wage-earner, his incarceration ended the family's cash flow. Maria's mother, who had never worked outside the home and spoke very little English, was forced to give up many of her household duties in order to secure paid employment. "It was like, 'What are we going to do?' I go to school, my brothers go to school. We live in a house. It's a lot of rent to pay. This is where I stepped into the real world and realized how difficult life really was." Maria stopped working at Students Together. "I had to help my mom. I couldn't spare time to go help the community." Instead of participating in structured extracurricular activities, Maria's out-of-school time was now dedicated to helping out at home. "It was very hard for me because before when I would come home, everything was clean, the food was made, it was just sort of let's sit down and have dinner. Now I realized all the things my mom had to do. I was only fifteen, I had to come home and clean and call my grandma, 'How do you make this?' It was very, very hard, and I didn't know what to do." She struggled to quickly learn the household tasks she had previously taken for granted and grieved the loss of her former life. In fact, Maria, her mother, and her siblings moved so frequently over the next few years that Maria lost track of their different apartments.

This drastic lifestyle change had at least one positive consequence for Maria: she became even more committed to attaining a college degree.

> I realized how important education really was, because I felt like I never want to see myself in my mom's shoes, to feel like I have to be with somebody just because he is the one that brings money to the house. That's what I like about my mom, she always told me everything, and she told me she never loved him. She was scared because she had three kids and she never worked before. She was too dependent on him. I don't want to be like that. Not only that, I want to help my mom. I want to show her that because of her, this is who I am. I don't want to be another burden for her.

Maria accepted the lion's share of work around the house and stepped up to care for her siblings while her mother was at work. Rather than using these obligations as an excuse to let her schoolwork slide, Maria saw it as motivation to take her studies more seriously. She set her sights on becoming director of a youth program, like Carolina. She became goal-oriented and organized. Her grades improved, and her college ambitions strengthened.

Though she was less involved with Students Together and other extracurricular activities later in her high school years, Maria stayed in touch with her mentors from the program and valued the sanctuary these relationships provided. "I kept in contact with Carolina and Jennifer, and they were always there, very supportive. Sometimes when I really wanted to forget, I would just call and get myself involved somewhere else, in a whole different environment where it was always about trying to do the right thing and the positive thing. That's where I went when I felt really down." By the time she graduated from high school, Maria had been awarded a prestigious community leadership award and a college scholarship—both of which she learned about from Carolina. Carolina and Jennifer had given her practical advice on applying to colleges and generous encouragement for her academic accomplishments. Overall, participating in Students Together began a cascade of opportunities that supported Maria through some of her darkest days and helped her attain her college ambitions.

After High School

Although Maria applied to and was accepted at a handful of four-year universities, her family's financial status prevented her from attending. "The problem was the money. There was no way to get around it." Even with a scholarship, community college was the only feasible option for continuing her education. Maria lived with her mother and helped care for her siblings, even as she took a full course-load and worked a full-time job.

Rather than thinking about her broader career goals, Maria "got a job, 'cause I had to get a job." She had worked at a relative's taco stand for a summer during high school and knew she did not want to return to food service. At the suggestion of a friend, she applied to an upscale hotel chain. Maria's experiences in Students Together not only helped her land the job but also facilitated her subsequent mobility.

> It's very hard when you've just graduated from high school to try to get a job—I told them about Students Together, how I did all these things, and we organized. That's a lot what helped me get the job, because I had more experience than just school. I had experience with people. I started working there, and I liked it but I got really bored of it after a couple of months because I felt like I knew everything that I need to know. I started to get more involved, like, "Let's try this," and, "Let's put the menus this way." And [my manager's] like, "Where in the world do you get all these things from?" But, honestly, what I was doing was bringing everything I learned from Students Together in to work.

Even as a high school graduate, Maria continued to benefit from the concrete skills and cultural capital she acquired in Students Together. Though

Maria excelled at her first hotel job, she became restless and began to look for a more satisfying position. Before long, a competing upscale hotel hired her, and after only six months the management promoted her to a supervisory role.

The logistics of keeping up with a demanding job, coursework, and her home life soon became overwhelming. Without a car, the commute required multiple bus and train transfers and consumed hours out of her day. She could not afford to cut back at work so she was forced to cut back at school. "I was like, 'This is too much for me.' I dropped out of school for one semester, which was the worst semester off ever in my life because I felt bored." Maria again reached out to her mentors from Students Together. "I was calling Carolina, 'Do you have anything for me to do, 'cause I'm not going to school?'" In addition to reengaging with Students Together, Maria took steps to simplify her life. She reenrolled at a community college closer to her apartment and negotiated a transfer within the hotel chain to a nearby property. She changed her schedule so that she worked days and attended school at night. This proved to be a better fit academically and facilitated new professional opportunities.

After about a year, Maria was recruited into the human resources department at the hotel. "I got really excited because I had never done HR before; I had only been with the company one year. Not only that, but I was really young. I was only twenty; all of the other HR ladies were in their forties." Maria was thrilled for the promotion and the change of pace. She liked her new job enough that she began to weigh advancing within the field of HR and turning her attention back to her long-time dream of a more civically engaged career.

My original plan was to become a director, like Jennifer and Carolina. Just because it's so fulfilling, not only professionally but personally. My goal was to go to school, get good grades, graduate, and do that. But there's so much in between that, in reality. I come home really tired sometimes and I don't want to do anything. But I can't go to sleep and wake up and go to work and go to sleep and go to school—that's not enough for me. I have a pretty stable job and I have a lot of opportunity to grow. I hope that I can get my certificate in HR, because I think it's going to be easier for me to find another job eventually, if one day I want to. But in reality, that's not who I am. Right now, I'm working because I have to get money. I go to school because I like going to school and because I want to do something more than just work. I think at this point in my life I need something more than just a job. I need to find a place where I can feel comfortable, where I can feel like it's something that I want to do the rest of my life. I've thought about a lot of things to do in my life, and part of it is how do I mix in the fact that I like to talk in front of people and, at the same time, I'm really organized and, at the same time, I can work on my own if I have to, and I'm able to work with people, too. And at the same time, how do I manage to make a difference? What I like doing is helping people and being involved in making decisions and planning and organizing. I think I'm heading more, like, a government-level kind of thing, where you're involved with the city and how do you get every single member of the community involved, just by how different their neighborhoods are and the language barriers? That's something that I feel like I would love to know and be able to work on.

Maria wrestled with her sense of wanting to make a difference in the world and follow the passion that was first sparked by Students Together and her appreciation of the relative security of her current position, all within the very real time and financial constraints of adult life. While she felt satisfied with her work in human resources and saw opportunity there, she hoped to eventually move to something more inspiring.

At the time of our final interview, Maria was three years out of high school and within one term of completing the requirements to transfer from community college to a four-year university to complete her degree. She had decided on a major but was still unclear about her long-term goals. "I want to major in communications, but I still want to do something else, so I'm still like, 'What is that something else I'm going to do?'" For a while she had been thinking about attending university in a different part of the state; however, she ultimately decided to stay closer to home, due to her job and her boyfriend.

Looking back, Maria saw clear inflection points in her life: migrating to the United States, joining Students Together, and standing up to her stepfather. She remained close with her mother and a small group of friends and continued to keep in touch with her mentors from Students Together for support and advice. She spent most of her time at school or at work and maintained a staunch commitment to attaining a bachelor's degree in the near future. Because she endured so much turmoil at home and negative peer influence at school, Students Together had the opportunity to provide a transformative influence on Maria's educational trajectory. Through teaching new skills, supporting positive identity development, and introducing long-term relationships with caring and knowledgeable adults, Students Together participation produced a significant and lasting influence on Maria's pathway to college.

Victoria

Childhood and Elementary School

Victoria was born in Mexico City and moved as a young child with her mother and older sister Ana to join their father in Bayside. Upon arrival, Victoria and her family settled into a small apartment with her uncle and his family. With so many people under the same roof, the apartment soon filled with tension. "Our first year here was horrible! My mom and my uncle's wife didn't get along. Then my dad's niece would call my mom 'Mom,' and his mom by her name, so it was like they were competing with each other about who gets called 'Mom' or something. My uncle's wife was dirty, and my mom was always a clean freak. I don't remember much from our first year here, only all the bad stuff that happened between my parents and my uncles and my aunts." Victoria and her father, mother, and sister lived with their uncle for about a year before relocating to another apartment nearby.

The next few years were "mellow years," due to relative peace at home and Victoria's success at school. At home, Victoria treasured time with her mother:

> I was always with my mom; she was my favorite person to be around. She would go to the gym. [I would go] work out with her. We would eat, watch TV, and then she would let us go out to play. We would be home by eight o'clock, and then we would go to sleep. My mom was always cooking and my mom taught us how to clean and wash. In Mexico, I remember she would put us up in a little stool and she would have us rinse all the pots and dishes. Part of it was her culture, "Women have to clean, clean, clean." So she taught us how to do that when we were young.

Her parents, however, were at odds regarding how she and Ana would be raised. Victoria's father believed that the girls should be skilled at traditionally female tasks, such as cooking and cleaning house, but he also believed in teaching the girls to be self-sufficient and mature. Victoria's mother raised her girls to be helpful around the house, but she also believed children should have a chance to be children. "[My mother] always talked to us like little kids. Like, 'Oh, come eat.' My dad and her would fight, like, 'You can't talk to the girls like that.' My mom was like, 'But they're my babies.' 'Well, don't talk to them like they're your babies, they're too old,' at, like, eight [years old], we were old to my dad." The fighting between Victoria's parents escalated with regard to other philosophical differences as well. Coming from dissimilar religious traditions, her mother and father sparred over which church their children would be raised in. "They were trying to decide whether they were going to take us to one [church] and then to another. And that's when they both decided, 'The girls can both come to the two churches and have them decide when they grow older.'" As her elementary school years continued, for these reasons among others, Victoria began to characterize her mother and father as "difficult parents to deal with."

At school and with peers, Victoria experienced a similar downward spiral from the "mellow years" into more difficult times. Victoria started first grade speaking only Spanish and attended bilingual classes during her first two years of elementary school. "Back then there still were bilingual teachers. So Spanish [to] English, it wasn't that hard. I was still young and I was absorbing everything like a sponge." Victoria quickly gained English fluency and, in third grade, started attending English-only classes.

From that time on, Victoria had primarily negative memories of her elementary school teachers. "All the teachers would tell my parents, 'I don't know if your daughters have a future.'" The only exception was a teacher's assistant Victoria worked with during third grade—she describes the assistant as "like a mother"—who helped her transition from bilingual to English-only classes. "She was the nicest lady on Earth and she used to always talk to us like, 'You guys are so smart. I know you guys will be someone later in life!' She was the one who taught us how to speak and read, and I will remember her forever. She was so positive all the time, even though she knew we were not in good terms." Victoria emphasized the traits that set her teacher's assistant apart from the other teachers in the school: her positive attitude and persistence with regard to academic progress, personal warmth with regards to nonacademic matters, and high expectations in spite of pervasive negative stereotypes. At the time of our final interview, Victoria still kept in touch with her through casual encounters in the community.

Outside school, Victoria participated in school-based cheerleading and basketball and a community college–based summer enrichment program during fourth and fifth grades. Although Victoria did not remember how she became involved in these programs, she had positive—if limited—memories of each. From cheerleading and basketball, Victoria's college preferences were shaped: "I always dreamed of going to [college] when I was in [elementary school]. My teacher started talking about college like, 'Do you guys have an idea what college you want to go to?' I was in cheerleading, and the young woman who was teaching us was a student at Cal State, so I was like, 'Oh, I want to go there!' I think Cal State was always the one I had in mind since I was a little kid, because there were a couple helpers and they all went to State." In the summer enrichment program, Victoria explored a variety of subjects. "I took karate, math, [and] poetry. It was fun!" While these extra-curricular opportunities helped round out Victoria's elementary school experience, they had little impact on her social world.

Victoria established a peer group when she started first grade, and many of those children continued through school with her for the next twelve years. "We don't keep in touch like we talk every day, but I see them and we still MySpace each other and stuff." These early connections, however, did not develop into supportive relationships. Victoria "never really socialized with friends" and struggled to spend time with peers outside school. "My mom was totally overprotective. It was hard for me to socialize because my parents wouldn't allow me to do sleepovers, even at my uncle's." In spite of everything, Victoria met Maria, her best friend, in fourth grade. "She's my total friend, like forever." Maria proved to be a perpetually positive influence for Victoria, even during rough times.

Given her early college aspirations, blossoming friendship, strong relationship with her mother, and extracurricular involvement, things should have been looking up for Victoria, but, with continuing tension at home and lack of teacher support at school, Victoria began to fall in with older, gang-affiliated youth. By fifth grade, Victoria started getting into serious trouble at school. "It was a harsh time, like, 'I'm going to beat some girl's ass because I don't like her.' Even today, I see teachers that were [at my elementary school], and they look at me now like, 'I can't believe you're doing [well],' because everyone had a negative connotation from me." Although she maintained good grades, Victoria's behavior continued to get worse.

Middle School

As a sixth grader at Adams, Victoria's trouble-making ways progressed. "My first two years in [middle school], they were a disaster. I think those were the years that I didn't care." She continued to get into physical fights with both boys and girls, during and after school. Lacking positive peer influences, she fell in easily with a seventh- and eighth-grade crowd. "Most of my friends were already in eighth grade, and I was a sixth grader. I wanted to be just like them. I was getting into fights. That was peer pressure from my older friends, like how they were acting." From these older peers and many of her older cousins, Victoria learned what it meant to become affiliated with a gang. Although Victoria never officially joined a gang or did drugs, she found a sense of belonging and an outlet for her frustrations. "It was just crazy, crazy, crazy times. Most of my older cousins were gang-affiliated, and that's who I grew up with, so I was going the wrong way. I was never a true gangster, but I was affiliated with them. If you're in a gang, you have to do everything the leader says. If you're gang-affiliated, you just hang out and you don't have to go beat up someone." Even though Victoria was constantly being reprimanded at school for behavioral issues, her schoolwork did not suffer. "I was never a bad student. I always turned in homework, even though I was gang affiliated." Many of her teachers reached out to establish trusting relationships with her. "It just happened that most of my teachers and I got personal, they worried about me." Meanwhile, other teachers maintained a more authoritarian stance. "A couple teachers were always like authority figures. I didn't like that." Overall, the adults by whom Victoria felt most supported were warmly encouraging without being authoritarian.

At home, family dynamics began to change. Victoria's mother was diagnosed with a fatal illness and passed away during her seventh-grade year.

> I remember [my mother] always telling me, "I want you to make me proud." Every time she would go to school it was because I was in trouble. She always told me, "I want you to one day change and be called to that school because you're in honors or something, not because you're in trouble. I come and I'm embarrassed that you're doing this." She never actually put me down, but she always kept saying, "Don't embarrass your family, because you reflect what we teach you and we'd never teach you to be like this." So when she passed away, it was really hard.

Victoria and her sister Ana were profoundly impacted by their mother's untimely death, both emotionally and logistically. As the women of the house, their father now expected them to assume full responsibility for household chores, including cooking, shopping, and cleaning.

> My dad is very macho. He made us learn how to cook when we were twelve, 'cause my mom passed away. He's like, "You guys need to cook for me because I'm the man of the house and I'm not cooking." I'm like, "Are you shitting me? I'm only twelve! I can't even do cereal." I had to learn how to cook. And he would send us to go pay the bills at the actual store, like AT&T, "Go to the store and pay this bill," and "Deposit this money in the bank and withdraw a hundred." I feel like that made us stronger now; that made us learn how to do stuff on our own. I had a grudge on him, "I didn't even have a childhood because you taught us how to cook and do all these things young." So, he was harsh, but it was also for our own good.

Almost overnight the girls went from a home where they were cared for by their mother to a living situation where they were upholding adult responsibilities. Although they resented this new role at the time, the hardship began to prepare them for the difficulties still ahead.

Victoria's father noticed her gang affiliations and tendency for getting into trouble, and, contrary to her mother, he approached her behavior with a heavy hand. "When I was gang affiliated, he used to tell me, 'If you want to be a gangster, then you better be the best gangster in the whole world, because you have to be the best at everything you do. If they call me and you're dead, I'm not even going to shed a tear. I'll go, bury you, and that's it.' He used to be so strong with those words!" Now missing her mother's warmth at home, Victoria sought out encouraging adults elsewhere.

As a sixth grader, Victoria knew of the Students Together program because her sister Ana was involved. Often, Victoria would hang out in the Students Together room after school. "I would go in there and wait for Ana and we would snack. So I just knew, 'Students Together, I get snacks,' in sixth grade." Even though she did not know much about the content of the program, Victoria decided to join when she was old enough: "I remember signing up late, so [the staff leader] told me, 'We're not taking any more applications.' But because I knew [the staff leader] since I was in sixth grade and she knew we were not in good shape [at home] and so she said, 'You know what, I'm going to get you in.'" Victoria credited Students

Together as being the most influential part of her middle school years and for helping her transition from a gang-affiliate to an engaged member of the community. Victoria stayed involved with Students Together for six years—first as a participant, then as a mentor, and finally as a mentor to the mentors—by working her way up Students Together's ladder of opportunities. Although, like others, Victoria did not recall which topic her cohort researched by the time of her final interview, she remembered many of the staff members and the ways that participating in Students Together helped her engage with her community in a positive way. To Victoria, Students Together offered three main things: the setting where she learned how to listen, speak, and socialize; a way to keep busy and a gateway to further civic engagement; and a connection to positive adult mentors.

First, Students Together taught Victoria skills for speaking her mind and helping others speak theirs. Students Together explicitly taught these skills through activities as well as the program structure: "[I learned] public speaking, being social, listening to others' different points of view. Because I didn't even learn that in school. I guess it's a class structure, so someone's speaking but you don't care; you're talking to your neighbor. But here I learned that you should listen to what others have to say, and you don't have to accept it but listening is good." In Students Together participants sat on couches in a circle, rather than in rows of desks like a traditional classroom. Each session began and ended with a check-in question where everyone in the circle had a chance to speak in turn while the rest of the group listened silently. The curriculum also included activities focused on listening skills, such as eye contact and body language, and speaking skills, through rehearsed presentations as well as improvisational skits. "I was so shy. I never spoke my mind. I was insecure of myself. When I joined Students Together, I think the first year I was quiet, but I was opening [up] more. In high school, I was just doing it. Like, I'm confident, I know this, and I can talk more and speak my mind a lot more." Victoria gained new skills through Students Together's structures and activities, and her confidence blossomed over time. Her experiences suggest the benefits for some students of having the opportunity to remain involved in the same program for multiple consecutive years.

Second, Students Together staff members assisted Victoria in getting involved with other organizations, even as she continued her involvement with Students Together. Like Maria, Victoria compared Students Together to "the trunk of a giant tree, with all of the other opportunities and advice as the branches." For example, "From Students Together I started going to [other] meetings. I went to the Youth Council. There were eight sessions with the city manager, where four youths were chosen among say a hundred people that were adults." Once Victoria got a taste of what it felt like to be positively engaged with her peers and her community, she started leaving her trouble-making days behind. In many ways, Students Together provided the same benefits that gang affiliation offered—belonging and autonomy—but without the violent drawbacks. "As soon as I started seeing opportunities that were approaching, I can't just say no. That's how I started leaving my gang stuff behind. I got involved with my community, and that kept me busy and kept me saying no to my [gang] friends. I think that's when my whole life changed. It was hard for me to leave my [gang] friends, because I felt like they were going to be like, 'Oh my God, you are a square.' You know? But it was easy to get involved with programs and staying busy." Being engaged in various out-of-school time programs that provided opportunities for leadership, skill development, and affirmation provided an alternative to the gang affiliation that Victoria had sought earlier. Participation allowed Victoria to reflect on her former life and how much she had changed. "I broadened my horizons after I joined Students Together. I felt like I was just in this little world and that was it. As a gang-affiliate I never did drugs, thank God, but I always just kept in mind that lifestyle. Once I joined Students Together, I was beyond gangs. I mean, that was an issue in the communities that everyone would talk about, and I just felt like, wow it's a problem and why was I in it?" Participation impacted how Victoria saw herself: from part of the problem to part of the solution. Participation also changed how Victoria presented herself. "I even started dressing differently since I was going to meetings, and I needed to be a little bit more presentable than my baggy jeans." In this and other ways, Victoria's persona shifted as a result of the programs available to her and the choices she made to engage in them.

Third, the adult staff members at Students Together took on a meaningful role in Victoria's life. At the time of participation, Victoria did not have many other positive role models to emulate. In her eighth-grade interview she reported that her older sister was a role model. "She is a role model for me to study because I see her study and get good grades." When asked about the other important adults in her life, Victoria responded, "My dad, of course, because he is my dad." She also responded, "My friends. They are nineteen, so they are adults already." The interviewer then asked Victoria how it came to be that at the age of thirteen, she had friends who were nineteen. "Because I have a young cousin/friend, she is fourteen and she has a sister and she is sixteen and she has a sister, she's nineteen. My friends are important to me because every time I have a problem with my dad and my sister or in fights or homework, they will be there for me. They will never let me down." Students Together provided positive adult role models at a time when Victoria needed them.

Across the six years she participated Victoria remembers forming tight relationships with all the adults who worked at Students Together. As a participant, she reported her favorite part of the program was the staff because they "made us feel comfortable." As a young adult, she elaborated. "The [staff] were really nice. I got to a personal level with them, with every single person. I think the people managing Students Together were more like a friend than director. I saw [Students Together] like a home. I felt protected there." She especially remembered the staff member who admitted her to the program, Carolina, because "she was the first one there that I actually talked to about personal stuff." Like many of the other adults Victoria remembered as influential across her life, the adults at Students Together were warm, encouraging, and supportive.

Overall, Students Together had a transformative influence on Victoria. The program and the relationships stemming from it served as a bridge from a rocky childhood toward a brighter future. "Students Together was one of the programs that kind of changed my whole life. If I never were involved in Students Together, I don't know what else I would have been doing. I have no idea what my life would be without Students Together." Although Students Together helped Victoria begin to develop her confidence and garner a more positively engaged peer group, Victoria continued to struggle as she continued her journey into adulthood.

High School

When it was time for Victoria to go to high school, her father opted to send her to Ridgetop High School rather than Arroyo, where she had been assigned. Although the two high schools were similarly sized, had similar student demographics, and were both on a public bus line, the high school he chose for the girls was located in a more affluent part of town. "My dad never wanted us to go to Arroyo because he knew we were not so studious. We didn't want to go anyway. Ridgetop was good." While the two high schools differed only slightly, Victoria's father's interest and attention to his daughters' choice of schools demonstrated his investment in and commitment to their attaining the best public education. Victoria attended the same high school for all four years, graduating with her class.

The transition from middle school to high school proved difficult as Victoria found herself in an entirely new environment, without many of her familiar supports, and again in the company of her older gang-affiliated peer group. While Victoria looked back on her middle school years as "fun," she says she "could regret" high school: "I'm like, ugh. I don't really care about high school." Her academic progress, which had remained strong even through her most violent middle school years, now began to fall by the wayside. "My freshman year was horrible. I don't know what the hell I was thinking my freshman year. I was getting Fs, Fs, Fs. It was a huge transition for me, middle school [to] high school." One of the hardest parts of the transition to high school for Victoria was once again learning to rebuff the negative influences of her peers.

Over time, continued participation in Students Together and other extracurricular activities helped Victoria regain her focus. "I was still in Students Together, so I was like, 'I'm doing good in my community, but what am I doing with me, academically? I have to do better.' So, that's when I started doing better stuff. I was so involved with Students Together I didn't have time to really hang out and go to parties and not do my homework. I was going to Students Together Monday through Thursday and I had homework and essays and reading." Throughout high school she worked with Students Together and even attended retreats and field trips across the state. "I did a lot of stuff with Students Together. That's why I feel like Students Together was like my savior." Victoria credited staying busy with organized programming as her saving grace.

Students Together was also a safe space for Victoria. Like Selena and Miguel, she felt discriminated against at her high school. For Victoria, this discrimination made her feel like she had to work harder than her peers. At Students Together, she felt differently. During an interview conducted during her junior year of high school, Victoria reflected: "In Students Together I feel like it doesn't matter whether I'm purple, white, pink—it doesn't matter. I don't feel like I need to prove myself. But in school I see a lot of discrimination and racism, everything put together in one. I feel that I have to prove myself to teachers and students and staff and everything at school. I need to prove to them that I'm an educated Latina and that

I'm a successful Latina, and that I'm not just any kind of Latina." While Selena reacted to the discrimination she experienced with fury and a call to action, Victoria sympathized with the people discriminating against her. "I understand why they're acting like that—because there's a lot of Latino and most of the Latinos are gangsters, most of the Latino are doing stuff that they shouldn't be doing. I understand why we get discriminated. But then again it's like why? I don't like it." As Ricardo Stanton-Salazar (2001) notes, it is quite common for the disadvantaged within our society to actually unknowingly and unintentionally contribute to their own oppression. The structures and networks that support discrimination are so powerful that even those who are discriminated against buy into them. In this case, Victoria bought into the stereotype that most Latino/as are gangsters and thus viewed her own oppression as justified. In Students Together, however, she felt and acted differently.

From Students Together, Victoria learned of other extracurricular participation opportunities. As a freshman she participated in a community-building group on the weekends. As a sophomore she joined a lunchtime support group for civically minded Latinas. This group not only built on the lessons Victoria had learned in Students Together but also filled a more culturally and gender-specific need.

> We went for a workshop where it talked about how relationships work and healthy relationships. They showed us a picture where there was a girl leaning on the guy's shoulder. That was really powerful because everyone said, "Oh, it's a romantic date." Then, the people teaching the workshop were like, "It's funny how you all think that it looks romantic, but what if she was just drunk and he was just trying to get into her pants, and that's where he took her?" We talked about how Latinas suffer from domestic violence more than any other race because we're afraid to speak up, or at least that's how our culture functions. Like if they hit you, you don't have to say anything, you just have to stay with that person because once you're married, you can't divorce.

For Victoria, this message hit very close to home: "Most of the women in my family have gotten beat up by their husbands. But I am different: I could never have a man lay any hands on me. I would leave him, I don't care. I'm more independent. All the women in my family are dependent on their husbands. I'm a little different. I think that's how I started thinking, since I joined Students Together. I felt like it liberated me a little bit, like I don't have to follow my father's rules or his customs and my family's customs, especially when they're so harsh for women." Victoria had always struggled with her father's gendered household roles and harbored her own independent spirit. Participation in activities like the Latina support group and Students Together provided an environment supportive of the ways that her gender and cultural identities diverged from her upbringing, introduced her to independent and educated Latina mentors, and helped develop her sense of confidence surrounding her ideals.

In addition to her extracurricular activities, Victoria worked hourly wage jobs throughout high school to support her family. None of her employment experiences was either memorable or long lasting. While her jobs contributed to helping her stay busy, none impacted her life in the same ways as participation in organized activities.

As the upheaval of her freshman year passed, Victoria's routine began to fall into place. In an interview conducted during her junior year of high school she said, "I'm looking forward to college, and I don't want a messed up grade that's going to ruin my educational reputation. I worry a lot about college and my grades." She made time for socializing, school-work, employment, and extracurricular activities, all the while beginning to think ahead to college. "I was just so busy. I needed to get this done, that done. I was just kind of finding myself during high school, I think. It was fun. I would go to all the afterschool dances at school, but it was mostly getting my stuff together and figuring out what was I going to do after high school." During this process, she continued to rely on her adult mentors from Students Together. In the same junior year interview, Victoria explained how Jennifer had played a role in her educational pathway. "We have a really personal relationship outside of Students Together. I feel like I can come back to her and ask her for help or support in anything, and she'll be there. Even if she's not the director, I feel like I can continue having that relationship with her." As Victoria and Maria prepared for college, neither received concrete guidance from their parents or family members. Jennifer, a college graduate, was able to help the girls navigate the process of choosing a college, applying to that institution, and finding scholarships. Simply aspiring to attend college was not enough to make it happen; the girls needed information and support during this process.

Like Maria, financial constraints were a big factor in choosing a college. "Money-wise, it was bad." But Victoria's family also influenced her choice.

She applied to a number of four-year state universities with her eye on a psychology major.

> My sister was the first one to go to college, but I'm the first one to go to a four-year college in my family. My family in Mexico, all of my cousins have a career and all of them have a degree, either a master's [or a] B.A. I just felt like we migrated to America for a better life and higher education, because it's so hard to do it in Mexico, and it would be stupid of me to not go to college. Also I wanted to see if I could get in at a four-year college. I just kind of took the chance like, "If I get accepted, I'll go." I applied to a couple [state colleges], but the first one that accepted me was Cal State. Also, I knew they had a really good program for psychology. It was hard for me to tell my dad I wanted to go to college. I mean, obviously, I was going to go but I felt like, "He's not going to be able to afford it, I don't know if it's going to be good or not." But then I had a $10,000 scholarship that a local community organization gave me, and so I could totally afford it.

Victoria had been admitted to her first choice school—Cal State—and won a substantial scholarship to support her education. Students Together staff members helped Victoria learn about and apply for the scholarship, an award "honoring volunteerism" in Bayside. By the time she graduated from high school, Victoria remembers feeling "so stable" and excited to be "planning all this for my future."

Despite Victoria's incredible transformation from troublemaker to community leader, she still encountered naysayers. Late in her senior year of high school, Victoria ran into her elementary school principal during a visit to her old school. "He saw me and he recognized me and we talked. I told him everything I was doing with Students Together and all the things I had planned and stuff. And he's just like, 'I thought you'd be pregnant by now. I really didn't think you could be what you are now.' I was so young [when he knew me]; I was in third or fourth grade. Are you serious? I just looked at him like: you're an asshole." Victoria took pride in her scholastic achievements, her civic engagement, and the contributions she made to her family. She also took pride in the fact the she had emerged from a history of gang affiliation into a life of confidence and positive contributions. As a young adult, she no longer heeded either negative stereotypes or low expectations. Rather, she reveled in being a success story.

After High School

It was unfortunate for Victoria, but graduating from high school did not mark a passage into less tumultuous times. By the time Victoria graduated, her sister Ana was pregnant and had moved in with the baby's father. Victoria was living alone with her father. During the summer before she started college, she shifted from an eclectic series of part-time jobs into restaurant work. Her first foray into the industry was short-lived. "I quit because they treated you like shit." She quickly found a more respectful employer and continued to work in the restaurant industry to help pay for school.

When fall arrived, the first big challenge in Victoria's college career was simply getting from Bayside to Cal State, a sixty-mile round-trip trek. By car, the commute would take about an hour each way. But on the public bus it took much longer. In the end, Victoria managed to make this long ride work to her advantage. "[For every] five hours in school, [I spent] ten hours in the bus. I finished all my homework on the bus. If I took the commuter train, I would go home and sit around. There's Internet, there's radio, there's food. I'm like, I'll stick to the bus, and I'll just do my homework there. So I had really good grades at State." Victoria chose the lengthy bus ride over the more efficient train commute because it allowed her a distraction-free zone in which to complete her homework. Before long, however, Victoria's transportation trials seemed minor compared to the struggles she faced at home.

When Victoria started at Cal State, her father was simultaneously protective and supportive. "My first day, my dad would walk me to the bus stop, and I'm like, 'Dad, you never did this when I was six, I'm twenty! What are you doing?' He's like, 'You know in Mexico, five in the morning is the time when everyone is stealing cars and the bad people are out doing their stuff. I just don't want to keep it in my conscience, if something happened to you and I didn't walk you.' So, he kept walking me from week to week." The emergence of her father's protectiveness relatively late in her life both annoyed and pleased Victoria. Yet with a sudden turn of events, Victoria began to see her father's ways in a new light.

About six months after Victoria graduated from high school, Victoria's father got deported. Victoria did not even contemplate returning to Mexico with her father. "That never crossed my head. My dad, even though he's very traditional, he also taught us to be independent. He always told us, 'If something ever happens to me, you guys need to learn how to live on your own.'

And [when he got deported] I felt like okay, let's put all of my dad's advice to practice now." Victoria was born in Mexico City but spent most of her childhood and adolescence in the United States. Like many 1.5 generation immigrants, she identified more strongly with American culture than her parents had. As a young adult, she harbored no resentment toward her father and blamed many of their past disagreements on cultural differences.

> He was very harsh, and I used to hate him. Now I understand him. Now I thank him. I'm independent and I do stuff for myself and if I need help, I ask. But once I learn it, I'm going to do it on my own. I was so mad at him for so many years, but I kind of have to understand him because he comes from a different culture from here. I am Mexican, but I feel like I am more Americanized than he is. Here you don't teach your children by hitting them. You teach them by talking. But he is totally different; he grew up in Mexico. He has that Mexican set of mind and I feel like I have to understand him, even though I never accepted his treatment. He was harsh, but now I understand it was for the good.

Although Victoria resented her father's conduct for many years, his absence helped her realize that his actions may have made her stronger.

Staying in the United States without him, however, proved arduous. Because Victoria had been living with her father, she had to find a new place to live. Lacking other options, she moved in with her sister Ana, Ana's boyfriend, and their newborn baby. Victoria had been financially dependent on her dad for many things so now Victoria also had to take on a full-time job. "I used to always say, 'I'm independent, I work for myself.' But I never thought it would be so expensive, like toothpaste and toilet paper and everything else. I was always depending on my dad because he paid all the bills. Everything. Food. Toothpaste. Shampoo. I would just buy my clothes, and that's it. I didn't have a cell phone forever because I can't afford it." Ana's boyfriend soon moved out, and Victoria and her sister lived together for nearly a year. They supported each other emotionally and shared household expenses as they coped with the realities of raising a newborn while missing their parents. Both Victoria and her sister dropped out of college due to the personal and financial strain.

> I kept telling myself, "My sister, she's a strong woman," but I feel like if she sees me cry or be like, "we're not going to make it," she will totally just collaborate

with me. We can't both be weak; someone has to be strong. So, even though I'm so weak, I had to show strength. I felt like I needed to show her that this is easy, we're going to get through it, and that's it. Because as this was happening, her boyfriend left. It's only me and her and the baby. And it was like, I don't have a stable job, it was just part-time. I need to find another job that's full-time. That's why I left school. Everything was so crazy for a moment in life; I felt like everything was falling apart and I didn't know how to put it back together.

After about a year, Victoria decided to move out of her sister's apartment and into a nearby apartment with some of her older cousins. While Victoria had her sights set on resuming her college education, her cousins instead stayed up late drinking with their friends. "Me and Ana started fighting a lot, and I moved out. Then I got evicted from my house because my cousins who were living with me are party, party, party. So I moved back in with my sister. I have to say that being with my nephew and my sister, I enjoy that very much. When I'm about to go out and my nephew's crying for me, I'm like, 'I don't want to go out anymore, I want to stay.'" At the time of Victoria's final interview, life had settled down for Victoria and Ana, and they looked back on all they had endured over the last few years with awe.

Victoria saw how much she had grown from being forced to live independent of her parents and had established a new sense of normalcy in her life. "Now I know how much I could spend for entertainment and how much I have to keep for rent and bills. I'm back on my own two feet. I'm touching the ground now. I'm doing it. I feel like I think I can breathe." After only one semester off, Victoria enrolled at the local community college because "State is way too expensive for me to afford now." Although she was not entirely pleased with her college pathway, Victoria remained determined to complete her four-year degree. "I'm working full-time, so I'm only able to go to school twice a week. I was actually talking to my counselor, she said, "I can probably get you out of here in three years." It's a semester of classes I need and it's going to take me that long! So, I'm working for general education requirements and my associate's, and then transfer back [to State] in my B.A. to major in psychology and minor in criminal justice." Victoria remained frustrated with how long it would take to achieve her A.A. degree and ultimately her bachelor's.

Given the extent of the personal difficulties with which she has had to deal, Victoria had not maintained the same engagement with community issues that she achieved during her adolescent years. She had a strong desire to mentor youth and contribute to her community, but she did not have the time. Although she had previously volunteered to help the current Students Together director, Amy, on a weekly basis, scheduling proved too difficult. "I feel like I am so disconnected with my community. I don't even know what the issues are. I'm absorbed by working and going to school now, that's why I asked Amy if I can volunteer, just to go back and feel like I'm doing something useful. I don't even know how kids are doing and what are their points of view or what are the issues we need to fix." Despite her current distance from the issues, connecting with young people remained part of Victoria's long-term plan. After college, Victoria hoped to use her psychology degree to work with at-risk children.

> I definitely want to be a probation officer with students or youth that are gang affiliated. I experienced it, maybe not as much because it was just for a short period of time, but I have cousins that have been through it and have been in prison and in jail for doing stupid stuff. I think as adults we don't have much hope. Once you're adult and you have your mind set to something and that's how you are. I think it's harder to change an adult than a kid. Children have hope. So I would want to work with teens, being a probation officer.

She was the first to recognize the irony in her chosen career, joking good-naturedly about the journey she has traveled since she began elementary school nearly fifteen years ago. "It's funny because when I was younger, I was like, 'Authority figures, I hate them!' And now, I'm like, 'I want to be an authority figure!'"

Overall, many factors set Victoria on a pathway toward delinquency from a young age. Her parents fought frequently, and her authoritarian father insisted she and her sister take up traditional gender roles. In part, due to her extended family, she became embedded in negative peer and neighborhood networks as early as her elementary years. Most of her teachers viewed her as a troublemaker who routinely acted out at school. When her mother died she had no supportive adults on whom to rely and instead relied on the sense of security she had found in gang life.

Students Together marked a drastic change in Victoria's life. The program taught her valuable skills for listening, speaking, and resolving conflict. Staff members linked Victoria with a cascade of constructive out-of-school activities that enabled her to leave behind her gang-affiliated friends. In addition, the close relationships she developed and sustained with the adult leaders throughout her high school years provided a safety net and a sanctuary, which offered both nurturing care as well as practical advice for the road to college. Students Together had a transformative influence on Victoria's educational trajectory by helping her turn from making trouble to achieving academically and by supporting her to continue along that path into her young adult years.

Relationships, Structures, and Agency

Prior to joining an out-of-school time program, students who experience a transformative degree of influence tend to be engaged in unsupportive relationships and embedded in structures that constrain their available courses of action. Yet at the confluence of limiting relationships and structures, these students exhibit a high degree of personal agency by choosing to become active in a high-quality program: engaging in program activities, seeking out connections with staff members, and continuing to involve themselves in affiliated relationships and events over a sustained period of time.

Because students in this category tend to be battling swarms of adversity, to achieve a transformative degree of influence an out-of-school time program must make new courses of action available across multiple contexts. And because out-of-school time staff members rarely have the authority to alter students' family situations, participation is most likely to influence students' choice of peer groups, dedication to their academic work, interactions with school personnel, and contributions within the broader community. By offering adolescents opportunities to opt out of social networks that limit access to higher education—such as gangs—and become embedded in relationships with peers and adults that facilitate school success and healthy development, extracurricular activities can act as a critical source of support as students begin to construct their pathways to college. The choice, however, of whether and how to engage the resources available through a high-quality out-of-school time program ultimately lies with the student.

Like their peers in the auxiliary influence category, Maria, Victoria, and Felicia gained fond memories and concrete skills from their time in

Students Together. Also like their peers in the distinguishable influence category, they built a new sense of identity centered on scholastic achievement and good deeds in the community. Moreover, because they developed deep bonds with staff members and remained involved in Students Together long after their eighth-grade year, the participants who experienced a transformative degree of influence also benefited from becoming embedded in relationships and networks that provided sanctuary, support, and advice. Without family backing, these students' college pathways were riddled with complications, from tuition payments to transportation. Yet they managed to stay in school—Maria with the goal of becoming a youth worker and Victoria with hopes of becoming a probation officer—and have never lost sight of their college dreams. These students capitalized on the opportunity offered by Students Together to undertake a drastic and positive change in their lives.

Relationships

Youth who experience a transformative influence from out-of-school time participation lack a consistent, warm, and supportive parental influence at the time of participation. Felicia's aunt, who had been like a mother to her, moved out during her sixth-grade year. While Felicia continued to live with her mother, Felicia's mother was neither supportive nor attentive. Victoria's mother passed away during her seventh-grade year. Her father provided financial support but was neither emotionally warm nor available. Maria's mother was overwhelmed by her abusive husband and thus unable to tend to Maria's needs. In addition to lacking positive adult role models at home, these young women were all in close contact with multiple negative adult role models, including uncles, cousins, or stepfathers.

Furthermore, in this category of influence the young women, starting at an early age, experienced pressure from their families to conform to restrictive gender roles and responsibilities. These responsibilities included cooking and cleaning house as well as looking out for younger siblings. At different moments in time, each of these young women also took on the responsibility of caring for a parent: Maria cared for her mother as she recovered from physical abuse, Victoria cared for her father after her mother passed away, and Felicia cared for her mother as she struggled with mental health issues. Their time in Students Together separated these respondents from the auxiliary influence respondents saddled with similar expectations; Felicia, Maria, and Victoria drew inspiration from the program to actively categorize the responsibilities they were assigned as gendered and unfair, and they fought back in various ways against the biased standards.

Although the students in this category had friends during middle school, these friends tended to exert a negative influence. Felicia refused to "choose a color" (gang affiliation) and did not feel like she fit in because she was smart. As she put it, "Latina women are expected to wear tight clothes and sit around, not get good grades." To rebel against these expectations at the intersection of ethnicity and gender, she hung out with the "alternative crowd," dying her hair and getting body piercings. Maria and Victoria entered middle school with blossoming gang affiliations and found themselves frequently in trouble. Students Together provided these young women with a positive peer culture and recognized their good acts, support that they were not receiving anywhere else.

Like participants in the distinguishable influence category, the adult leaders at Students Together were important to Felicia, Victoria, and Maria, but, instead of simply being held up as inspiring role models, staff members were considered "family," acting as a primary support system. Respondents' relationships with them were deep and long lasting, such that all the respondents in this category were still in touch with at least one staff member at the time of our final interview. Such caring bonds helped buffer students from the negative pressures they were experiencing at home and with peers.

Structures

Overall, youth in the transformative category were not seen positively within the primary structures in their lives at the time they joined the program. They tended to be capable but frequently in trouble at school. They did not look to teachers as positive mentors; rather, each respondent recalled one or more examples of teachers who told them they could not possibly succeed. Participation in an extracurricular program motivated these teens to keep up with their studies and incentivized appropriate classroom behavior. After joining, these students got in trouble less frequently and began to build a positive rapport with teachers. Yet their improved academic habits did not tend to endure without consistent support, and youth in this category of influence continually returned to Students Together for structure and encouragement throughout their high school years.

Other societal structures also proved limiting. For example, while the students in this group, starting in high school, were employed, their experiences tended to be negative, and each respondent reported being treated poorly at one or more jobs. In addition, Victoria and Maria both struggled with the immigration system deporting family members at different points in time. The school, employment, and legal systems exemplify social structures that tend to limit low-income and minority adolescents' available courses of action and obscure pathways to college. Out-of-school time programs, however, may have the potential to counteract these negative forces.

For participants who experience a transformative influence, extracurricular participation comprises an important structure in their lives. First, it gives students something to do after school instead of being on the streets or at home. Because of their blossoming gang ties and difficult home environments, no respondent in this category would probably have been involved in a structured program after school if it were not for Students Together. Second, programs can connect young people with continuing opportunities to participate. All the respondents in this category persisted with Students Together for multiple years as paid mentors, and they also participated in at least two other organizations that they learned about through Students Together staff members. This network of supports was likely crucial in keeping them on the college track. Students Together acted as the first rung on a ladder of opportunities for structured out-of-school time engagement.

Personal Agency

Social capital theorists argue that low achievement has structural roots, but they nonetheless locate the route to academic success in a student's ability to navigate the system and build beneficial relationships. Although the nature of an adolescent's social embeddedness dictates his or her available courses of action, individuals actively negotiate within available opportunities and constraints. In other words, in the face of macrolevel structures that restrict students' social networks, studies have shown that successful Latino/a youth are those who actively seek out supportive adults within their schools, families, and communities (Furstenberg and Hughes 1995; Granovetter 1985; Stanton-Salazar 1997, 2001; Stanton-Salazar and Dornbusch 1995).

The profiles presented in chapter 5 suggest that, if a program is to achieve a transformative degree of influence, personal agency is particularly important for young people who are struggling with violent or abusive contexts in and out of school. As noted earlier in this chapter, adult staff members can make themselves open to building lasting bonds with participants, and program structures must enable youth to remain involved and/or in contact over multiple years. Students, however, must also actively pursue relationships with adult staff members, maintain those relationships over time, and willingly return to the program for support as adversity arises.

Part of encouraging students to exercise agency and sustain involvement may rest on finding a good match between a student's personality and interests and a program's goals and content. No program can or should be expected to provide an appropriate fit for every student. Schools and communities should collaborate to create a diverse network of out-of-school time programs and work together to shepherd each student in the right direction. Students Together focused on topics of interest to the young people profiled in this chapter—youth activism and city governance—a large part of the reason they were able to experience a transformative influence from participation.

In sum, participants who experience a transformative degree of influence benefit from out-of-school time program participation through three primary processes. Like the auxiliary and distinguishable groups, they gain skills that are valued by institutional gatekeepers and act as cultural capital along the pathway to college. Like the distinguishable group, these participants also feel a strong sense of belonging and identification with program content, thereby establishing an affirmative sense of self tied to educational attainment. Moreover, these students engaged in deep relationships with staff members and became embedded in social networks that facilitated new opportunities to succeed.

6

The Differential Role of Extracurricular Activity Participation

Latino youth are the fastest growing segment of the US population, yet their academic achievement has lagged significantly behind other ethnic groups. Scholars have looked to demographic, structural, cultural, and psychological factors to explain this gap; however, few existing theories recognize the role that structured out-of-school time programs can play in Latino, or specifically Mexican American, students' school success. In national samples, participation in extracurricular activities has been associated with a host of positive outcomes, but research on the experiences of Mexican American and other marginalized students is scarce. As the number of Latina/o children in our public schools climbs and as evidence on the pivotal role that out-of-school time can play continues to accumulate, practitioners, policymakers, and researchers will require a better understanding of exactly how programs influence participants' pathways to college. Rather than mimicking quantitative studies that isolate links between specific activity combinations and educational outcomes, this book introduces a comprehensive framework for understanding how and why out-of-school time programs influence educational attainment among Mexican American youth.

Through the stories of Graciela, Julio, Teresa, Selena, Maria, Victoria, and their Students Together cohorts, this book defines the processes through which extracurricular participation may influence students' pathways to college—concrete skills, identity development, and supportive relationships—as well as the complex reasons why some participants may benefit more than others. Spanning auxiliary, distinguishable, and transformative degrees of influence, this chapter develops a theory of *embedded influence* of out-of-school time programs by emphasizing the ways that relationships, school and community structures and personal agency overlap and interact. Thus, the embedded influence of a particular program takes into account the holistic landscape of adolescents' experiences and the multitude of ways organized activities can matter in young people's lives.

Theoretical Explanations for Academic Success and Failure

Most existing theoretical explanations for Mexican American students' academic successes seek to isolate a single explanatory factor, such as parental education or teacher training. By examining students' educational trajectories over time, however, the case studies presented in this book illustrate the complex interactions between home, school, out-of-school, and community influences. This complexity, pervasive in students' lived experiences, suggests the need for a more nuanced theoretical framework.

Asset and deficit explanations focus on individual, family, or cultural factors to predict educational outcomes, perhaps thus oversimplifying the college process and leaving little room for extracurricular activities to occupy a significant role in students' academic attainment. We see both support and counterevidence for these theoretical approaches among the Students Together participants profiled in this book. Many respondents cited their parents as their biggest supporters, and out-of-school time programs served to complement parental love with college-oriented knowledge and skills. Other respondents did not experience any family characteristics that have been linked with school success, such as parental support of students' growth into areas of their own interest and parents' influences on educational aspirations (Cornelius-White, Garza, and Hoey 2004; Trusty,

Plata, and Salazar 2003); these students made it to college because of the layered and consistent support available via extracurricular participation. Although each participant's story offers examples of the ways that family, individual, and cultural factors exerted a profound influence on his or her college trajectory, these case studies also reveal the inadequacy of relying on asset or deficit theories to explain academic success.

The case studies in this book also reveal the role of structural factors in students' pathways to educational attainment. Structural theorists argue that support and critical information can be intentionally combined within a school setting to promote academic success among marginalized students (Sanchez, Reyes, and Singh 2006) by addressing the most common barriers between Latino/a youth and college (Immerwahr 2003; Zalaquett 2006). Social capital theorists add an element of agency to this argument by claiming that successful Mexican American students seek supportive adults within their schools (Stanton-Salazar 1997, 2001; Stanton-Salazar and Dornbusch 1995). Certainly the students profiled in this book illustrate the ways that teachers and schools can impact educational pathways as well as the variation in student agency. For some respondents, however, extracurricular activities provided the same combination of support and information outside the traditional school day. On the surface, out-of-school time programs could be considered another structural explanation for educational attainment among some Mexican American students, particularly those who remain involved in a program for multiple years.

Yet young people do not experience extracurricular activities in a uniform manner. Programs like Students Together have the potential to provide a safe and supportive environment, with opportunities for skill building and belonging. Staff members can provide support, encouragement, and vital information along the path to college. In addition, staff members with local knowledge can network participants into subsequent opportunities when they age out of the program or their interests change. Depending on the alignment of participants' personal characteristics, their networks of school, community, and home supports, and the quality and fit of resources and relationships available in a particular program, out-of-school time participation may act as either a stopover after school or a life-changing opportunity. A high-quality out-of-school time program can exert great influence, ranging from auxiliary to distinguishable to transformative, on the lives of Mexican American students. This typology of degrees of influence, presented in earlier chapters, illustrates both the commonalities and wide diversity among participating adolescents.

Embedded Influence

Rather than attempting to isolate a single variable that explains why some marginalized students succeed in school while others flounder and fail, this book develops a theory of *embedded influence* of out-of-school time programs. The theory builds on John Laub and Robert Sampson's (2003) theory of embedded agency, grounded in the life course perspective, which positions personal agency as an environmentally and temporally situated process. The theory of embedded influence locates the relationship over time between extracurricular participation and educational attainment within the overlapping and evolving contexts of students' homes, schools, and communities.

In existing studies, academic attainment is too often portrayed as a static destination to which one arrives, without attention to transgressions and redemption along the way. Adolescents' pathways to college are modeled as straight lines by theorists seeking significant factors in childhood that will predict adult outcomes. For some students, the journey to academic success or failure may indeed be as predictable as existing theories posit. But for many marginalized youth, including most respondents in this study, the journey through school resembles more of a zig-zag than a straight line. Young people do not predictably adhere to aggregated national patterns based solely on demographic categories, nor do they enact behaviors based entirely on fixed individual traits. The theory of embedded influence recognizes that participants' and their social settings change over time, and, owing to the complex interactions between social embeddedness in multilayered contexts and personal agency, the ways an out-of-school time program can influence participants and the degree to which that influence is felt will inevitably vary.

By situating adolescents' educational trajectories within multiple overlapping spheres of impact, including but not limited to out-of-school time, the theory of embedded influence further recognizes that no single intervention is capable of advancing every child to college. Rather, this theory argues that behind each successful student lies an ecosystem of supports and buffers, working symbiotically to overcome the challenges presented by systemic and microlevel factors, ranging from poverty and addiction to bullying and abuse. For some students, extracurricular activities may feature prominently in their constellation of supports. For others, organized activities supplement an already robust network.

Even students who experience a transformative degree of influence from an out-of-school time program cannot succeed by relying on that program alone. Part of the reason the influence can be described as transformative is indeed because the program, weaving a broader and deeper network of supports, connects the participant with outside resources. For example, when Maria was in high school, immigration officials threatened to deport her mother. With family members providing little help, Maria would probably have dropped out of school to care for her younger siblings if her mother had been deported. Through her participation in Students Together and at the suggestion of the group's staff members, however, Maria had joined a Latina support group and a youth activism program. Although none of these youth-serving organizations could have provided all the emotional and material capital Maria required to help her mother fight the threat, this trio of supports worked together to link her with resources. Because of their cumulative support, she was ultimately able to continue along a positive trajectory toward high school graduation and college matriculation. Like Maria, each student profiled in this book leaned on a dynamic network of social, emotional, and academic supports throughout the educational journey. The multifaceted nature of these networks likely plays a central role in enabling attainment.

By locating out-of-school time participation within these various and overlapping contexts and systems, the theory of embedded influence calls out a pivotal, yet rarely recognized, factor in explaining educational success: the timing of extracurricular participation in relation to life events. For example, two youth in the auxiliary group, Julio and Rosa, did well academically and socially throughout middle school and did not maintain affiliations with Students Together after their transition to high school. By the end of each respondent's sophomore year, however, Julio and Rosa had taken up with delinquent crowds and fallen behind academically. Neither student was participating in a structured extracurricular activity at the time. During this time of greater social need perhaps participation in Students Together could have prevented Julio and Rosa from getting off track, as it had done for Maria and Victoria, It was fortunate for Julio and Rosa, however, that a close relationship with a supportive adult—for Julio reconnecting with his father and for Rosa finding a mentor at church—pulled them back on the trajectory toward high school graduation. Each student experienced an auxiliary degree of influence in part because the timing of participation in Students Together did not align with their periods of greater adversity.

In another example, this study included a pair of sisters who were close in age: Ana and Victoria. While Victoria experienced a transformative influence from participating in Students Together, Ana experienced an auxiliary influence. The difference cannot likely be attributed to differences in cultural background, socioeconomic status, or parenting. Rather, the sisters varied in other ways: timing of participation, peer influences, and length of affiliation. Ana maintained an academically oriented peer group throughout school, while Victoria began associating with gang members as early as fifth grade. Ana was actively involved in Students Together when the girls' mother passed way. Victoria was not yet involved at the time and instead sought refuge in her gang-affiliated crowd. By the following year, Ana had adapted to high school life, and Victoria was considering dropping out of seventh grade. Involvement in Students Together turned Victoria's academic trajectory around, and her continued involvement with the program as a mentor for three years helped keep her on a positive pathway after eighth grade. She also participated in other community organizations that had strong ties with Students Together. Around the time of her high school graduation, she kept in contact with two former Students Together staff members through e-mail, phone calls, and encounters at community events. Those staff members raised money for a scholarship fund to assist Victoria with the costs of books, a computer, transportation, and college tuition. At the time of the final follow-up interview she was still in touch with those two staff members on a monthly basis. Meanwhile, Ana only participated in Students Together for one year and did not communicate with staff members after her advancement to high school. She transitioned in and out of college, with no financial support outside her family. Clearly no single factor contributed to the differing influence of the program between the sisters. Only by looking across multiple overlapping contexts can we see the embedded influence of participation and the role that timing of participation might play.

The theory of embedded influence posits that Mexican American students can benefit through different processes and to varying degrees from extracurricular participation. The ways that participants benefit both aligns with and builds upon existing theoretical explanations for academic attainment among low-income and minority youth. The former participants interviewed for this book all acquired concrete skills from out-of-school time participation that acted as education-related cultural capital by gaining them favor with an array of institutional gatekeepers. Participants who experienced a distinguishable or transformative influence also began to develop positive identities bridging their home and school lives through skill building, community participation, and a sense of belonging. Furthermore, students who experienced a transformative degree of influence built social capital and became embedded in more advantageous social networks through relationships with supportive and knowledgeable staff members. The processes through which a high-quality out-of-school time program may benefit participants build on cultural capital, role identity, and social capital theories; no single theory accounts for the role of extracurricular participation across all students.

By joining these theories, the theory of embedded influence comes closer to a cohesive explanation for educational attainment while recognizing the ways that young people's social contexts change over time and evaluating the range of roles that organized activities might assume in youth's educational trajectories. The case studies in this book affirm that out-of-school time participation is by no means the only factor influencing participants' academic attainment, even for students who experience a transformative degree of influence. Instead, extracurricular participation is but one element—with a range of potential influences—that should be woven together with family, school, peer, and community variables to establish a holistic portrayal of development among Latina/o students.

Intersectional Identities and Embedded Influence

The theory of embedded influence not only takes into account the ways that overlapping social contexts interact with personal agency over time, but it also considers the role of broader societal structures and identities, including race, ethnicity, and gender. Because the primary focus of this book is the educational experiences of Mexican American students, none of the interviews explicitly inquired about topics related to racial or ethnic identity. Not surprisingly, however, given our society's history of systemic oppression based on racial categories and the ways this history intertwines with contemporary policy and mythology around immigration, race and ethnicity clearly emerged as meaningful forces in adolescents' college pathways. Coming of age in California, a primary receiving destination for immigrants, during a time when xenophobia and Mexican immigration reached its height in the American collective conscience, racial and ethnic identities influenced the young people in this study in both positive and negative ways. Rather than reducing race and ethnicity to control variables, the case studies in this book reveal the ways that these socially constructed categories exert dynamic and multidimensional influences on students' educational attainment over time.

Though all respondents strongly identified as American rather than Mexican—regardless of immigrant generation—they often drew strength from the values and cultural practices linking them to their Mexican heritage. With regard to food and music, as well as frequent gatherings of extended kin, participants tended to feel grounded in the familiarity of a vibrant coethnic community. Students who were native Spanish speakers used their bilingual skills when volunteering in the community and for career advancement across a variety of fields. In addition, the value placed on hard work, respect for elders, and familism engendered a sense of dedication, responsibility, and, for many, emotional support. For a few, however, the prevailing cultural orientation toward family systems proved dangerous, such as in cases of abuse or instances when older cousins introduced respondents to gang life.

Though families were largely a positive influence, participants experienced the negative stigma of their marginalized status within broader social structures. Some respondents were "othered" in school contexts and subjected to low expectations and other forms of symbolic violence. Although most students felt supported during their elementary school years, especially within their bilingual classrooms, their academic environments grew more diverse and more hostile as they entered adolescence. For example, Selena and Miguel felt ostracized as token students of color at predominantly white private high schools. Victoria and Felicia felt as though teachers and school personnel expected them to drop out and get pregnant just because they were Mexican American. Some students also experienced discrimination at the hands of law enforcement, in dealings with employers, and when participating in other organized activities, such as sports teams. The role that racial and ethnic identities played for students varied over time and across contexts.

For many, the immigrant experience also impacted their daily lives. Most of the 1.5- and second-generation respondents enrolled in elementary school speaking no English and thrived in bilingual classrooms. Those with strong family support practiced English at home with their parents, who were also learning, while those without strong family support relied more heavily on peers and teachers. Many respondents watched their parents and extended family members relegated to service work and menial labor because of their limited cultural and social capital, and the long hours and unpredictable schedules impacted young people's perceptions of parental availability and support. Those with undocumented parents took on increased responsibilities, such as caring for younger siblings, running errands, providing transportation, and interacting with public officials (including teachers and doctors), especially when Immigration and Customs Enforcement raids reached peak levels. Those who were also undocumented themselves saw their struggles further increase when they went to apply for and enroll in college, in large part because they were ineligible for most sources of financial aid. Immigration status impacted students differently, but it grew particularly salient during the transition from adolescence into adulthood.

Race, ethnicity, and immigration status further intersected with gender to influence young people's educational trajectories in meaningful ways. For example, Julio and many of the other young men in this sample felt increased pressure to provide financially for their children, girlfriends, and parents, thus motivating and enabling their plans for higher education. Yet most of the young women felt burdened with gendered caretaking expectations at home that interfered with their academic aspirations. Because the majority of the respondents in this study were women, this discussion focuses on their experiences. Future research, however, should investigate in more depth the role of gender as it relates to the embedded influence of extracurricular programs.

The embedded influence of out-of-school time participation for Latina students varied, partly based on their level of frustration with and rebellion against gendered cultural norms, as well as the extent of their relationships with women staff members in Students Together. Many of the Latina respondents who experienced a distinguishable and transformative degree of influence specifically cited the gender of staff members as an important element identifying why those leaders were so inspirational. These same respondents spoke about the pressures to take on weighty household tasks imposed by family members. In the context of a culture that privileges men as breadwinners and women as homemakers, having college-educated female role models helped these young people see that it was possible for women to attain an academic degree and a meaningful professional career.

For example, as early as her middle school years Felicia did not feel as though she fit in with her peers because she was smart and would never fit the stereotype of Latinas that "wear tight pants and sit around." Her connections with staff members in Students Together helped her continue to resist the stereotypes she saw, move through high school and community college, and progress toward a bachelor's degree. She did not take on substantial responsibilities at home, in part because the abusive environment motivated her to avoid her immediate family as much as possible. Rosa, however, adapted to what was culturally expected of her at home. As the oldest daughter with six younger siblings, an absent father, and a mother who spoke no English and could not drive, she took on the responsibility of helping her siblings with their schoolwork, teaching them English, and doing the household shopping, cooking, and cleaning. But this allegiance to her family cost her. She barely graduated from high school and completed only one quarter of community college in the following year. Unlike Felicia's situation, Rosa's family circumstances and sense of obligation caused her schoolwork to suffer. Because she did not harbor any desire to distance herself from her family, she was not experiencing an unmet need for support, and there was less room for Students Together to influence her trajectory.

Sisters Ana and Victoria provide another example. The girls were responsible for all the cooking and cleaning at home after their mother passed away, yet their reactions to these expectations diverged. As the eldest daughter, Ana accepted these duties, curbed her extracurricular involvement, and completed all of her schoolwork. Victoria also helped at home, but she pushed to establish herself as independent. After observing that all the women in her family were dependent on their husbands, she wanted to be different. Students Together "liberated her a little bit" and helped her see there was an alternative to following her father's customs, "especially when they're so harsh for women." Unlike Ana, Victoria developed strong relationships with women staff members in the program and relied on those connections for support into her young adult years.

After high school, Ana had a baby and took a break from her community college classes. Like Julio's girlfriend, Ana became the baby's full-time caregiver while her boyfriend had the freedom to work, go to school, and eventually exit their lives altogether. Victoria also took time off from her college classes to work and help her sister with the baby, primarily so that her sister did not have to depend on her boyfriend for support. Victoria remained steadfast in her insistence that she would never be governed by a man in a way that compromised her integrity or independence. Although their family circumstances were similar, Ana and Victoria varied with regard to their personal agency and the depth of their relationships with Students Together staff members. Because Victoria wanted to break free from the cultural norms of her family, she held tightly to the opportunities offered by Students Together, opted to sustain lasting relationships with inspiring and supportive staff members, and remained steadfast to her college aspirations.

The ways that race, ethnicity, and gender interact differently for each student, even within the same family, underscore the importance of the embedded influence framework. In addition to highlighting the ways that personal agency and overlapping social contexts influence students' educational attainment over time, the theory of embedded influence calls out the ways that intersectional identities matter throughout adolescence and into adulthood, particularly for marginalized students. This framework carries important implications for researchers, policymakers, and practitioners.

Directions for Future Research

Continued study of Mexican American adolescents' extracurricular participation has the potential to bring us closer to eliminating the achievement gap that has plagued our society for decades. The case studies in this book reveal the processes and degrees to which out-of-school time participation may influence students' academic attainment and carve out a theoretical framework for longitudinal research on extracurricular experiences. Future studies should seek not only to test this framework empirically but also to expand its scope.

While the research methodology used in this study has many strengths, it also has important drawbacks. In-depth interviews with participants over an extended period of time provided detailed portraits of respondents' lives and supported the development of a theoretical framework. Yet the sample size is small; thus, the generalizability is quite limited. In addition, the young adult interviews focused on retrospective data, which are subject to memory selectivity and bias. A number of other methodologies have been used to successfully study extracurricular activities and triangulate the findings of interview-based studies such as this one, including surveys, observations, and experience sampling and time diaries (Vandell et al. 2015). As discussed in chapter 1, much of the existing research on organized activities relies on survey measures. These studies, given the benefit of large sample sizes and numerous control variables, have the potential to assess the relationship between participation intensity and duration or program characteristics and academic or developmental outcomes over time. Observational studies offer setting-level assessments of program quality and rich descriptions of young people's experiences (see Yohalem et al. 2009 for an analysis of systemic observational tools). Experience sampling and time diaries have the benefit of reducing the effects of retrospective bias while gathering valid data on students' time use and subjective states (e.g., Vandell et al. 2005). In particular, mixed methods research may offer promising avenues for understanding the role of organized activities for young people in context and over time.

Across methodologies, more research is needed on out-of-school time participation patterns among marginalized students. Prior research indicates that because disadvantaged students benefit more from organized activities than their privileged peers, out-of-school time participation is one way to narrow the achievement gap. Yet understanding why adolescents do or do not choose to participate is key to leveraging the potential of out-of-school time programs. Is the low rate of participation among Latino/as nationally due to the lack of opportunities to participate, lack of resources, or lack of desire? What can schools, families, and program staff members do to encourage more young people to join out-of-school time programs? A better understanding of who participates and why will provide the necessary foundation for further development of the embedded influence framework.

Building on these questions, researchers should also explore the factors that predict which degree of influence a student might experience in a given program. How much of the influence a program has over time can be attributed to alignment between students' interests and program resources? How much of the influence can be attributed to either the presence or the lack of other opportunities and supports in a student's life? Finally, what role, if any, do race, ethnicity, gender, and socioeconomic status play in determining what influence participation will have? If alignment turns out to be an important factor, it would follow that each community should have a wide variety of programs and a way of making these varied options known to students. If out-of-school time programs, however, fill a void for certain youth, regardless of program content, then access to any high-quality program would make a difference. All respondents in this study indicated that they originally became involved with Students Together because they were interested in making their community a better place; these responses suggest that program alignment with students' interests may be an important factor in generating participation, while the presence or lack of other support systems may ultimately determine a program's degree of influence on a young person's pathway. By using multiple methodologies, future studies should test this hypothesis among diverse student populations.

Further research should also explore a single program's possible or desirable range of influences across participating youth. Is the distribution of degrees of influence this study found in Students Together similar to the distribution of embedded influences within other programs? Can a program have a transformative influence for the majority of its participants, or is it more desirable to have a smaller percentage of participants with a heightened need for intervention? And what would a program look like for students who are already on a college pathway to experience transformative influence in an extracurricular program? In addition, future research should expand the theory of embedded influence to encompass a wider range of student experiences. For example, this book did not include profiles of participants who were negatively influenced by a program or students whose families actively discouraged them from participating.

Furthermore, this book suggests a need for research on networks of referral among organized activities within the same community. Although most programs do not have the resources to provide age-appropriate programming for all students, studies should explore how young people who age out of a program get referred to other programs within a community. For example, how do graduating middle school youth get referred to high school programs? Research on strategies for linking elementary programs with middle school programs and middle school programs with high school programs could aid more young people in following the "ladder of opportunities" that respondents who experienced a transformative influence describe in this study. These questions could be examined by drawing on techniques common among social networks researchers.

Finally, the case studies in this book demonstrate that some participants can be influenced by extracurricular programs long after participation has ended. Out-of-school time researchers need to branch out from the narrow world of before-and-after evaluation studies. Examining participation in the context of other experiences over time provides a broader view of how and to what extent programs impact students. Quantitative studies in particular should not rest on the assumption that family influences, peer networks, and the level of adversity a participant encounters due to race, class, gender, or immigration status are static over time. A stronger focus in the out-of-school time field on longitudinal research across all methodologies may have much to teach us about how programs influence young people's trajectories during adolescence and into adulthood.

Implications for Out-of-School Time Policy

Although the scope of this study did not include analysis of systems-level data, the embedded influence framework suggests clear directions for local and national policymakers. At the macrolevel, just as organized activities must be incorporated into theoretical explanations for school success among marginalized students, such programs ought to be recognized as part of a holistic policy approach to closing the achievement gap that includes family, school, peer, and community influences. By recognizing structured out-of-school time activities as a key component to promoting educational attainment among marginalized youth, policymakers have the potential to pave the way for increased funding and professionalization. In fact, the case studies presented in this book more specifically suggest three areas where policy interventions might bolster the out-of-school time field: training and support for youth workers, community networks of youth-serving organizations, and funding.

Training and Support for Youth Workers

Because skilled staff members are critical to high-quality programs, we should pay attention to increasing the availability of and access to training opportunities, including but not limited to four-year degree programs. Staff members ought to be well-trained in the tenets and practices of the PYD philosophy, have hands-on experience working with young people, and be sensitive to the opportunities and constraints offered by students' cultural dispositions and neighborhood environments. They ought to be supported to develop an intimate knowledge of the local community, including connections with other afterschool programs. Furthermore, if proponents hope to encourage participants along the pathway to college, staff members should be college graduates with detailed knowledge of the college search and application process as well as relevant resources, such as scholarships, transportation services, and childcare options. In short, staff members must possess the skills to create a nurturing environment where students feel welcomed and empowered and engage the network to help sustain supports for students after they leave the program.

For adult leaders to maintain emotional availability to students, program structures ought to support staff members in self-care and program development. Programs should offer professional wages commensurate with the employee's level of education and experience, affordable health care, and a safe work environment. Programs should also provide staff members with time to prepare for each session, occasions to reflect on challenges and successes, a culturally responsive and developmentally appropriate curriculum, professional development opportunities, and avenues for networking within the local community. Finally, low youth-adult ratios allow staff members to get to know each participant on a personal level and seek additional resources befitting each student's specific needs. Other structural supports may vary depending on the nature of the program, student demographics, and available resources.

Additionally, program structures ought to support staff members to develop long-term relationships with students. For example, a program may serve multiple age groups, a feature that allows students to continue taking part in the same program for consecutive years. Alternately, a program may serve only one age cohort but may have opportunities for alumni to continue participating as mentors or youth staff. Practices that encourage low rates of staff turnover may also increase the likelihood that the staff can sustain longer-term relationships with the students.

Community Networks of Youth-Serving Organizations

In the case of out-of-school time activities, adolescents are drawn to programs that cater to their particular age cohort (Strobel et al. 2008), and participation begets participation. Many respondents in this study learned of subsequent opportunities for meaningful extracurricular engagement from Students Together-related contacts. For some students, those subsequent experiences were more influential on their pathway to college than Students Together. For youth to progress through a community's ladder of opportunities, those opportunities must exist for every age cohort, and staff members at each rung must be knowledgeable of and connected to programs that serve both older and younger students. Communities can support this process by mapping existing opportunities and working to fill in gaps. In addition, communities must be intentional about developing systems and structures that network among youth-serving organizations.

Funding

Part of enabling marginalized youth to participate in out-of-school time programs depends on decreasing barriers to participation, including fees for participation, specialized equipment, and transportation. Yet high-quality programs cost money to staff, operate, and supply. Creating funding streams that take the burden off participants while allocating ample resources to maintaining low youth-adult ratios, as well as staff training, salaries, and benefits, will be critical to unlocking the potential for extracurricular activities to influence educational outcomes. Furthermore, funding streams that allow programs to maintain a consistent meeting space, phone number or other mode of contact, and visibility within the local community will enable them to be more accessible to former participants who stop attending for a period of time and wish to return.

Lessons for Practitioners

Although out-of-school time programs vary with regard to their goals and scope, the case studies presented in this book offer core lessons for practitioners regarding the processes through which participation may influence students' pathways to college and the positive program traits associated with these processes.

Concrete Skills

Participants across all degrees of embedded influence reported learning concrete skills from participation in Students Together. Students sharpened their public speaking skills by presenting to their peers as well as in front of community and school audiences. They also developed their abilities to communicate with others in small group settings; more outgoing participants practiced skills in active listening, and more reserved participants learned to speak up with confidence. Because participants applied and were selected into the program by staff members, most had only one prior friend also participating. Thus, students learned to work among a diverse group of peers with whom they might otherwise not have come into contact, honing skills for teamwork, compromise, and collaboration.

These skills proved beneficial outside the program by helping participants gain advantages with teachers, employers, and other institutional gatekeepers. Maria used activities from Students Together in her human relations job. Selena employed her inquiry skills to write college papers. Miguel reflected on his achievements in Students Together during high school admissions interviews. Rosa put her leadership skills to work when she started an anti-litter group at her high school. Out-of-school time participation instilled the kinds of skills valued by the middle and upper classes and signaled students' upwardly mobile ambitions. Indeed, some students reported joining Students Together and other extracurricular activities because they knew colleges looked favorably on such activities. Through access to and participation in out-of-school time programs, working-class and Mexican American youth accumulated advantages otherwise reserved for their more affluent peers.

Because participation in and of itself acted as an important credential with institutional gatekeepers, practitioners must first focus on enabling marginalized students to access a broad spectrum of extracurricular activities within their communities. To counteract the range of obstacles that often block young people from taking part in organized activities, programs should work to make participation available at no cost to interested youth. Though the evidence on effectiveness is mixed, programs that pay students for their time may attract and enable even more young people to participate. Although high school students are often saddled by the obligation to engage in paid work and contribute to their family's financial well-being, middle school students are more likely to be unencumbered.

Yet low-income students across age cohorts lack disposable income for program fees, supplies, field trips, and transportation. Programs can work around these constraints by supplying snacks and required equipment, considering students' transportation options with regard to convening times and locations, and accommodating students' work schedules and family obligations.

In addition to attending to logistical and financial obstacles to participation, programs must focus on maintaining an affirming stance toward students' home and neighborhood cultures. This requires hiring staff members who are familiar with the local community, native or accustomed to students' backgrounds, and conversant in participants' first languages. It also requires structuring the program and using a curriculum in culturally responsive ways.

While they cater to students' ethnic and socioeconomic backgrounds, programs can still provide beneficial skills to youth by simultaneously teaching the kinds of skills that are valued by institutional gatekeepers— the kinds of cultural capital privileged children tend to learn at home. To engender the feelings of entitlement that enable middle- and upper-class students to deftly advocate for themselves in a variety of settings, programs can focus on developing students' strengths and encouraging positive outcomes—such as college graduation—rather than taking a deficit-oriented approach. Although programs may vary in their topical specialties, every program should incorporate a curriculum layered with more generalizable skills and dispositions, such as communication, teamwork, and leadership. Furthermore, to empower students to believe that their voices are valuable, programs should embrace participants as decision-making partners and active leaders within both the program and the broader community. Not only were feelings of empowerment key to adolescents' engagement in the Students Together program, but they also enabled participants to confront negative influences in their lives, including gendered stereotypes, unfavorable peer groups, and systemic injustices. This multidimensional emphasis—positive outcomes, teamwork and communication, student voice and leadership, and empowerment through community engagement—has the potential to influence participants' college pathways by instilling the kinds of cultural capital valued by many social institutions.

Supportive Environment for Identity Development

In addition to gaining concrete skills and cultural capital, students for whom participation had a greater influence—distinguishable or transformative—were also touched in other ways by out-of-school time participation. Extracurricular activities helped them find their voices, find themselves, or feel as if they mattered. This sense of self carried into their school lives and home lives, as students were praised by teachers for their extracurricular involvement and their increased dedication to schoolwork and positively regarded by their families for contributing to the community. For example, Maria's mother did not complete elementary school and thus rarely took interest in her daughter's academics; however, when Maria had the opportunity to present to the city council, her mother was bursting with pride. In keeping with role-identity theory, out-of-school time programs can help participants develop identities as committed students, confident peers, and engaged citizens that allow them to bridge the divergent school and home worlds between which they travel. In the case studies presented in this book, we see this to be especially true for students who did not have a constructive peer group prior to program participation.

To support development toward an identity that is positively received across divergent contexts, programs must reward constructive engagement at school and in the community and offer opportunities for identity-enhancing experiences. Many of the same practices and activities that engender cultural capital also facilitate this process, such as focusing on positive outcomes and empowering students' voices. But enabling students to develop a "school kid" identity necessitates going beyond teaching valued skills and requires that a program provide the social ties, emotional support, and experiential incentives for students to confidently take on a new persona.

Programs can support and reward the "good kid" identity in a variety of ways. For example, Students Together enforced a minimum grade point average required for participation; thus, inclusion in the program was itself a reward for achievement. Programs might also reward academic aspirations by encouraging students to pursue higher education and regularly involving them in conversations about college. Outside school, programs can create opportunities for other kinds of socially appropriate engagement by building on their academic skills yet allowing accessibility to a broader audience. For example, Students Together participants made public presentations based on original empirical data to city council members, school officials, and university students. Participants also traveled to youth development conferences, policy briefings, and other events. These opportunities both supported and rewarded students as they established positively received identities and learned to sustain them across school, home, and community contexts.

Out-of-school time programs must also provide social supports, including engagement with others who support the "school kid" identity. To facilitate compassionate peer interactions, practitioners should proactively attend to the interpersonal dynamics within their programs. Low youth-adult ratios are key to this process. If admission to the program is selective, staff members may have the opportunity to create a diverse cohort of participants, thereby forcing students out of their preexisting cliques, disrupting established patterns of communication, and maximizing students' opportunities to learn from others who are different from themselves. If admission to the program is not selective, then enforcing diversity by breaking up established crowds within supervised subgroups may induce the same results. Either way, intentionally scaffolding peer interactions provides support for students struggling to develop a positive sense of self by teaching healthy communication skills, introducing diverse points of view, and developing a sense of belonging.

Relationships with Supportive Adults

Many factors contribute to creating a high-quality out-of-school time program, but trained and skillful staff members are critical to any program's ability to instill cultural capital, scaffold a supportive environment, and influence students' educational trajectories. For young people in the distinguishable influence category, staff members provide emotional support, academic encouragement, and cultural capital regarding pathways to college—important contributions, given the literature claiming that academic success among Latino/as arises from the combined influences of loving parents and supportive nonparent adults (Immerwahr 2003; Sanchez, Reyes, and Singh 2006; Zalaquett 2006). For those who experience a transformative degree of influence, the role of staff members is even more pronounced. Because they draw on relationships with staff members for support and guidance long after their tenure in the program has ended, participation has the potential to significantly change the students' educational trajectories.

Given the essential role that staff members can play in facilitating all three processes and degrees of influence outlined in this book, the importance of hiring and retaining caring and knowledgeable program leaders cannot be overstated. Attracting staff members with these qualifications requires adequate compensation and a stable work environment. As described earlier in chapter 6, staff members must be trained in the principles of PYD and have experience executing developmentally appropriate and culturally responsive curricula that teach institutionally valued skills. Staff members must be able to scaffold compassionate peer environments and create opportunities for meaningful community engagement. Furthermore, staff members must have the skills and motivation to establish and maintain supportive and long-term relationships with participants.

In addition, programs must be structured in ways that enable program leaders to attend to students' needs as well as their own. Adult-student ratios are part of the equation, but the balance of students within each cohort also matters. Because students come into a program with varying support networks and confront different issues at different times, constructing cohorts with dissimilar needs may help create a more manageable workload for staff members. Although it might seem most efficient to allocate spaces in extracurricular programs to the neediest students first, program quality may suffer, and the likelihood of participants experiencing a transformative degree of influence may drop if staff members are overloaded. The case studies in this book suggest that even students with strong networks of support across multiple contexts benefit from out-of-school time participation and that the benefits stem in part from interacting with a diverse peer group. Therefore, to the extent that it is possible within a given school or neighborhood, balancing students' needs within each cohort likely offers benefits for both participants and adult leaders.

Part of a program's ability to wield influence on students' educational trajectories is also likely to rest in staff members' connections with other out-of-school time programs and practitioners. Staff members should engage with the professional community, build awareness of best practices, and share expertise by cultivating connections nationally. Meanwhile, developing contacts within nearby programs enables staff members to refer students into continuing opportunities as they either age or develop changing needs and interests. Because achieving a compatible fit between a student and an out-of-school time program depends on myriad factors, staff members should be connected to many different kinds of local programs, serving a variety of age groups.

Beyond these critical traits, staffing needs may vary according to program goals and participant demographics. For example, if increasing educational attainment is a goal, staff members should have graduated from college and be familiar with the landscape of higher education such that they can encourage students—especially first-generation and low-income students—to think beyond what they may have heard from peers about the college search and application process. For example, students should be prompted to consider the differences between public and private institutions, small and large campuses, community colleges versus four-year schools, and other key factors. In addition, given that many low-income and minority students are inclined to stay close to home as they earn their degrees, staff members should be familiar with local possibilities. Students Together was situated in a metropolitan area with a vast array of higher education choices; therefore, students could attain a degree from virtually any kind of institution and remain within easy commuting distance of their families. Other locales are not as rich with options, and staff members should be competent at advising participants with regard to opportunities, while respecting students' values and family obligations.

Overall, out-of-school time programs should seek to offer a developmentally appropriate and culturally responsive curriculum in the context of positive peer and adult relationships. Program design should attend to adolescents' need for belonging, while teaching skills for leadership and community engagement. Such a balance is hard to strike and requires the expertise of trained and talented staff members who are supported generously and connected thoroughly.

The case studies in this book illuminate the ways that variation in young people's family, school, peer, and community support systems, as well as their personalities and interests, leave different openings for extracurricular programs to influence their educational trajectories. By examining multiple interconnected contexts over an extended period of time, this book documents the distinct differences among the roles a high-quality out-of-school time program can play for diverse participants, including the processes through which participation might impact students' pathways to college. Building on this critical examination of the Students Together program, this book suggests a new embedded influence framework for understanding the relationship between extracurricular participation and academic attainment: depicting that influence as dependent upon preexisting resources and supports and having the potential to alter future availability of resources and supports through new attitudes, behaviors, and social networks.

Appendix

Methodological Reflections

In order to collect longitudinal data for this book, I adapted and applied the life history calendar (LHC), a quantitative methodology, to qualitative research (for more detail, see Nelson 2010). The LHC has emerged as a reliable method for collecting retrospective data on multiple simultaneous event histories (Belli, Stafford, and Alwin 2009; Freedman et al. 1988), by using a printed matrix with temporal cues running horizontally and domain cues listed vertically. Use of the matrix eases respondents' event timing recall (Caspi et al. 1996; Freedman et al. 1988), and it elicits more accurate retrospective data than traditional questionnaires (Belli, Shay, and Stafford 2001; van der Vaart 2004; van der Vaart and Glasner 2007; Yoshihama et al. 2005). My semistructured qualitative LHC allowed for many of the same benefits of the traditional LHC: capturing the process of becoming involved in and disengaging from activities, networks, and behaviors; uncovering complex patterns of continuity and change in individual behavior over time; and allowing respondents to cross-reference multiple domains to ease recall of event timing. Yet, unlike the traditional LHC, the semistructured qualitative LHC also captured the hows and whys behind each transition.

I began by pilot testing a structured LHC protocol coupled with open-ended questioning (Harris and Parisi 2007). Pilot interviews, however, failed to elicit in-depth responses from young adults of working-class backgrounds. The participants took the structure of the LHC matrix as a cue to limit their responses to event-timing information. Open-ended questioning following completion of the LHC matrix revealed that participants omitted major life events—such as a transition from birth parents to a foster family or the deportation of a parent by immigration authorities—because they were not explicitly part of the matrix. Although limiting the categories of response eases data coding, entry, and analysis, and thus may be desirable in quantitative studies, qualitative research depends on the unhindered breadth and depth of respondents' narratives within researchers' preconceived categories. As the purpose of this study was to generate in-depth qualitative data on a small number of young adults, I began testing a less structured LHC.

After multiple rounds of testing, each with less structure to the matrix, the most detailed data emerged from interviews I began with a large blank page. The respondent and I subsequently coconstructed time cues horizontally—from birth to present day—and substantive cues vertically. Because of the age of the respondents, I used school transitions as the most salient landmarks across the temporal line of the LHC. Thus, the LHC, like the interview questions, was divided into five sections: before elementary school, elementary school, middle school, high school, and after high school. Not all participants started elementary school on time or completed high school so it made sense to add the school landmarks in the presence of the interviewee. There were three domains for this study: school (across the upper third of the page), home (across the bottom third of the page), and "everything that is not school and not home" (across the middle third of the page). The middle band primarily encompassed extracurricular activities, but leaving this domain cue open to interpretation also provided a space to include other domains, such as religious involvement, gang affiliations, and chronic illnesses.

As in previous incarnations of the LHC, the size of the paper was important (e.g., Freedman et al. 1988). I found in pilot interviews that respondents began to truncate their responses when the paper appeared to be full; the larger the paper (and the more blank space), the more detailed the respondents' answers became. I chose to use a standard easel pad consisting of large, high-quality paper with a cardboard backing. Instead of pencils, the respondent and I used colored markers and children's stickers to map out the respondent's life. Unlike Deborah Freedman et al. (1988), we did not use these materials in a uniform manner across interviews. Rather, each respondent was free to use the materials as he or she saw fit.

Table A.1

Student Characteristics

	Respondent	Gender	Self-identified ethnicity[a]	ELL in elementary school[b]	High school type	Employment[a]	Current school[a]	Career goal[a]
Transformative	Maria	Female	Mexican	Y	Large public	Human relations FT	Community college PT	Unsure
	Felicia	Female	Mexican	Y	Large public/ community college	Afterschool program PT	Community college FT	Researcher
	Victoria	Female	Mexican	Y	Large public	Food service FT	Community college PT	Unsure
Distinguishable	Selena	Female	Mexican	N	Small private	Community organizing PT	Private university FT	Lawyer
	Teresa	Female	Mexican	N	Large public	Grocery FT	Community college FT	Nurse
	Molly	Female	White	N	Large public	None	Private university FT	Photographer
Auxiliary	Julio	Male	Mexican	Y	Large public/ continuation	Delivery FT	Trade school PT	Firefighter
	Miguel	Male	Mexican	Y	Small private	Research PT	Private university FT	Doctor
	Rosa	Female	Mexican	Y	Large public	Public relations PT	Community college PT	Unsure
	Benjamin	Male	White	N	Large public	None	Trade school FT	Electrician
	Graciela	Female	Mexican	Y	Large public	Retail PT	Private college FT	Doctor
	Ana	Female	Mexican	Y	Large public	Food service FT	Community college PT	Unsure

[a]At time of final interview.

[b]Self-report.

This variation on the LHC method helped build rapport, allowed for more in-depth narratives, and placed respondents' pathways to college within the broad contexts of family, school, and community. For instance, this method helped build rapport because the respondent steered the sequence of the interview. Instead of having a prescribed order of questions, the interviewer laid out the scope of the LHC, including time periods and topics of interest. The interviewer then granted the respondent permission to begin with any topic and time period. By initially outlining the scope of the interview and allowing the respondent to dictate its progression, respondents became engaged and assumed ownership of their own narratives. The interviewer asked probing questions when necessary and used the LHC as a visible reminder to explore all time periods and topic domains.

This semistructured LHC protocol provides a specific benefit to researchers studying emotion-laden topics because respondents may opt to delay mentioning emotionally difficult experiences until they have established rapport. For example, Victoria—who immigrated from Mexico as a young child and whose mother died while she was in eighth grade—chose to begin with her elementary school years, followed by high school, returning to her early childhood and middle school years—her most difficult times—near the end of the interview. Because the interviewer usually does not know which periods of a respondent's life were most difficult, allowing respondents to dictate their own sequence of events within the structure of the LHC provides researchers with an opportunity to build rapport and capture detailed narratives of emotionally sensitive events.

References

American Youth Policy Forum. 2004. *Outcomes for children and youth in the out-of-school time: What the evidence says.* Accessed November 23, 2005. http://www.aypf.org/forumbriefs/2004/fb043004.htm.

Barber, Bonnie, Jacquelynne Eccles, and Margaret Stone. 2001. "Whatever happened to the jock, the brain, and the princess? Young adult pathways linked to adolescent activity involvement and social identity." *Journal of Adolescent Research* 16 (5): 429–455.

Barrington, Byron, and Bryan Hendricks. 1989. "Differentiating characteristics of high school graduates, dropouts, and nongraduates." *Journal of Educational Research* 82 (6): 309–319.

Baumrind, Diana. 1966. "Effects of authoritative control on child behavior." *Child Development* 37: 887–907.

Bean, Frank, and Marta Tienda. 1987. *The Hispanic population of the U.S.* New York: Russell Sage Foundation.

Belli, Robert, William Shay, and Frank Stafford. 2001. "Event history calendars and question list surveys: A direct comparison of interviewing methods." *Public Opinion Quarterly* 65 (1): 45–74.

Belli, Robert, Frank Stafford, and Duane Alwin, eds. 2009. *Calendar and time diary methods in life course research.* Thousand Oaks, CA: Sage.

Bennett, Pamela, Amy Lutz, and Lakshmi Jayaram. 2012. "Beyond the schoolyard: The role of parenting logics, financial resources, and social institutions in the social class gap in structured activity participation." *Sociology of Education* 85 (2): 131–157.

Bernstein, Basil. 1958. "Some sociological determinants of perception: An enquiry into subcultural differences." *British Journal of Sociology* 9 (1): 159–174.

Blazevski, Juliane, and Charles Smith. 2007. *Afterschool quality and school-day outcomes.* Ypsilanti, MI: High/Scope Educational Research Foundation.

Blum, Robert. 2003. "Positive youth development: A strategy for improving adolescent health." In *Handbook of applied developmental science: Promoting positive child, adolescent, and family development through research, policies, and programs,* vol. 2, edited by Richard Lerner, F. Jacobs, and D. Wertlieb, 237–252. Thousand Oaks, CA: Sage.

Bodilly, Susan, and Megan Beckett. 2005. *Making out-of-school time matter: Evidence for an action agenda.* Santa Monica, CA: RAND Corporation.

Bohnert, Amy, Jennifer Fredricks, and Edin Randall. 2010. "Capturing unique dimensions of youth organized activity involvement: Theoretical and methodological considerations." *Review of Educational Research* 80 (4): 576–610.

Bohnert, Amy, and Judy Garber. 2007. "Prospective relations between organized activity participation and psychopathology during adolescence." *Journal of Abnormal Child Psychology* 35 (6): 1021–1033.

Bouffard, Suzanne, C. Wimer, P. Caronongan, P. Little, E. Dearing, and S. D. Simpkins. 2006. "Demographic differences in patterns of youth out-of-school time activity participation." *Journal of Youth Development* 1 (1).

Bourdieu, Pierre. 1973. "Cultural reproduction and social reproduction." In *Knowledge, education, and cultural change,* edited by Robert Brown, 71–112. London: Tavistock.

———. 1986. "The forms of capital." In *Handbook of theory and research for the sociology of education,* edited by John Richardson. Westport, CT: Greenwood.

Bowles, Samuel, and Herbert Gintis. 1976. *Schooling in capitalist America: Educational reform and the contradictions of economic life.* New York: Basic Books.

Broh, Beckett. 2002. "Linking extracurricular programming to academic achievement: Who benefits and why?" *Sociology of Education* 75 (1): 69–95.

Bronfenbrenner, Urie. 1979. *The ecology of human development.* Cambridge, MA: Harvard University Press.

Bronfenbrenner, Urie, and Pamela Morris. 2006. "The bioecological model of human development." In *Handbook of child psychology,* 6th ed., edited by William Damon and Richard M. Lerner, 793–828. Hoboken, NJ: Wiley.

Brooks-Gunn, Jeanne, and Lisa Markman. 2005. "The contribution of parenting to ethnic and racial gaps in school readiness." *The Future of Children* 15 (1): 139–168.

Busseri, Michael, and Linda Rose-Krasnor. 2009. "Breadth and intensity: Salient, separable, and developmentally significant dimensions of structured youth activity involvement." *British Journal of Developmental Psychology* 27 (4): 907–933.

Busseri, Michael, Linda Rose-Krasnor, Teena Willoughby, and Heather Chalmers. 2006. "A longitudinal examination of breadth and intensity of youth activity involvement and successful development." *Developmental Psychology* 42 (6): 1313–1326.

Camp, William. 1990. "Participation in student activities and achievement: A covariance structural analysis." *Journal of Educational Research* 83 (5): 272–278.

Carnegie Council on Adolescent Development. 1992. *A matter of time: Risk and opportunity in the nonschool hours.* New York: Carnegie Corporation of New York.

Carnevale, Anthony, Nicole Smith, James Stone III, Pradeep Kotamraju, Bruce Steuernagel, and Kimberly Green. 2011. *Career clusters: Forecasting demand for high school through college jobs 2008–2018.* Washington, DC: Georgetown University Center on Education and the Workforce.

Carnevale, Anthony, and Jeff Strohl. 2013. *Separate and unequal: How higher education reinforces the intergenerational reproduction of white racial privilege.* Washington, DC: Georgetown Public Policy Institute Center on Education and the Workforce.

Carter, Prudence. 2005. *Keepin' it real: School success beyond black and white.* New York: Oxford University Press.

Casey, David, Marika Ripke, and Aletha Huston. 2005. "Activity participation and the well-being of children and adolescents in the context of welfare reform." In *Organized activities as contexts of development: Extracurricular activities, after-school and community programs*, edited by Joseph L. Mahoney, Reed W. Larson, and Jacquelynne S. Eccles, 65–84. Mahwah, NJ: Erlbaum.

Caspi, Avshalom, Terrie Moffitt, Arland Thornton, Deborah Freedman, James Amell, Honalee Harrington, Judith Smeijers, and Phil Silva. 1996. "The life history calendar: A research and clinical assessment method for collecting retrospective event-history data." *International Journal of Methods in Psychiatric Research* 6: 101–114.

Catalano, Richard, M. Lisa Berglund, Jean Ryan, Heather S. Lonczak, and J. David Hawkins. 2004. "Positive youth development in the United States: Research findings on evaluations of positive youth development programs." *Annals of the American Academy of Political and Social Science* 591 (1): 98–124.

Chin, Tiffini, and Meredith Phillips. 2004. "Social reproduction and child-rearing practices: social class, children's agency, and the summer activity gap." *Sociology of Education* 77 (3): 185–210.

Coleman, James. 1988. "Social capital in the creation of human capital." *American Journal of Sociology* 94: 95–120.

Coleman, James, Ernest Campbell, Carol Hobson, James McPartland, Alexander Mood, Frederic Weinfeld, and Robert York. 1966. *Equality of educational opportunity*. Washington, DC: US Government Printing Office.

Conchas, Gilberto. 2001. "Structuring failure and success: Understanding the variability in Latino school engagement." *Harvard Educational Review* 71 (3): 475–504.

Cornelius-White, Jeffrey, Aida Garza, and Ann Hoey. 2004. "Personality, family satisfaction, and demographic factors that help Mexican American students succeed academically." *Journal of Hispanic Higher Education* 3 (3): 270–283.

Covay, Elizabeth, and William Carbonaro. 2010. "After the bell: Participation in extracurricular activities, classroom behavior, and academic achievement." *Sociology of Education* 83 (1): 20–45.

Csikszentmihalyi, Mihaly, and Reed Larson 1984. *Being adolescent*. New York: Basic Books.

Dahl, R. E. 2005. "Brain biology, pubertal maturation, and adolescence: New insights from a developmental framework." Paper presented at the National Academies of Science/Institute of Medicine/National Research Council Workshop on the Science of Adolescent Health and Development, Washington, DC, September 8.

Darling, Nancy, Linda Caldwell, and Robert Smith. 2005. "Participation in school-based extracurricular activities and adolescent adjustment." *Journal of Leisure Research* 37 (1): 51–76.

Delgado-Gaitan, Concha. 1988. "The value of conformity: Learning to stay in school, an ethnographic study." *Anthropology and Education Quarterly* 19 (4): 354–382.

Denault, Anne-Sophie, and François Poulin. 2009. "Intensity and breadth of participation in organized activities during the adolescent years: Multiple associations with youth outcomes." *Journal of Youth and Adolescence* 38 (9): 1199–1213.

Deutsch, Martin. 1967. *The disadvantaged child: Selected papers of Martin Deutsch and Associates*. New York: Basic Books.

Dotterer, Aryn, Susan McHale, and Ann Crouter. 2007. "Implications of out-of-school activities for school engagement in African American adolescents." *Journal of Youth and Adolescence* 36 (4): 391–401.

Dukakis, Kara, Rebecca London, Milbrey McLaughlin, and Devon Williamson. 2009. *Positive youth development: Individual, setting, and system-level indicators*. Stanford, CA: John W. Gardner Center for Youth and Their Communities.

Dumais, Susan. 2006. "Elementary school students' extracurricular activities: The effects of participation on achievement and teachers' evaluations." *Sociological Spectrum* 26 (2): 117–1147.

———. 2008. "Adolescents' time use and academic achievement: A test of the reproduction and mobility models." *Social Science Quarterly* 89 (4): 867–886.

Duncan, Greg, and Richard Murnane. 2011. "Introduction: The American Dream, then and now." In *Whither opportunity: Rising inequality, schools, and children's life chances*, edited by Greg J. Duncan and Richard J. Murnane. New York: Russell Sage.

Durlak, Joseph, Roger Weissberg, and Molly Pachan. 2010. "A meta-analysis of after-school programs that seek to promote personal and social skills in children and adolescents." *American Journal of Community Psychology* 45: 294–309.

Eccles, Jacquelynne, and Bonnie Barber. 1999. "Student council, volunteering, basketball, or marching band: What kind of extracurricular involvement matters?" *Journal of Adolescent Research* 14 (1): 10–43.

Eccles, Jacquelynne, Bonnie Barber, Margaret Stone, and James Hunt. 2003. "Extracurricular activities and adolescent development." *Journal of Social Issues* 59 (4): 865–889.

Eccles, Jacquelynne, and Jennifer Gootman, eds. 2002. *Community programs to promote youth development.* Washington, DC: National Academies Press.

Elder, Glen Jr. 1974. *Children of the Great Depression: Social change in life experience.* Chicago: University of Chicago Press.

Elder, Glen Jr., Michael Shanahan, and Julia Jennings. 2015. "Human development in time and place." In *Handbook of child psychology and developmental science*, vol. 4, edited by Richard M. Lerner, 6–54. Hoboken, NJ: Wiley.

Entwistle, Doris, and Karl Alexander. 1992. "Summer setback: race, poverty, school composition, and educational stratification in the U.S." *American Sociological Review* 57: 72–84.

Feldman, Amy, and Jennifer Matjasko. 2005. "The role of school-based extracurricular activities in adolescent development: A comprehensive review and future directions." *Review of Educational Research* 75 (2): 159–210.

———. 2007. "Profiles and portfolios of adolescent school-based extracurricular activity participation." *Journal of Adolescence* 30: 313–332.

———. 2012. "Recent advances in research on school-based extracurricular activities and adolescent development." *Developmental Review* 32: 1–48.

Fernandez, Ricardo, and Gangjian Shu. 1988. "School dropouts: New approaches to an enduring problem." *Education and Urban Society* 20 (4): 363–386.

Fine, Michelle. 1991. *Framing dropouts: Notes on the politics of an urban public high school.* Albany: State University of New York Press.

Flores-González, Nilda. 2002. *School kids/street kids: Identity development in Latino students.* New York: Teachers College Press.

Foley, Douglas. 1997. "Deficit thinking models based on culture: The anthropological protest." In *The evolution of deficit thinking: Educational thought and practice*, edited by Richard R. Valencia. Bristol, PA: Falmer Press.

Fordham, Signithia, and John Ogbu. 1986. "Black students' school success: Coping with the 'burden of acting white.'" *Urban Review* 18 (3): 176–206.

Frankenberg, Erica, Chungmei Lee, and Gary Orfield. 2003. *A multiracial society with segregated schools: Are we losing the dream?* Cambridge, MA: Civil Rights Project, Harvard University.

Fredricks, Jennifer. 2012. "Extracurricular participation and academic outcomes: Testing the over-scheduling hypothesis." *Journal of Youth and Adolescence* 41 (3): 295–306.

Fredricks, Jennifer, and Jacquelynne Eccles. 2005. "Developmental benefits of extracurricular involvement: Do peer characteristics mediate the link between activities and youth outcomes?" *Journal of Youth and Adolescence* 34 (6): 507–520.

———. 2006a. "Extracurricular involvement and adolescent adjustment: Impact of duration, number of activities, and breadth of participation." *Applied Developmental Science* 10 (3): 132–146.

———. 2006b. "Is extracurricular participation associated with beneficial outcomes? Concurrent and longitudinal relations." *Developmental Psychology* 42 (4): 698–713.

Freedman, Deborah, Arland Thornton, Donald Camburn, Duane Alwin, and Linda Young-DeMarco. 1988. "The life history calendar: A technique for collecting retrospective data." *Sociological Methodology* 18: 37–68.

Frey, William. 2011. *America reaches its demographic tipping point.* Washington, DC: Brookings Institution. Accessed January 19, 2016. http://www.brookings.edu/blogs/up-front/posts/2011/08/26-census-race-frey.

Frost, Joe, and Glenn Hawkes, eds. 1966. *The disadvantaged child: Issues and innovations.* New York: Houghton Mifflin.

Fry, Richard, and Rakesh Kochhar. 2014. *America's wealth gap between middle-income and upper-income families is widest on record.* Washington, DC: Pew Research Center. Accessed January 20, 2016. http://pewrsr.ch/1GPTiiP.

Fry, Richard, and Kim Parker. 2012. *Record shares of young adults have finished both high school and college.* Washington, DC: Pew Research Center. Accessed January 20, 2016. http://www.pewsocialtrends.org/2012/11/05/record-shares-of-young-adults-have-finished-both-high-school-and-college/.

Furstenberg, Frank Jr., and Mary Elizabeth Hughes. 1995. "Social capital and successful development among at-risk youth." *Journal of Marriage and the Family* 57: 580–592.

Gamoran, Adam, and Daniel Long. 2006. *Equality of educational opportunity: A 40-year retrospective* (WCER Working Paper No. 2006–9). Madison: University of Wisconsin–Madison, Wisconsin Center for Education Research.

Gandara, Patricia. 1995. *Over the ivy walls: The educational mobility of low-income Chicanos.* Albany: State University of New York Press.

Gandara, Patricia, and Frances Contreras. 2009. *The Latino education crisis: The consequences of failed social policies.* Cambridge, MA: Harvard University Press.

Gardner, Margo, Jodie Roth, and Jeanne Brooks-Gunn. 2009. "Can after-school programs help level the academic playing field for disadvantaged youth?" *Equity Matters: Research Review No. 4.* New York: Campaign for Educational Equity, Teachers College, Columbia University.

Gerber, Susan. 1996. "Extracurricular activities and academic achievement." *Journal of Research and Development in Education* 30 (1): 42–50.

Ginwright, Shawn. 2010. *Black youth rising: Activism and radical healing in urban America.* New York: Teachers College Press.

Glaser, Barney, and Anselm Strauss. 1967. *The discovery of grounded theory: Strategies for qualitative research.* Chicago: Aldine.

Gordon, Edmund, Beatrice Bridglall, and Aundra Saa Meroe. 2005. *Supplementary education: The hidden curriculum of high academic achievement.* Lanham, MD: Rowman and Littlefield.

Granovetter, Mark. 1985. "Economic action and social structure: The problem of social embeddedness." *American Journal of Sociology* 91: 481–510.

Halpern, Robert. 2003. *Making play work: The promise of after-school programs for low-income children.* New York: Teachers College Press.

Hansen, David, Reed Larson, and Jodi Dworkin. 2003. "What adolescents learn in organized youth activities: A survey of self-reported developmental experiences." *Journal of Research on Adolescence* 13: 25–55.

Hanson, Sandra, and Rebecca Kraus. 1998. "Women, sports, and science: Do female athletes have an advantage?" *Sociology of Education* 71: 93–110.

Harris, Deborah, and Domenico Parisi. 2007. "Adapting life history calendars for qualitative research on welfare transitions." *Field Methods* 19: 40–58.

Harris, Kathleen Mullan. 1993. "Work and welfare among single mothers in poverty." *American Journal of Sociology* 99: 317–352.

Hellmuth, Jerome, ed. 1967. *Disadvantaged child*, vol. 1. New York: Brunner/Mazel.

Holloway, John. 2000. "Extracurricular activities: The path to academic success." *Educational Leadership* 57 (4): 87–88.

Hultsman, Wendy. 1992. "Constraints to activity participation in early adolescence." *Journal of Early Adolescence* 12 (3): 280–299.

Immerwahr, John. 2003. *With diploma in hand: Hispanic high school seniors talk about their future.* Washington, DC: National Center for Public Policy and Higher Education.

Jencks, Christopher, and Meredith Phillips. 1998. "The black-white test score gap: An introduction." In *The black-white test score gap*, edited by Christopher Jencks and Meredith Phillips, 1–51. Washington, DC: Brookings Institution Press.

Jerrim, John. 2014. "The unrealistic educational expectations of high school pupils: Is America exceptional?" *Sociological Quarterly* 55 (1): 196–231.

Jordan, Will, and Saundra Murray Nettles. 2000. "How students invest their time outside of school: Effects on school-related outcomes." *Social Psychology of Education* 3: 217–243.

Kao, Grace, and Jennifer Thompson. 2003. "Racial and ethnic stratification in educational achievement and attainment." *Annual Review of Sociology* 29: 417–442.

Kao, Grace, and Marta Tienda. 1995. "Optimism and achievement: The educational performance of immigrant youth." *Social Science Quarterly* 76 (1): 1–19.

Kataoka, Sabrina, and Deborah Lowe Vandell. 2013. "Quality of afterschool activities and relative change in adolescent functioning over two years." *Applied Developmental Science* 17 (3): 123–134.

Kaufman, Jason, and Jay Gabler. 2004. "Cultural capital and the extracurricular activities of girls and boys in the college attainment process." *Poetics* 32 (2): 145–168.

Krogstad, Jens M. and Richard Fry. 2014. "More Hispanics, blacks enrolling in college, but lag in bachelor's degrees." *Fact tank: News in the numbers.* Washington, DC: Pew Research Center. Accessed January 21, 2016. http://www.pewresearch.org/fact-tank/2014/04/24/more-hispanics-blacks-enrolling-in-college-but-lag-in-bachelors-degrees/.

Kwon, Soo Ah. 2008. "Moving from complaints to action: Oppositional consciousness and collective action in a political community." *Anthropology and Education Quarterly* 39: 59–76.

———. 2013. *Uncivil youth: Race, activism, and affirmative governmentality.* Durham, NC: Duke University Press.

Lareau, Annette. 2003. *Unequal childhoods: Class, race, and family life.* Berkeley: University of California Press.

Lareau, Annette, and Elliot Weininger. 2003. "Cultural capital in educational research: A critical assessment." *Theory and Society* 32: 567–606.

Larson, Reed. 2000. "Toward a psychology of positive youth development." *American Psychologist* 55: 170–183.

Larson, Reed, and Rachel Angus. 2011. "Pursuing paradox: The role of adults in creating empowering settings for youth." In *Empowering settings and voices for social change*, edited by Mark S. Aber, Kenneth I. Maton, and Edward Seidman, 65–93. New York: Oxford University Press.

Larson, Reed, and David Hansen. 2005. "The development of strategic thinking: Learning to impact human systems in a youth activism program." *Human Development* 48 (6): 327–349.

Larson, Reed, David Hansen, and Giovanni Moneta. 2006. "Differing profiles of developmental experiences across types of organized youth activities." *Developmental Psychology* 42 (5): 849–863.

Larson, Reed, Robin Jarrett, David Hansen, Nickki Pearce, Patrick Sullivan, Kathrin Walker, Natasha Watkins, and Dustin Wood. 2004. "Organized youth activities as contexts for positive development." In *Positive psychology in practice*, edited by P. A. Linley and S. Joseph, 540–560. Hoboken, NJ: Wiley.

Larson, Reed, and Douglas Kleiber. 1993. "Structured leisure as a context for the development of attention during adolescence." *Society and Leisure* 16: 77–98.

Larson, Reed, and Suman Verma. 1999. "How children and adolescents spend time across the world: Work, play, and developmental opportunities." *Psychological Bulletin* 125: 701–736.

Larson, Reed, and Kathrin Walker. 2006. "Learning about the "real world" in an urban arts youth program." *Journal of Adolescent Research* 21 (3): 244–268.

Larson, Reed, Kathrin Walker, and Nickki Pearce. 2005. "A comparison of youth-driven and adult-driven youth programs: balancing inputs from youth and adults." *Journal of Community Psychology* 33 (1): 57–74.

Laub, John, and Robert Sampson. 2003. *Shared beginnings, divergent lives: Delinquent boys to age 70.* Cambridge, MA: Harvard University Press.

Lauer, Patricia, Motoko Akiba, Stephanie Wilkerson, Helen Apthorp, David Snow, and Mya Martin-Glenn. 2006. "Out-of-school-time programs: A meta-analysis of effects for at-risk students." *Review of Educational Research* 76 (2): 275–313.

Laughlin, Lynda. 2013. "Who's minding the kids? Child care arrangements: Spring 2011." In *Current population reports*, 70–135. Washington, DC: US Census Bureau.

Lerner, Richard. 2004. *Thriving and civic engagement among America's youth.* Thousand Oaks, CA: Sage.

———. 2005. "Understanding and enhancing adolescent health and development." Paper presented at the National Academies of Science/Institute of Medicine/National Research Council Workshop on the Science of Adolescent Health and Development, Washington, DC, September 9.

Lerner, Richard, Jacqueline Lerner, Edmond Bowers, and John Geldhof. 2015. "Positive youth development and relational developmental systems." In *Handbook of child psychology and developmental science*, vol. 1, edited by Richard Lerner, 607–651. Hoboken, NJ: Wiley.

Lewis, Oscar. 1966. "The culture of poverty." *Scientific American* 215: 19–25.

Linver, Miriam, Jodie Roth, and Jeanne Brooks-Gunn. 2009. "Patterns of adolescents' participation in organized activities: Are sports best when combined with other activities?" *Developmental Psychology* 45 (2): 354–367.

Lleras, Christy. 2008. "Do skills and behaviors in high school matter? The contribution of noncognitive factors in explaining differences in educational attainment and earnings." *Social Science Research* 37: 888–902.

Lowell, Lindsay, and Roberto Suro. 2002. *The improving educational profile of Latino immigrants.* Washington, DC: Pew Hispanic Center.

MacLeod, Jay. 1995. *Ain't no makin' it: Aspirations and attainment in a low-income neighborhood.* 2nd ed. Boulder, CO: Westview Press.

Mahoney, Joseph. 2000. "School extracurricular participation as a moderator in the development of antisocial patterns." *Child Development* 71: 502–516.

Mahoney, Joseph, and Robert Cairns. 1997. "Do extracurricular activities protect against early school drop out?" *Developmental Psychology* 33: 195–217.

Mahoney, Joseph, Beverley Cairns, and Thomas Farmer. 2003. "Promoting interpersonal competence and educational success through extracurricular activity participation." *Journal of Educational Psychology* 95 (2): 409–418.

Mahoney, Joseph, Angel Harris, and Jacquelynne Eccles. 2006. "Organized activity participation, positive youth development, and the over-scheduling hypothesis." *Society for Research in Child Development Social Policy Report* 20 (4): 1–31.

Mahoney, Joseph, and Andrea Vest. 2012. "The over-scheduling hypothesis revisited: Intensity of organized activity participation during adolescence and young adult outcomes." *Journal of Research on Adolescence* 22 (3): 409–418.

Margonis, Frank. 1992. "The cooptation of 'at risk': Paradoxes of policy criticism." *Teachers College Record* 94: 343–364.

Marsh, Herbert, and Sabina Kleitman. 2002. "Extracurricular school activities: The good, the bad, and the nonlinear." *Harvard Educational Review* 72 (4): 464–514.

McGee, Rob, Sheila Williams, Philippa Howden-Chapman, Jennifer Martin, and Ichiro Kawachi. 2006. "Participation in clubs and groups from childhood to adolescence and its effects on attachment and self-esteem." *Journal of Adolescence* 29 (1): 1–17.

McNeal, Ralph Jr. 1995. "Extracurricular activities and high school dropouts." *Sociology of Education* 68: 62–81.

Mehan, Hugh, Lea Hubbard, and Irene Villanueva. 1994. "Forming academic identities: Accommodation without assimilation among involuntary minorities." *Anthropology and Education Quarterly* 25 (2): 91–117.

Mehan, Hugh, Lea Hubbard, Irene Villanueva, and Angela Lintz. 1996. *Constructing school success: The consequences of untracking low achieving students.* Cambridge: Cambridge University Press.

Melnick, Merrill, Donald Sabo, and Beth Vanfossen. 1992a. "Educational effects of interscholastic athletic participation on African American and Hispanic youth." *Adolescence* 27: 295–308.

———. 1992b. "Effects of interscholastic athletic participation on the social, educational, and career mobility of Hispanic girls and boys." *International Review for the Sociology of Sport* 27: 57–73.

Miller, Kathleen, Merrill Melnick, Grace Barnes, Michael Farrell, and Don Sabo. 2005. "Untangling the links among athletic involvement, gender, race, and adolescent academic outcomes." *Sociology of Sport Journal* 22: 178–193.

Mills, C. Wright. 2000. *The sociological imagination.* New York: Oxford University Press.

Mondale, Sarah, and Sarah Patton. 2001. *School: The story of American public education.* Boston: Beacon Press.

Morris, David. 2015. "Actively closing the gap? Social class, organized activities, and academic achievement in high school." *Youth and Society* 47(2):267–90.

National Center for Education Statistics. 2013. *The nation's report card: Trends in academic progress 2012* (NCES 2013–456. National Center for Education Statistics, Institute of Education Sciences). Washington, DC: US Department of Education.

National Research Council. 2006a. *Hispanics and the future of America.* Washington, DC: National Academies Press.

———. 2006b. *Multiple origins, uncertain destinies: Hispanics and the American future.* Washington, DC: National Academies Press.

Nelson, Ingrid A. 2010. "From quantitative to qualitative: Adapting the life history calendar method." *Field Methods* 22 (4): 413–428.

Nelson, Ingrid A., and Billie Gastic. 2009. "Street ball, swim team, and the sour cream machine: A cluster analysis of out-of-school time participation portfolios." *Journal of Youth and Adolescence* 38 (9): 1172–1186.

Oakes, Jeanne. 2005. *Keeping track: How schools structure inequality.* 2nd ed. New Haven, CT: Yale University Press.

Ogbu, John. 1978. *Minority education and caste.* New York: Academic Press.

Overton, Willis F. 2015. "Relational developmental systems and developmental science." In *Handbook of child psychology and developmental science*, vol. 1, edited by Richard M. Lerner. Hoboken, NJ: Wiley.

Pearl, Arthur. 1991. "Systemic and institutional factors in Chicano school failure." In *Chicano school failure and success: Research and policy agendas for the 1990s*, edited by Richard R. Valencia, 273–320. London: Falmer Press.

———. 1997. "Cultural and accumulated environmental deficit models." In *The evolution of deficit thinking: Educational thought and practice*, edited by Richard R. Valencia, 132–159. London: Falmer Press.

Perez, William. 2012. *Americans by heart: Undocumented Latino students and the promise of higher education.* New York: Teachers College Press.

Perie, Marianne, Rebecca Moran, and Anthony Lutkus. 2005. *NAEP 2004 trends in academic progress: Three decades of student performance in reading and mathematics* (NCES 2005–464). Washington, DC: US Government Printing Office.

Perreira, Krista, Kathleen Mullan Harris, and Dohoon Lee. 2006. "Making it in America: High school completion by immigrant and native youth." *Demography* 43 (3): 511–536.

Pew Research Center. 2011. *Demographic profile of Hispanics in California, 2011.* Washington, DC: Pew Research Center, Hispanic Trends. Accessed January 20, 2016. http://www.pewhispanic.org/states/state/ca/.

Phelan, Patricia, Ann Locke Davidson, and Hanh Thanh Cao. 1991. "Students' multiple worlds: Negotiating the boundaries of family, peer, and school cultures." *Anthropology and Education Quarterly* 22 (3): 224–250.

Pierce, Kim, Daniel Bolt, and Deborah Lowe Vandell. 2010. "Specific features of after-school program quality: Associations with children's functioning in middle childhood." *American Journal of Community Psychology* 45: 381–393.

Pittman, Karen, et al. 2003. *Preventing problems, promoting development, encouraging engagement: Competing priorities or inseparable goals.* Washington, DC: Forum for Youth Investment, Impact Strategies.

Portes, Alejandro, and Min Zhou. 1993. "The new second generation: Segmented assimilation and its variants." *Annals of the American Academy of Political and Social Science* 530: 74–96.

Quinn, Jane. 1999. "Where need meets opportunity: Youth development programs for early teens." *The Future of Children* 1999: 96–116.

Quiroz, Pamela Anne, Nilda Flores-González, and Kenneth Frank. 1996. "Carving a niche in the high school social structure: Formal and informal constraints on participation in the extra curriculum." In *Research in sociology of education and socialization*, vol. 11, edited by Aaron Pallas, 93–120. Greenwich, CT: JAI Press.

Ream, Robert. 2005. *Uprooting children: Mobility, social capital, and Mexican American underachievement*. New York: LFB Scholarly Publishing.

Ream, Robert, and Russell Rumberger. 2008. "Student engagement, peer social capital, and school dropout among Mexican American and non-Latino white students." *Sociology of Education* 81 (2): 109–139.

Reardon, Sean. 2011. "The widening academic achievement gap between the rich and the poor: New evidence and possible explanations." In *Whither opportunity? Rising inequality, schools, and children's life chances*, edited by Greg J. Duncan and Richard J. Murnane, 91–116. New York: Russell Sage Foundation.

Reardon, Sean, and Kendra Bischoff. 2011. *Growth in the residential segregation of families by income, 1970–2009*. US 2010 Project. Accessed December 10, 2015. http://www .russellsage.org/blog/r-mascarenhas/new-us-2010-report-residential-income -segregation-america.

Reardon, Sean, Elena Tej Grewal, Demetra Kalogrides, and Erica Greenberg. 2012. "Brown fades: The end of court-ordered school desegregation and the resegregation of American public schools." *Journal of Policy Analysis and Management* 31 (4): 876–904.

Riggs, Nathaniel, Amy Bohnert, Maria Guzman, and Denise Davidson. 2010. "Examining the potential of community-based after-school programs for Latino youth." *American Journal of Community Psychology* 45: 417–429.

Rose-Krasnor, Linda, Michael Busseri, Teena Willoughby, and Heather Chalmers. 2006. "Breadth and intensity of youth activity involvement as contexts for positive development." *Journal of Youth and Adolescence* 35 (3): 365–379.

Roth, Jodie, and Jeanne Brooks-Gunn. 2003. "What exactly is a youth development program? Answers from research and practice." *Applied Developmental Science* 7 (2): 94–111.

Rumberger, Russell. 1995. "Dropping out of middle school: A multilevel analysis of students and schools." *American Educational Research Journal* 32: 583–625.

Rutten, Esther, Maja Deković, Geert Jan Stams, Carlo Schuengel, Jan Hoeksma, and Gert Biesta. 2008. "On-and off-field antisocial and prosocial behavior in adolescent soccer players: A multilevel study." *Journal of Adolescence* 31 (3): 371–387.

Sabo, Donald, Merrill Melnick, and Beth Vanfossen. 1993. "High school athletic participation and post-secondary educational and occupational mobility: A focus on race and gender." *Sociology of Sport Journal* 10: 44–56.

Salusky, Ida, Reed Larson, Aisha Griffith, Joanna Wu, Marcela Raffaelli, Niwako Sugimura, and Maria Guzman. 2014. "How adolescents develop responsibility: What can be learned from youth programs." *Journal of Research on Adolescence* 24 (3): 417–430.

Sánchez, Bernadette, Olga Reyes, and Joshua Singh. 2006. "Makin' it in college: The value of significant individuals in the lives of Mexican American adolescents." *Journal of Hispanic Higher Education* 5 (1): 48–67.

Schreiber, James, and Elisha Chambers. 2002. "After-school pursuits, ethnicity, and achievement for 8th and 10th grade students." *Journal of Educational Research* 96 (2): 90–100.

Shernoff, David. 2013. *Optimal learning environments to promote student engagement*. New York: Springer.

Shernoff, David, and Deborah Lowe Vandell. 2008. "Youth engagement and quality of experience in afterschool programs." *Afterschool Matters Occasional Paper Series* 2008: 1–14.

Simpkins, Sandra, Melissa Delgado, Chara Price, Alex Quach, and Elizabeth Starbuck. 2013. "Socioeconomic status, ethnicity, culture, and immigration: Examining the potential mechanisms underlying Mexican-origin adolescents' organized activity participation." *Developmental Psychology* 49 (4): 706–721.

Simpkins, Sandra, Jacquelynne Eccles, and Jennifer Becnel. 2008. "The mediational role of adolescents' friends in relations between activity breadth and adjustment." *Developmental Psychology* 44 (4): 1081–1094.

Simpkins, Sandra, Jennifer Fredricks, and Jacquelynne Eccles. 2012. "Charting the Eccles' expectancy-value model from mothers' beliefs in childhood to youths' activities in adolescence." *Developmental Psychology* 48 (4): 1019–1032.

Simpkins, Sandra, Megan O'Donnell, Melissa Delgado, and Jennifer Becnel. 2011. "Latino adolescents' participation in extracurricular activities: How important are family resources and cultural orientation?" *Applied Developmental Science* 15 (1): 37–50.

Spreitzer, Elmer. 1994. "Does participation in interscholastic athletics affect adult development? A longitudinal analysis of an 18–24 age cohort." *Youth and Society* 25 (3): 368–387.

Stanton-Salazar, Ricardo. 1997. "A social capital framework for understanding the socialization of racial minority children and youths." *Harvard Educational Review* 67 (1): 1–40.

———. 2001. *Manufacturing hope and despair: The school and kin support networks of U.S.-Mexican youth.* New York: Teachers College Press.

Stanton-Salazar, Ricardo, and Sanford Dornbusch. 1995. "Social capital and the reproduction of inequality: Information networks among Mexican-origin high school students." *Sociology of Education* 68 (2): 116–135.

Steinberg, Laurence, Sanford Dornbusch, and Bradford Brown. 1992. "Ethnic differences in adolescent achievement: An ecological perspective." *American Psychologist* 47 (6): 723–729.

Stevens, Mitchell. 2007. *Creating a class: College admissions and the education of elites.* Cambridge, MA: Harvard University Press.

Strobel, Karen, Ben Kirshner, Jennifer O'Donoghue, and Milbrey McLaughlin. 2008. "Qualities that attract urban youth to after-school settings and promote continued participation." *Teachers College Record* 110 (8): 1677–1705.

Taylor, Paul. 2011. *Is college worth it? College presidents, public assess value, quality, and mission of higher education.* Washington, DC: Pew Research Center.

Thompson, Douglas, Ronaldo Iachan, Mary Overpeck, James Ross, and Lori Gross. 2006. "School connectedness in the health behavior in school-aged children study: The role of student, school, and school neighborhood characteristics." *Journal of School Health* 76 (7): 379–386.

Trusty, Jerry, Maximino Plata, and Carmen Salazar. 2003. "Modeling Mexican Americans' educational expectations: Longitudinal effects of variables across adolescence." *Journal of Adolescent Research* 18 (2): 131.

Valdes, Guadalupe. 1996. *Con respeto: Bridging the distances between culturally diverse families and schools.* New York: Teachers College Press.

Valencia, Ricardo. 1997. *The evolution of deficit thinking: Educational thought and practice.* Bristol, PA: Falmer Press.

———. 2002. *Chicano school failure and success: Past, present, and future.* 2nd ed. London: Routledge Falmer.

Valenzuela, Angela. 1999. *Subtractive schooling: U.S.-Mexican youth and the politics of caring.* Albany: State University of New York Press.

Valverde, Leonard, and Kent Scribner. 2001. "Latino students: Organizing schools for greater achievement." *NASSP Bulletin* 85 (624): 22–31.

Vandell, Deborah Lowe, Reed Larson, Joseph Mahoney, and Tyler Watts. 2015. "Children's organized activities." In *Handbook of child psychology and developmental science*, vol. 4, edited by Richard M. Lerner, 305–344. Hoboken, NJ: Wiley.

Vandell, Deborah Lowe, Kim Pierce, and Kimberly Dadisman. 2005. "Out-of-school settings as a developmental context for children and youth." In *Advances in child development and behavior*, vol. 33, edited by R. V. Kail, 43–77. New York: Academic Press.

Vandell, Deborah Lowe, and Jill Posner. 1999. "Conceptualization and measurement of children's after-school environments." In *Measuring environment across the life span: Emerging methods and concepts*, edited by S. L. Friedman and T. D. Wachs, 167–196. Washington, DC: American Psychological Association Press.

Vandell, Deborah Lowe, David Shernoff, Kim Pierce, Daniel Bolt, Kimberly Dadisman, and Bradford Brown. 2005. "Activities, engagement, and emotion in after-school programs (and elsewhere)." *New Directions for Youth Development* 2005 (105): 121–129.

van der Vaart, Wander. 2004. "The time-line as a device to enhance recall in standardized research interviews: A split ballot study." *Journal of Official Statistics* 20: 301–317.

van der Vaart, Wander, and Tina Glasner. 2007. "Applying a timeline as a recall aid in a telephone survey: A record check study." *Applied Cognitive Psychology* 21: 217–238.

Weininger, Elliot, Annette Lareau, and Dalton Conley. 2015. "What money doesn't buy: Class resources and children's participation in organized extracurricular activities." *Social Forces* 94: 479–503.

Willer, Barbara, S. L. Hofferth, E. Kisker, P. Divine-Hawkins, E. Farquhar, and F. Glantz. 1991. *The demand and supply of child care in 1990: Joint findings from the National Child Care Survey 1990 and a profile of child care settings*. Washington, DC: National Association for the Education of Young Children.

Willis, Paul. 1979. *Learning to labor: How working class kids get working class jobs*. Adlershot, Hampshire, UK: Saxon House.

Yohalem, Nicole, A. Wilson-Ahlstrom, S. Fischer, and M. Shinn. 2009. *Measuring youth program quality: A guide to assessment tools*. 2nd ed. Washington, DC: Forum for Youth Investment.

Yoshihama, Mieko, Brenda Gillespie, Amy Hammock, Robert Belli, and Richard Tolman. 2005. "Does the life-history calendar method facilitate the recall of domestic violence victimization? Comparison of two methods of data collection." *Social Work Research* 29 (3): 151–163.

Zaff, Jonathan, Kristin Moore, Angela Romano Papillo, and Stephanie Williams. 2003. "Implications of extracurricular activity participation during adolescence on positive outcomes." *Journal of Adolescent Research* 18 (6): 599–630.

Zalaquett, Carlos. 2006. "Study of successful Latina/o students." *Journal of Hispanic Higher Education* 5 (1): 35–47.

Index

academic achievement: asset theory on high, 43–44; benefits of organized activity to, xvi, 12–15, 18; class-based differences in, xii–xiii; deficit explanations of, 33–35; among Latino/as, 10–11; processes of influence on, 49–57; reproduction theory on, 38–40; resistance theory on, 40–43; role-identity theory on high, 45, 47–49; social capital and social embeddedness theory on high, 45–47; structural theory on high, 44; structural theory on low, 35–37; theoretical explanations for high, 43–49; theoretical explanations for low, 33–43

academic attainment, of Latino/as, 10

accomplishment of natural growth, 39, 60

achievement gap, xii, 31, 32

achievement test scores, among Latino/as, 10

active listening skills, 5, 141, 151–152, 173

additive/subtractive school experience, 37

Advancement Via Individual Determination (AVID), 44

African Americans: and academic achievement gap, xii, 31, 32; dropout rates of, xii, 35; racial disparity in educational outcomes and, xi–xii; stereotypes of attitude toward education, 42

agency. *See* personal agency

American Dream, ix, x, xiv

arts activities, 12

asset theory, 43–44, 158–159

at-risk label, 34, 35, 44

auxiliary degree of influence, 28, 59–63, 162; during childhood and elementary school, 63–64, 73–74; and early support with adversity, 61–62; Graciela (participant), 63–73; during high school, 67–71, 76–79; after high school, 71–73, 79–82; Julio (participant), 73–82; during middle school, 65–66, 74–76; overview of, 28, 59–63; and personal agency, 86–87; and relationships, 83–84; and structures, 84–86. *See also* distinguishable influence; transformative influence

awards, 8, 133, 147

Bayside Youth Council, 95, 96, 97, 102, 106–107, 119, 142

bilingual instruction, 62, 63–64, 137, 164–165

bioecological theory, 20

blacks. *See* African Americans

Bourdieu, Pierre, 15, 16–17, 60

Broh, Beckett, 13

Bronfenbrenner, Urie, 20, 21

Brooks-Gunn, Jeanne, 14–15, 33

Brown v. Board of Education, xi, 40

bullying, 17, 121, 122, 161

Carter, Prudence, 42–43, 47

civic leader program, 2

cliques, 45, 51, 102, 176

About the Author

INGRID A. NELSON is an assistant professor of sociology at Bowdoin College. Her research focuses on the ways that families, schools, and communities influence marginalized young people as they transition from high school to college and into adulthood. Her research has been published in *Educational Researcher, Journal of Youth and Adolescence, Afterschool Matters, Field Methods,* and *Rural Sociology.* A graduate of Wellesley College, Professor Nelson earned her MA and PhD from Stanford University